If It Be Thy Will

Thoughts On. . .

If It Be Thy Will

Book 5 in the "Thoughts On" Series

by David M. Arns

First Edition
Copyright © 2015 David M. Arns
Ninth Printing, July 2015
All rights reserved.
ISBN 978-1-50850-314-9

Books in the "THOUGHTS ON" Series, by David Arns

BOOK 1: *Prophets vs. Seers: Is There a Difference?* This book looks at that question from a Biblical viewpoint. There are Bible teachers teaching that prophets and seers are fundamentally different, and they offer some supporting evidence, while others say they merely variations in manifestation of fundamentally the same gift and calling. Is there enough Scriptural evidence to conclude that they are the same kind of person, or the same kind of calling, or are they indeed different? An in-depth analysis of related Scriptures leads the author to a solid conclusion.

BOOK 2: *Is It Possible to Stop Sinning?* There are a couple common beliefs in Christianity today: one holds that Christians living on earth will inevitably continue to sin until they graduate to heaven, and the other holds that it is possible for Christians to be without sin even while living on earth. Of course, the major factor in this discussion is what the Bible says. For example, What is sin? What does God say about it? What does God tell us to do about it? What did Jesus provide in the atonement? This book delves into great detail on the subject and includes Biblical support from many relevant Scriptures, showing God's heart on the matter, in a way that is both theologically relevant and practical in everyday life.

BOOK 3: *Extra-Biblical Truth: A Valid Concept?* There is a theory that says that God will not do nor say anything for which there is not a Biblical precedent, nor would He reveal a doctrine that was hitherto unheard of. Is this theory reasonable? Does the Bible itself address the question of God doing or saying things that are not already exemplified in the Bible itself? Actually, the Bible does address this question very

clearly, and in several different ways. This book illustrates how to analyze and discern, from a Scriptural point of view, events and practices for which the Bible doesn't have specific examples.

BOOK 4: ***Gold Dust, Jewels, and More: Manifestations of God?*** For the last couple of decades, there have been more and more reports of "unusual" occurrences taking place at meetings in which the Holy Spirit is allowed to moved freely. These occurrences include gold dust appearing on people and things, jewels suddenly popping into existence, people "falling under the power" (a.k.a., being "slain in the Spirit"), glory clouds hovering or swirling, oil coming from people's hands, and more. Are these real manifestations of God, or just the result of overzealous but unethical leaders? Is there a Biblical basis for any of these? This books delves into the Scriptures and analyzes passages that are often overlooked, to give a thoughtful and Biblically sound response to these reports of unusual manifestations.

BOOK 5: ***If It Be Thy Will*** Many people in the Body of Christ, when they pray for physical healing, end their prayers with ". . .if it be Thy will." That brings up a very important point: *Is it* God's will to heal us? Never, sometimes, or always? How do we know? What does the Bible say? So often, Jesus said to the people He just healed, "Your faith has made you well." Where did they get that faith, and can we learn from them? This book goes into great detail about what the Bible says—and does *not* say—about physical healing, and whether praying for it is something we are forbidden, discouraged, permitted, encouraged, or commanded to do. The Bible has much to say on this subject, and we can learn a great deal by just looking at what it says, and noting the obvious implications.

BOOK 6: *Free to Choose?* One of the most hotly debated concepts in the last 500 years or so has been that of whether or not people actually have a free will to choose their eternal destiny. People debate each other with—shall we say, *religious* fervor—and people on both sides of the debate offer Scriptures to support their viewpoints. On the one hand, we have people who believe that God offers us a choice to voluntarily repent and turn to Him. On the other hand, we have people who believe that God is sovereign, and that sovereignty necessarily means that God determines the eternal destination of everyone, with no regard to our choices. These two viewpoints can't both be correct, because they say mutually exclusive things. But fortunately, the Bible is remarkably unambiguous in its teachings: reading Scriptures in context and thinking about how various passages relate to each other make it abundantly clear which one of these viewpoints is actually the Biblical position.

BOOK 7: *Be Filled With the Spirit* In the last fifty years or so, there has been a tremendous resurgence of interest in the baptism of the Holy Spirit and the accompanying gifts of the Spirit. In some, the interest is entirely academic; in others, it is a passionate hunger to experience it firsthand. But there are people who claim that such things faded away around the end of the first century, and are therefore no longer available. Did they really fade away? We need to know because other people claim to have been baptized in the Holy Spirit and use the gifts of the Spirit every day, as a normal part of Christian life. As always, the Bible is the normative standard for living the Christian life, so what does the Bible say on this topic? Quite a lot, and if we follow what the Bible says, our Christian lives will become much more exciting and fruitful in the things of the Kingdom.

All of the above books are available in electronic form and/or as paperback, and are available from the sources mentioned on the website BibleAuthor.DaveArns.com.

Table of Contents

Preface 15
   Typographical Conventions 19
   Endorsements 20
Chapter 1: "If It Be Thy Will. . ." 21
   Bible-Study Practices 22
      Multiple Translations 22
      Multiple References 23
      The Preponderance of Scripture 23
      The Plain, Surface Meaning 24
      The Bible Itself Defining Its Terms 25
Chapter 2: God's Original Intent 27
   The Beginning of It All 27
   The End of It All 29
Chapter 3: Biblical Promises 31
   "None of These Diseases" 31
   "If You Worship Me" 34
   Fertility Is a Blessing 35
   The Secret Place of the Most High 36
   Forget Not All His Benefits 40
   Attend Unto My Words 40
   God's Vengeance 42
   Wounded for Our Transgressions 44
      By His Stripes We Are What? 48
      How Reliable Is It? 49
   God's Preferred Fast 50
   The "Jehovah" Names 51
   How Fares Your Soul? 53
Chapter 4: Jesus' Examples 55
   Examples of Jesus Healing Individuals 58
      The Royal Official's Son 58
      Demoniac in the Synagogue 58
      Peter's Mother-in-Law 59
      The Leper 60
      Would God Do the Same for Me? 61

The Paralytic with Four Good Friends 61
The Lame Man at the Pool of Bethesda 63
The Man with the Withered Hand. 65
The Centurion's Servant. 66
The Son of the Widow of Nain 67
The Mute Demoniacs 68
The Gadarene Demoniacs 70
Jairus' Daughter Raised from the Dead 73
The Woman with the Issue of Blood 74
The Two Blind Men. 75
The Canaanite Woman's Daughter. 77
Healing the Deaf Mute. 81
Healing the Blind Man. 82
The Deaf Mute Epileptic Boy. 83
    Mark's Account 87
The Ten Lepers. 88
The Man Born Blind 90
Raising Lazarus 92
The Woman with the Spirit of Infirmity. 97
The Man with Dropsy 99
Blind Bartimaeus and Friend 100
    Matthew's Account. 100
    Mark's Account 101
    Luke's Account. 104
Malchus' Ear 106
Your Faith has Made You Well 108
What Is Faith, Anyway? 109
Jesus Healing Large Crowds 112
    Before the Sermon on the Mount. 112
    In the Evening 113
    After Healing the Mute Demoniac. 115
    After Healing the Man with the Withered Hand 115
    Peter's Sermon to Cornelius 116
Why Did Jesus Heal? 117

Chapter 5: Are All Christians Supposed to Heal the Sick? 119
   The Disciples 120
   The Seventy-Two 122
   The Great Commission 123
   Being Christlike 124
   "So Send I You" 125
Chapter 6: Post-Ascension Examples of Healing 127
   The Apostles at Solomon's Porch 127
   Philip in Samaria 130
   Peter Meets Aeneas at Lydda 131
   Peter Meets Tabitha at Joppa 131
   The Apostle Paul 132
Chapter 7: Hindrances to Healing 139
   What If It Doesn't Work? 140
      How Do You Know It Didn't Work? 140
         Why Would God Delay a Healing Like That? 141
      Did Something Else Get Healed? 141
      Is It In Process? 142
      Is That Really the Issue? 143
      What If It Actually Doesn't Work? 143
   Insufficient Faith in the Prayee 145
   "God Wants Me Sick to Teach Me Something" 148
      "God Used My Sickness For His Glory" 149
      Couldn't I Have a Sickness for a Greater Good? 150
   Insufficient Faith in the Prayer 152
   Sin in the Prayee's Life 153
   A Spiritual Hindrance 156
      Fear 157
      Giving Satan an Opportunity 160
   God is Sovereign 161
      Co-Laboring With Christ 163
   The Fellowship of Christ's Suffering 168
      Good Suffering 169
      Bad Suffering 169
   What About Paul's "Thorn?" 174
      What Does "Thorn" Mean, Anyway? 174
      Why Did Paul Have His Thorn? 178

What Did Paul Say His "Thorn" Was?	178
What Did Not Paul Say His "Thorn" Was?	183
An Eye Disease?	184
Where Did Paul's Thorn Come From?	185
"My Grace is Sufficient For You. . ."	187
The Parable of the College Student	188
Paul's "Infirmities"	192
What About Trophimus?	197
So-and-So Got Prayed For, But Didn't Get Healed	199
The Common Thread	203
"The Healing Didn't Last Very Long"	203
Chapter 8: The Atonement	**207**
The Passover Lamb	209
The Healing of the Leper	210
Korah's Rebellion	211
The Caduceus	212
Forgiveness and Healing Together	216
The Curse of the Law	219
Wounded for Our Transgressions, Take 2	228
It Just Makes Sense	228
Chapter 9: Personal Testimonies	**231**
Aspergillosis	232
Neuropathy of the Feet	233
Kidney Failure	234
Left Ankle and Back	235
Frozen Neck, Internal Organs, and Asthma	236
Others	237
Chapter 10: What Shall We Say, Then?	**239**
The Kingdom of God	239
The Lord's Prayer	241
Applying God's Will In Our Lives	241
About the Author	**245**
The "Thoughts On" Series of Books	245

Preface

All Scripture references are from the public-domain King James Version (KJV) of the Bible unless otherwise noted. Other versions of the Bible that may be quoted are as follows:

- Amplified Bible (AMP): Copyright © 1954, 1958, 1962, 1964, 1965, and 1987 by the Lockman Foundation, La Habra, CA, 90631. All rights reserved. www.lockman.org.
- American Standard Version (ASV) of 1901: Public Domain.
- Bible in Basic English (BBE): This text is in the public domain and has no copyright. The Bible In Basic English was printed in 1965 by Cambridge Press in England. Published without any copyright notice and distributed in America, this work fell immediately and irretrievably into the Public Domain in the United States according to the UCC convention of that time.
- Common English Bible (CEB): All rights reserved.
- Contemporary English Version (CEV): Copyright © 1995 by American Bible Society. All rights reserved.
- Complete Jewish Bible (CJB): Copyright © 1998 by David H. Stern. All rights reserved.
- Darby Translation (DARBY): Public domain. First published in 1890 by John Nelson Darby, an Anglo-Irish Bible teacher associated with the early years of the Plymouth Brethren.
- Douay-Rheims Bible (DOUAY), translated from the Latin Vulgate. Rheims New Testament, 1582; Douay Old Testament, 1610.
- Easy-to-Read Version (ERV): Copyright © 2006 by World Bible Translation Center.
- The Holy Bible, English Standard Version (ESV): Copyright © 2001, 2006, 2011 by Crossway Bibles, a division of Good News Publishers. All rights reserved.
- The Expanded Bible (EXB): Scripture taken from The Expanded Bible. Copyright © 2011 by Thomas Nelson, Inc. Used by permission. All rights reserved.

- Geneva Bible (GNV): The Geneva Bible (1599), Public Domain.
- Good News Translation (GNT): Copyright © 1992 by American Bible Society. All rights reserved.
- God's Word Translation (GWORD): Copyright © 2010 by Baker Publishing Group, © 1995 by God's Words to the Nations. All Rights reserved.
- Holman Christian Standard Bible (HCSB): Copyright © 1999, 2000, 2002, 2003 by Holman Bible Publishers. Holman Christian Standard Bible®, Holman CSB®, and HCSB® are federally registered trademarks of Holman Bible Publishers. Used by permission.
- International Standard Version (ISV): The Holy Bible: International Standard Version. Release 2.0, Build 2014.07.18. Copyright © 1995–2014 by ISV Foundation. All Rights Reserved Internationally. Used by permission of Davidson Press, LLC.
- The Jubilee Bible (JUB): The Jubilee Bible (from the Scriptures of the Reformation), edited by Russell M. Stendal; Copyright © 2000, 2001, 2010.
- Lexham English Bible (LEB): Scripture quotations marked (LEB) are from the Lexham English Bible. Copyright © 2012 Logos Bible Software. Lexham is a registered trademark of Logos Bible Software.
- The Message (MSG): Scripture taken from The Message. Copyright © 1993, 1994, 1995, 1996, 2000, 2001, 2002. Used by permission of NavPress Publishing Group.
- New American Bible, Revised Edition (NABRE): © 2010, 1991, 1986, 1970 Confraternity of Christian Doctrine, Inc., Washington, DC. All Rights Reserved.
- New American Standard Bible (NASB): Copyright © 1960, 1962, 1963, 1968, 1971, 1972, 1973, 1975, 1977, 1995 by The Lockman Foundation. All rights reserved.

- New Century Version (NCV): Scripture taken from the New Century Version®. Copyright © 2005 by Thomas Nelson, Inc. Used by permission. All rights reserved.
- New English Translation (NET). The NET Bible®, First Edition (NET); New English Translation, The Translation That Explains Itself™; Copyright © 1996–2005 by Biblical Studies Press, L.L.C. All rights reserved.
- New International Readers' Version (NIRV): Copyright © 1996, 1998 by Biblica.
- New Life Version (NLV): Copyright © 1969 Christian Literature International.
- New Living Translation (NLT): Holy Bible, New Living Translation, Copyright © 1996, 2004 by Tyndale Charitable Trust. Used by permission of Tyndale House Publishers, Inc., Wheaton Illinois 60189. All rights reserved.
- New International Version (NIV): Scripture quoted by permission. Quotations designated (NIV) are from The Holy Bible: New International Version (NIV). Copyright © 1973, 1978, 1984 by International Bible Society. Used by permission of Zondervan Publishing House. All rights reserved.
- New Revised Standard Version (NRSV): New Revised Standard Version Bible, Copyright © 1989 the Division of Christian Education of the National Council of the Churches of Christ in the United States of America. Used by permission. All rights reserved.
- Names of God Bible (NOG): The Names of God Bible (without notes) © 2011 by Baker Publishing Group. Scripture is taken from God's Word®, © 1995 God's Word to the Nations. Used by permission of Baker Publishing Group.
- J.B. Phillips New Testament (PHILLIPS): J. B. Phillips, "The New Testament in Modern English," 1962 edition by HarperCollins.
- Revised Standard Version (RSV): Copyright © 1971 by the Division of Christian Education of the National Council of the Churches of Christ in the United States of America

- Today's English Version (TEV): Today's English Version Bible. Copyright © American Bible Society, 1966, 1971, 1976, 1992. Used by permission.
- The Living Bible (TLB): Copyright © 1971 by Tyndale House Foundation. Used by permission of Tyndale House Publishers Inc., Carol Stream, Illinois 60188. All rights reserved.
- The Voice Bible (VOICE): The Voice Bible Copyright © 2012 Thomas Nelson, Inc. The Voice™ translation © 2012 Ecclesia Bible Society. All rights reserved.
- Worldwide English (WE): Copyright © 1969, 1971, 1996, 1998 by SOON Educational Publications, Willington, Derby, DE65 6BN, England. Taken from The Jesus Book—The Bible in Worldwide English. Copyright SOON Educational Publications, Derby DE65 6BN, UK. Used by permission.
- World English Bible (WEB): "World English Bible" is a trademark of Rainbow Missions, Inc. Permission is granted to use the name "World English Bible" and its logo only to identify faithful copies of the Public Domain translation of the Holy Bible of that name published by Rainbow Missions, Inc. The World English Bible is not copyrighted.
- Wycliffe Bible (WYC): Wycliffe Bible Copyright © 2001 by Terence P. Noble.
- Young's Literal Translation of the Holy Bible (YLT): This text is in the public domain and has no copyright.

Typographical Conventions

In Scriptural quotes in this book, emphasis (indicated by **boldface** type, and occasionally *italic* **within the boldface**) may be added by the author to draw attention to the portions of the passage that pertain to the topic currently under discussion. This applies throughout, so "emphasis added by author" doesn't need to be stated in every single instance.

In this book, the generic pronouns "he," "him," and "his" are used whenever explicit inclusion of both gender-specific pronouns would result in grammatical cumbersomeness. We know that in Christ, there is no difference between male and female (Galatians 3:28), so the pronouns used in this way should be read as generic, not masculine.

When you see a number prefixed by a "H" or a "G", it represents the word number Hebrew or Greek dictionaries of *Strong's Exhaustive Concordance,* one of the standard tools for Biblical study: *Strong's Hebrew and Chaldee Dictionary of the Old Testament* (Hebrew Strong's) and *Strong's Greek Dictionary of the New Testament* (Greek Strong's), both public domain. So, for example, "G256" indicates that English word being discussed was translated from the word defined in entry 256 in Strong's Greek Dictionary.

In Scripture quotations, the letter case of the English word "Lord" indicates the standard meanings when quoting from the Old Testament. Mixed Case, as in "Lord," indicates the Hebrew name אֲדֹנָי (*Adonay*, H136), while SMALL CAPS, as in "LORD" indicates the Hebrew name יְהֹוָה (*Yahweh*, H3068), also known as the Tetragrammaton, which literally means "four letters." And finally, when the original Hebrew uses the name יְהֹוָה אֱלֹהִים (*Yahweh Elohim*, H3068 H430), it is translated and letter-cased as "Lord GOD."

Cover image is in the Public Domain.

Endorsements

While contending for a total healing from ALS, I have read nearly every Christian book on healing. It wasn't until I found Dave's book, The "Thoughts On" Series, *If It Be Thy Will*, that I discovered truths so profound that I read the book once and immediately read it again. If you've ever had a question concerning God's will on healing, you will find the answers you need in this book. He not only addresses those questions, but he backs them up Scripturally using several different Bible translations as well as explaining the Hebrew meaning of key words. Dave lays out the truths so simply, that as you read, your faith builds and builds. It's so simple, yet so profound. I never found myself questioning if I had "done enough" for Jesus as I read the book. There was no condemnation about not having enough faith to be healed. God has given Dave a gift for telling the healing story like Jesus would tell it, so lovingly, so personal. I want to recommend this book to anyone; not just those needing healing in their body. I'm beginning my third reading because I know each time I read it, my faith grows by leaps and bounds. Romans 10:17, "Faith comes by hearing and hearing by the Word of God." I read much of the book out loud so I could "hear" the spoken Word contained within nearly every page. Thank you Dave, for writing this very timely book.

—*Diane Evans, M.A., Retired Language Arts Instructor*

I just finished your book on healing *If It Be Thy Will*. I found it to be an easy read; I enjoyed the Scripture references and to be able to look at different translations side by side. You brought things out that I had not seen or thought about before, which was fun. I loved how you covered the Bible from Genesis to Revelation and the flow from Old to New Covenant. It's very clear how God's will is to heal today, as it was in the past. . . if you feel led to share the book with somebody at the Healing Rooms, please do; I think it would bless him tremendously.

—*Tom Tyrrell, Director, Healing Rooms of Loveland, Colorado*

Chapter 1:

"If It Be Thy Will. . ."

Most people are at least familiar with (even if they're not comfortable with) the idea of praying for physical healing for someone. But many people, myself included, have on occasion ended such a prayer with ". . .if it be Thy will." What exactly does that mean? Should we pray that? Can we know God's will in this area? Why does prayer for healing not work sometimes? Does the Bible address this?

People have a whole range of beliefs on this subject, and those beliefs have been formed and shaped by a variety of things: their denominational backgrounds, teachings that they have heard on the radio, television, podcasts, and so forth, their own experiences, reports from friends or relatives, and more. Oh, yes: and the Bible. Obviously, some of these sources might disagree with each other, and just as obviously, one of these sources is more reliable than the others.

So how can we come to a logical, rational, well-thought-out, Scriptural conclusion that sits well with God's loving Father-heart? How can we know whether or not God wants to heal *in this particular case?* Because that is most often the question. Most people wouldn't dispute that God *could* heal people if He chose to, and most people wouldn't even argue with the idea that He actually does want to heal *at least sometimes*. But the $64,000 question is this: *Does He want to heal this person I'm praying for right now?* That is the Big Question this book addresses. But if you have any of the other questions I mentioned above, I think those too will be answered in the following pages.

Not surprisingly, the Bible does address all these questions, in a host of different ways. God knows that it is important to us as humans to be in good health, and it is important to Him as well. And, as we'll find out, it is even *more* important to Him than it is to us.

The various chapters in this book will cover questions relating to God's will (as it pertains to physical healing) from a variety of different aspects, and then address Biblical responses to those questions. My prayer is that you, the reader, will grow in understanding and faith as you read what God's Word says on this very important subject.

Bible-Study Practices

As I study the Bible, I employ quite a few different study techniques that I have found, over the decades, to be quite useful and reliable. I describe them here for two reasons. First, that you would see how I came to the conclusions I came to, and second, so you could start employing them in your own Bible study, should you so choose.

Multiple Translations

As you may have seen in other books in the "Thoughts On" series, I often include relevant verses from several different translations of the Bible. This seems prudent, and more reliable, because I have seen Bible teachings that were based entirely on a single translation of the Bible, and if the "wrong" translation was used, it failed to support, and sometimes even contradicted, the whole point of the teaching.

In those cases where a passage of Scripture is quoted out of several translations, and you may be tempted to read just the first one, and skip the rest. But, I encourage you to thoughtfully read each translation's rendering of the verses, and note the different shades of meaning. You will be pretty amazed at what the Bible says...

Multiple References

Also, you'll notice that when I make a doctrinal statement, I often support my statement with a series of Scriptures. Sometimes I use the same Scripture out of different translations as described above, but also I will often give a list of different Scriptures, all of which support the point I am trying to make. This also seems prudent, because it lessens the likelihood of misinterpretation. For example, if I make a statement and back it up with only a single Scripture, that's good, but someone could respond with "That's not what that says! You misinterpreted that verse!" And that is certainly possible.

But an even better approach is this: if I offer a list of *ten* different Scriptures, *all* of which support my point, it becomes more and more likely that I am understanding Scripture correctly, and less and less likely that I happened to misinterpret all of them in an identical manner. As a result, my assertions that are backed up with a larger number of Scriptures are probably more reliable than those backed up by only one or two. And since my goal is to understand as accurately as possible what God is saying through His Word, and communicate that as accurately as possible to the reader, please bear with me when I support a statement with a list of Scriptures that you may feel is excessively long. I, for one, am comforted when my doctrinal beliefs are supported by a plethora of Scriptures instead of just one or two.

The Preponderance of Scripture

This concept is similar, but not identical, to the one above, so I mention it separately.

The "preponderance of Scripture" is another good Bible-study tool. Basically, it looks at how many Scriptures can reasonably be interpreted one particular way, as opposed to how many can be interpreted in some alternate way. For example, if I have a verse that seems to say one thing, or at least it *could* be interpreted one particular way, but a dozen verses that say the opposite, and *couldn't* be interpreted in such a way as to support the other verse, it's not rocket science to conclude that the interpretation supported by the dozen Scriptures is more likely to be reliable than the interpretation supported by only the one.

For this reason, too, when I present a statement or doctrine that I believe to be true, I usually give quite a bit of supporting Scriptural evidence that upholds that statement or doctrine. It's all part of I Peter 3:15 (NIV): "Always be prepared to give an answer to everyone who asks you to give the reason for the hope that you have." And in doing so, I'd better have my doctrinal "ducks in a row," so to speak, because I, as a teacher, will be judged with a stricter judgment (James 3:1).

The Plain, Surface Meaning

While it is often valuable to refer back to Hebrew and Greek, the original languages in which the Bible was written, for clarification and/or subtle nuances of meaning in the text, it shouldn't be necessary to resort to the original languages for major doctrines. The Bible is for the purpose of God communicating with us, so reading it in our own language should give us plenty of understanding on the essential doctrines of Christianity.

As a result, you'll notice in this book that I refer to English translations of the Bible for most of my content, with only occasional excursions into the Hebrew or Greek, where such an excursion would be useful to clarify or reveal a nuance of meaning. In other words, I go in most cases by the plain, surface meaning of the text: the meaning that any unbiased, literate speaker of English would derive from the text.

If I am required to go to the original languages for some concept because there is insufficient evidence from plain, surface meaning at least somewhere in the Bible, it seems to me that that concept is either questionable or, if it is undisputable, it is relatively unimportant.

Basing major doctrines on things that can *only* be supported by a knowledge of Greek or Hebrew, sounds dangerously close to what the organized church in the Middle Ages did: keeping the Bible obscure, only in Latin, so the "common folk" were dependent upon trained religious leaders to interpret it for them. Wouldn't want them to get all confused by reading God's Word for themselves. . .

The Bible Itself Defining Its Terms

As you may have seen in other books in the "Thoughts On" series, one good way of finding out what the Bible means by a particular word or phrase in some verse is to see if the Bible uses, or even defines, that same word or phrase elsewhere. If it does, then you're more likely to have learned something that Bible actually intended, as opposed to some modern-day commentator or theologian's opinion on what the Bible meant.

There are many verses that refer to various Scriptural concepts. Of course, that's not a problem—they are obviously Scriptural words—but the problem arises when we apply a different meaning to the word than that which the Biblical authors (read: "God") intended. This is very easy to do; we, as modern-day Americans, don't typically know a lot about ancient Hebrew or Greek laws, customs, feasts, traditions, vocabulary, grammar, idioms, and so forth. Usually the resulting misinterpretation is not malicious; it's just a result of insufficient study. The problem that arises here is simply: How do we know what the correct meanings of Biblical words are?

In some cases, we need to go back to the original languages, and that's fine when necessary, but sometimes it's possible to learn what Biblical words mean because *the Bible itself defines them*. In such cases, the definition is usually in a different Scripture, because if it were in the same Scripture, there wouldn't be a question in the first place.

You may have seen that this approach was used to determine the Biblical meaning of the word "repent" in the section "Jonah Preaching in Nineveh," and the word "grace" in the section "Being Under Grace," both in Book 2 of the "Thoughts On" series: *Is It Possible to Stop Sinning?* (Both are available from the sources noted on BibleAuthor.DaveArns.com.) This approach will not work in every case, because not all controversial Biblical words are clearly defined in Scripture. But when it does, it is very enlightening, and very reliable.

Another thing that Biblical usage of words can often tell us is what a word does *not* mean. For example, I've heard it said that the "wine" back in Bible days was not actually alcoholic, but was only a kind of grape juice. It doesn't take too much deep thought to realize that the same Bible that refers to "wine" also warns us not to get drunk on it. And if we are willing to acknowledge that it would be silly and pointless for God to warn us away from a behavior that was impossible to do anyway, we are compelled to conclude that the wine in Bible days was indeed alcoholic.

Chapter 2:

God's Original Intent

We all know that there is sickness and disease and injury in the world nowadays; you would have to have lived under a rock your whole life to not realize that people often get sick. And they get sick in a variety of ways: from the common cold that is nothing more that a minor annoyance for a few days, to degenerative diseases that reduce healthy people to permanent paralysis, to fatal diseases that can take your life in a matter of days. But regardless of the seriousness of the sicknesses, they are not good.

The Beginning of It All

An important question is, Was it always this way? The answer, as we can see from the Bible, is No. When God created the heavens and the earth, the Bible says several times that "God saw that it was good" (Genesis 1:4, 10, 12, 18, 21, and 25). And then He created man, and "God saw that it was *very* good" (1:31). There was no sickness or disease the way God originally made everything.

So what happened? Adam and Even sinned by eating of the tree of the knowledge of good and evil, thereby switching their allegiance from

God to the serpent, Satan. Because of their rebellion, the ground was cursed, horticulture became hard work, weeds started growing and, just like God had said, they died. Spiritually, they died instantly upon sinning, and physically, they died over time. God addresses Adam:

> Genesis 3:17–19: And unto Adam he said, Because thou hast hearkened unto the voice of thy wife, and hast eaten of the tree, of which I commanded thee, saying, Thou shalt not eat of it: cursed is the ground for thy sake; in sorrow shalt thou eat of it all the days of thy life; ¹⁸Thorns also and thistles shall it bring forth to thee; and thou shalt eat the herb of the field; ¹⁹In the sweat of thy face shalt thou eat bread, **till thou return unto the ground**; for out of it wast thou taken: for dust thou art, and **unto dust shalt thou return**.

So why did God make it take so long to die physically? Wasn't that just prolonging the inevitable, now that sin, decay, disease, and death were in the world? Perhaps, but there's more to it than that. When God was pronouncing the curse on the serpent for tempting Adam and Eve into their sin, He said to the serpent:

> Genesis 3:14–16: And the LORD God said unto the serpent, Because thou hast done this, thou art cursed above all cattle, and above every beast of the field; upon thy belly shalt thou go, and dust shalt thou eat all the days of thy life: ¹⁵And **I will put enmity between thee and the woman, and between thy seed and her seed; it shall bruise thy head, and thou shalt bruise his heel**. ¹⁶Unto the woman he said, I will greatly multiply thy sorrow and thy conception; in sorrow thou shalt bring forth children; and thy desire shall be to thy husband, and he shall rule over thee.

Before sin was in the world, God told Adam and Eve to multiply; i.e., have children. That was part of the blessing of existence. And now that sin was in the world, the childbearing part became *really* necessary, because it was through one of the descendents of the woman that the Redeemer would come. In the first few hours, at most, after the first shockwave of sin had ravaged the universe, God had already announced His plan to redeem mankind.

So mankind had to have a lifespan long enough to have children so the species could be perpetuated until the fullness of time had come (Galatians 4:4), and at that point God would send His Son into the world, not to condemn it, but that the world, through Him, might be saved (John 3:16–17). But one of the side-effects of having a life long enough to bear and raise children, is that there is more time for the curse to cause damage, and for Satan to steal, kill, and destroy, which are the only reasons Satan even shows up (John 10:10). Hence, the environment of decay and disease we currently live in.

So sin introduced death into the universe when Adam gave his allegiance to Satan, but death is not that picky about *how* it gets its grisly job done. Death by the decay of old age, death by violent attack by other humans, death by sickness, death by accident—death (and Satan) aren't that particular *how* it gets done, they just want you dead. So sickness is just one method, one avenue, one tool the enemy uses to try to kill people. Again, it wasn't this way when God created it all, but it came later when Adam sinned.

The End of It All

At the end of history, God creates a new heaven and a new earth (Revelation 21:1). Here is a partial description of that time:

> Revelation 21:4: And God shall wipe away all tears from their eyes; and **there shall be no more death, neither sorrow, nor crying, neither shall there be any more pain:** for the former things are passed away.

Sickness and disease always cause some combination of sorrow, pain, crying, and/or death, so it sounds like sickness and disease will be things of the past at this point. When we read the verse again, we see that that is indeed true: it says very plainly "the former things are passed away."

During the description of the New Jerusalem, the Bible says:

> Revelation 21:27: And **there shall in no wise enter into it any thing that defileth**, neither whatsoever worketh abomination, or maketh a lie: but they which are written in the Lamb's book of life.

> AMP: But **nothing that defiles** or profanes or is unwashed **shall ever enter it**. . .
>
> CJB: **Nothing impure** may enter it. . .
>
> ERV: **Nothing unclean** will ever enter the city.
>
> TLB: **Nothing evil** will be permitted in it. . .
>
> NLT: **Nothing evil** will be allowed to enter. . .
>
> VOICE: **Nothing that defiles** or is defiled can enter into its glorious gates.
>
> WE: **Nothing that is not holy** will ever go in.

Sickness indeed will be done away with, because sickness undeniably defiles, it is evil, impure, unclean, unholy, and so forth. Then, in describing the Tree of Life:

> Revelation 22:2: In the midst of the street of it, and on either side of the river, was there the tree of life, which bare twelve manner of fruits, and yielded her fruit every month: and the **leaves of the tree were for the healing of the nations.**

So healing is provided through the leaves of the Tree of Life. But the real clincher is the very next verse:

> Revelation 22:3: And there shall be **no more curse**. . .

Ah! Remember the curse that went into effect in the Garden of Eden, when man sinned and gave his allegiance to Satan? In the New Jerusalem, it will not be around anymore! No more sickness, disease, decay, aging, senility, frailty, and death!

So healing—and its result, health—are definitely in God's will. We can see it in how He originally created things, and how He will ultimately restore things. But what good does that do us now? We aren't living in the time before Adam and Eve sinned anymore, and we're not in the new heavens or on the new earth yet, so how does the above help us right now? *It tells us what God's will is,* in regard to physical healing. And that, as you remember, is the topic of this entire book, entitled *If It Be Thy Will.*

Chapter 3:

Biblical Promises

Let's look at what God says, both in the Old and New Testaments, about the subjects of sickness and disease, and their opposite, health. Actually, God makes many promises in the Old Testament on this topic, and from them, we can see God's heart on the subject.

"None of These Diseases"

Immediately after God delivered the children of Israel from the Egyptian army at the Red Sea, Moses and the Israelites sang a song of worship to the Lord. Then they travelled three days' journey into the wilderness, found a source of bitter (non-potable) water, which God healed miraculously. God then told them He was testing them:

> Exodus 15:26: And said, If thou wilt diligently hearken to the voice of the LORD thy God, and wilt do that which is right in his sight, and wilt give ear to his commandments, and keep all his statutes, **I will put none of these diseases upon thee, which I have brought upon the Egyptians: for I am the LORD that healeth thee.**

So here God promises healing and health *if* they are obedient to His commands. God promises to put none of the diseases he put on the Egyptians on the Israelites if they follow His laws. What were the diseases God put on the Egyptians? The fifth plague (after water turning to blood, frogs, gnats/lice, and flies) was a disease on livestock, perhaps as a "warning shot across the bow," as if the first four weren't enough. Then the sixth plague was festering (rupturing/oozing) boils on all the animals and people; the seventh was a hailstorm with hailstones so large they would kill any animals or people out in it. Then finally locusts, darkness, and the death of the firstborn.

So actually, the only diseases that afflicted humans *during the ten plagues* were the festering boils (a sickness that, while very painful, was not fatal) and the death of the firstborn (some sickness that *was* fatal). So apparently, other diseases had already been afflicting the Egyptians before the "official" plagues started. This shouldn't be surprising; it is consistent with God's covenant with Abram/Abraham:

> Genesis 12:3 (NIV): I will bless those who bless you, and whoever curses you I will curse; and all peoples on earth will be blessed through you.

Since Egypt had already been enslaving Israel for four hundred years, it is very likely, in my estimation, that even before the official plagues started, the Egyptians were suffering a variety of diseases as they reaped what they were sowing. Hundreds of years before, when Pharaoh took Abram's wife Sarai into his harem, it didn't take long at all for the plagues to start:

> Genesis 12:14–20: And it came to pass, that, when Abram was come into Egypt, the Egyptians beheld the woman that she was very fair. ¹⁵The princes also of Pharaoh saw her, and commended her before Pharaoh: and the woman was taken into Pharaoh's house. ¹⁶And he entreated Abram well for her sake: and he had sheep, and oxen, and he asses, and menservants, and maidservants, and she asses, and camels. ¹⁷And **the LORD plagued Pharaoh and his house with great plagues because of Sarai Abram's wife.** ¹⁸And Pharaoh called Abram, and said, What is this that thou hast done unto me? why didst thou not tell me that she was thy wife? ¹⁹Why saidst thou, She is my sister? so I might have

taken her to me to wife: now therefore behold thy wife, take her, and go thy way. ²⁰And Pharaoh commanded his men concerning him: and they sent him away, and his wife, and all that he had.

But getting back to God's promise "I am the LORD that healeth thee," Israel had already seen this in action. God said that after they had been in the wilderness three days, which was after the Egyptian army was overthrown, which was after Moses led the Israelites out of Egypt.

When they came out of Egypt, *everyone* in the whole nation was healthy. *That's* pretty impressive. But how many people were in the nation at that time?

> Numbers 1:45–46 (NLT): They were registered by families—all the men of Israel who were twenty years old or older and able to go to war. ⁴⁶The total number was 603,550.

At this point, just a few days after they left Egypt, there were 603,550 men. What kind of men? "Twenty years old or older and able to go to war." In other words, of marriageable age. Considering that the Israelites understood that marriage was a blessing, we can safely conclude that there were very close to 603,550 wives of these men. That's more than 1.2 million people, *without even counting the children.*

How many children were typical in a Hebrew family back then? It's unlikely they had birth control, and even if they did, it's unlikely that they would have used it, because they realized that children were a blessing (Psalm 127:3–5). So it seems that a conservative estimate would be that each family had six children under twenty years old—less than one pregnancy every three years seems quite conservative. Obviously, many families had more than six, but let's assume six children per family for the moment. So if, for each man of marriageable age, there was a wife and six children, that would have made almost five million people in the nation at that time.

> Psalm 105 recounts the deliverance of Israel from Egypt, and it says:
> Psalm 105:37: He brought them forth also with silver and gold: and **there was not one feeble person among their tribes.**

GNT: Then he led the Israelites out; they carried silver and gold, and **all of them were healthy and strong.**

JUB: And he brought them forth with silver and gold, and **there was not one sick person among their tribes.**

TLB: . . .and brought his people safely out from Egypt, loaded with silver and gold; **there were no sick and feeble folk among them then.**

NLV: Then He brought Israel out with silver and gold. And **there was not one weak person among their families.**

WYC: And he led out them with silver and gold; and **none was sick** in the lineages of them. (And he led them out with silver and gold; and **no one was weak, or feeble, in all their tribes.**)

Not one single sick person in the whole nation! When you realize that nowadays, it is difficult to gather a mere *dozen* people, picked at random, and find not one single sick person among them, it becomes even more impressive that the whole nation of millions of people was healthy.

The Hebrew word translated "feeble" in the KJV is כָּשַׁל (*kashal*, H3782), whose definitions include "to totter or waver (through weakness of the legs, especially the ankle)," "to falter, stumble, faint, or fall," "be decayed," "be ruined," and "be weak." And not one of the people in the whole nation was this way! So again, the Israelites were already experiencing the reality of this promise even before God gave it.

"If You Worship Me"

When Moses went up Mount Sinai the first time, and he received the Ten Commandments verbally (he did not receive the Ten Commandments on the stone tablets during this trip; for more detail, see the chapter "The Glory Cloud" in Book 4 of the "Thoughts On" series: *Gold Dust, Jewels, and More: Manifestations of God?*, available from the sources noted on BibleAuthor.DaveArns.com).

During that trip, God gives Moses not only the Ten Commandments, but quite a few other commands that would ultimately be incorporated into what we now call The Law of Moses. And one little section in among all the rest is quite significant:

> Exodus 23:25–26 (NIV): Worship the LORD your God, and his blessing will be on your food and water. **I will take away sickness from among you,** [26]and **none will miscarry or be barren** in your land. **I will give you a full life span.**

Health, fertility, full-term pregnancies, long life. Good stuff, but why was it contingent upon the people worshipping God? Because God is the single, only, sole, unique, solitary, source of all life and health, and if we turn away from Him, *what else is there* but sickness and death? In other words, there is only one right answer for the source of life, and if you reject that one right answer, it doesn't much matter which wrong answer you choose—the results are the same.

Fertility Is a Blessing

In Deuteronomy, the Law of Moses is restated. Listen to the following and notice the strength of the blessings God puts on the people:

> Deuteronomy 7:12–15 (TEV): If you listen to these commands and obey them faithfully, then the LORD your God will continue to keep his covenant with you and will show you his constant love, as he promised your ancestors. [13]**He will love you and bless you, so that you will increase in number and have many children;** he will bless your fields, so that you will have grain, wine, and olive oil; and **he will bless you by giving you many cattle and sheep.** He will give you all these blessings in the land that he promised your ancestors he would give to you. [14]No people in the world will be as richly blessed as you. **None of you nor any of your livestock will be sterile.** [15]**The LORD will protect you from all sickness,** and he will not bring on you any of the dreadful diseases that you experienced in Egypt, but he will bring them on all your enemies.

So again, God promises health ("The LORD protect you from all sickness"), and one aspect of that is fertility, and it applies to their animals as well ("None of you nor any of your livestock will be sterile").

A sadly overlooked blessing in this day and age is that of children; so often they are considered a bother, a nuisance. What is the phrase that God uses to described the Promised Land? "A land flowing with milk and honey." Where does milk come from? Lactating females. How do females start lactating? Childbearing. Fruitfulness, in the sense of bearing young, is inextricably linked to health; sick animals and people don't reproduce well, and all sorts of problems result.

Flash back to when Jacob was pronouncing blessings over all his sons; he was speaking prophetically what God was saying. To Joseph, Jacob says:

> Genesis 49:25: Even by the God of thy father, who shall help thee; and by the Almighty, who shall bless thee with blessings of heaven above, blessings of the deep that lieth under, **blessings of the breasts, and of the womb**. . .

He specifically blesses Joseph with reproductive functionality. Hmm. Maybe healthy reproduction is a greater blessing than the modern world thinks. . .

The Secret Place of the Most High

One of the most beloved and reassuring passages in Christendom is Psalm 91: "He that dwelleth in the secret place of the most High shall abide under the shadow of the Almighty. I will say of the LORD, He is my refuge and my fortress: my God; in him will I trust," and so on. Very comforting, very reassuring, and many people claim its promises often.

But have you ever noticed that in no less than three different places, Psalm 91 explicitly states that God will provide healing and/or health to us? That He will protect us from sickness and disease? This is often overlooked, because the KJV uses the archaic words "pestilence" and "plague," but everybody knows what these words mean if they just think about it for a moment.

> Psalm 91:3, 5–6, 10: **Surely he shall deliver thee** from the snare of the fowler, and **from the noisome pestilence**. . . . ⁵**Thou shalt not be**

afraid for the terror by night; nor for the arrow that flieth by day; ⁶Nor **for the pestilence that walketh in darkness; nor for the destruction that wasteth at noonday.** . . . ¹⁰There shall no evil befall thee, **neither shall any plague come nigh thy dwelling.**

CEB: ³**God will save you** from the hunter's trap and **from deadly sickness.** . . . ⁶or sickness that prowls in the dark, destruction that ravages at noontime. . . . ¹⁰no evil will happen to you; **no disease will come close to your tent.**

CEV: ³**The Lord will keep you safe from** secret traps and **deadly diseases.** . . . ⁶And **you won't fear diseases that strike in the dark** or sudden disaster at noon. . . . ¹⁰and no terrible disasters will strike you or your home.

ERV: ³**God will save you** from hidden dangers and **from deadly diseases.** . . . ⁶**You will have no fear of diseases** that come in the dark or terrible suffering that comes at noon. . . . ¹⁰So nothing bad will happen to you. **No diseases will come near your home.**

EXB: ³**God will save [protect] you** from hidden traps [the snare of the fowler] and **from deadly diseases [pestilence].** . . . ⁶**You will not be afraid of diseases [. . .or the pestilence]** that come [walks; stalks] in the dark **or sickness [stings]** that strikes [devastates; overpowers] at noon. . . . ¹⁰Nothing bad [evil; harmful] will happen to [befall] you; **no disaster [blow; or plague] will come to [approach] your home [tent].**

GWORD: ³**He is the one who will rescue you** from hunters' traps and **from deadly plagues.** . . . ⁶plagues that roam the dark, epidemics that strike at noon. . . . ¹⁰No harm will come to you. **No sickness will come near your house.**

HCSB: ³**He Himself will deliver you** from the hunter's net, **from the destructive plague.** . . . ⁶the plague that stalks in darkness, or the pestilence that ravages at noon. . . . ¹⁰no harm will come to you; **no plague will come near your tent.**

TLB: ³**For he** rescues you from every trap and **protects you from the fatal plague.** . . . ⁶**nor dread the plagues of darkness,** nor disasters in the morning. . . . ¹⁰**How then can evil** overtake me or **any plague come near?**

NCV: ³**God will save you** from hidden traps and **from deadly diseases.** . .. ⁶**You will not be afraid of diseases that come in the dark or sickness that strikes at noon.** . . . ¹⁰**Nothing bad will happen to you**; no disaster will come to your home.

NET: ³**he will certainly rescue you** from the snare of the hunter and **from the destructive plague.** . .. ⁶**the plague that comes in the darkness, or the disease that comes at noon.** . . . ¹⁰No harm will overtake you; **no illness will come near your home.**

NIRV: ³**He will certainly save you** from hidden traps and **from deadly sickness.** . .. **You won't have to be afraid of the sickness that attacks in the darkness. You won't have to fear the plague that destroys at noon.** . . . ¹⁰Then no harm will come to you. **No terrible plague will come near your tent.**

NLV: ³For **it is He Who takes you away from** the trap, and from **the killing sickness.** . .. ⁶**You will not be afraid of the sickness that walks in darkness,** or of the trouble that destroys at noon. . . . ¹⁰**nothing will hurt you.** No trouble will come near your tent.

VOICE: ³For **He will rescue you** from the snares set by your enemies who entrap you and **from deadly plagues.** . .. ⁶Or **the plagues that lurk in darkness** or the disasters that wreak havoc at noon. . . . ¹⁰No evil will come to you; **plagues will be turned away at your door.**

This Psalm is even cooler than we had thought: The various translations above state that God will deliver us, save us, keep us safe from, protect us from, rescue us from, and take us away from pestilence, plagues, sicknesses, diseases, epidemics, and illnesses. How cool is that! But what's more, *how* in the world could we have ever misunderstood what it's saying?

If It Be Thy Will

Forget Not All His Benefits

In Psalm 103, David is extolling the goodness of God; there is verse after verse after verse of descriptions of how wonderful and loving and kind God is. And one of David's statements is:

> Psalm 103:2–3 (NIV): Praise the LORD, O my soul, and forget not all his benefits— ³who forgives all your sins and **heals all your diseases**. . .

David certainly categorized this attribute of God correctly: It is indeed a benefit to be healed of all our diseases. But notice that it also says: He "forgives all our sins." Now, examine your heart for a moment: Do you find it easier to believe that he could and would forgive all your sins, than that He could and would heal all your diseases? If so, why is there a discrepancy? Why is it harder to believe that God would be more willing or able to do one thing than another, especially when they are side by side in a single verse like this? This might betray some errant thinking, perhaps instilled by errant teaching, mightn't it?

Attend Unto My Words

In Proverbs, Solomon speaks wisdom which, since the Bible was God-breathed to the amanuenses to write down (II Timothy 3:16–17 and II Peter 1:21), is coming from the heart of God. He writes:

> Proverbs 4:20: My son, attend to my words; incline thine ear unto my sayings. ²¹Let them not depart from thine eyes; keep them in the midst of thine heart. ²²For they are life unto those that find them, and **health to all their flesh.**

Again, here is another way God is saying that if we obey Him, we will be healthier. But what does that mean? It could mean:

1. When we live according to God's principles, life is more peaceful; i.e., less stressful, and thus we will automatically avoid stress-related health problems. And this is a lot; some estimates state that 98% of degenerative diseases are caused by stress.

John 14:27 (TEV): **Peace is what I leave with you; it is my own peace that I give you.** I do not give it as the world does. Do not be worried and upset; do not be afraid.

2. When we live according to God's principles, we'll automatically avoid diseases and injuries caused by engaging in a sinful lifestyle.

   Galatians 6:7–8 (TEV): Do not deceive yourselves; no one makes a fool of God. **You will reap exactly what you plant.** [8]**If you plant in the field of your natural desires, from it you will gather the harvest of death;** if you plant in the field of the Spirit, from the Spirit you will gather the harvest of eternal life.

   For example, if we avoid the sin of drunkenness, we'll drastically reduce our incidence of anemia, cancer, cardiovascular disease, cirrhosis of the liver, dementia, depression, seizures, gout, high blood pressure, infectious diseases in general, nerve damage, and pancreatitis, not to mentioned injuries or death caused by the reduced coordination that accompanies being drunk.

   Another example is this: if we avoid sin related to sexual promiscuity, we're much less susceptible to STDs (chlamidia, gonorrhea, syphilis, genital herpes, etc.), HIV, AIDS, depression, and HPV (Human Papilloma Virus, which greatly increases likelihood of cervical cancer), PID (Pelvic Inflammatory Disease, which itself can cause ectopic pregnancy, chronic pelvic pain, and infertility), Hepatitis B, and on and on.

3. When we live according to God's principles, we'll realize that God has supernaturally provided for our health and healing (for more details, see the chapter on The Atonement, below):

   James 5:14–16 (NIV): Is any one of you sick? He should call the elders of the church to pray over him and anoint him with oil in the name of the Lord. [15]And **the prayer offered in faith will make the sick person well; the Lord will raise him up.** If he has sinned, he will be forgiven. [16]Therefore confess your sins to each other and **pray for each other so that you may be healed.** The prayer of a righteous man is powerful and effective.

   In practical terms, this means that when we start feeling ill, or are diagnosed with a disease, we don't have to pray, "Lord, help me accept this sickness," nor should we be in denial that the condition exists. We simply realize that God is stronger than the disease, and He is good, and He loves us, and we should pursue His miraculous healing, as well as medical attention if He so directs us.

So back to Proverbs. When the Holy Spirit, through Solomon, says to keep His words in the midst of our hearts, because "they are life unto those that find them, and health to all their flesh," is it talking about the mechanism in Item 1, 2, or 3, above? *Yes.* It's talking about all three of those ways listed above, and probably many more besides.

God's Vengeance

I believe it was Mike Bickle who said, "God's judgments are directed only at those things that interfere with His love." How true. God loves people so amazingly much that even when we were still spitting in His face, He was willing to die in our place to take our punishment so we wouldn't have to.

But what's all this about "God's judgment" and "God's vengeance" some people talk so much about? Well, let's look at the Bible for a moment:

> Isaiah 34:17–35:10 (NIV): He allots their portions; his hand distributes them by measure. They will possess it forever and dwell there from generation to generation. ¹The desert and the parched land will be glad; the wilderness will rejoice and blossom. Like the crocus, ²it will burst into bloom; it will rejoice greatly and shout for joy. The glory of Lebanon will be given to it, the splendor of Carmel and Sharon; they will see the glory of the LORD, the splendor of our God. ³Strengthen the feeble hands, steady the knees that give way; ⁴say to those with fearful hearts, "Be strong, do not fear; your God will come, **he will come with vengeance; with divine retribution he will come to save you.**" ⁵Then will the eyes of the blind be opened and the ears of the deaf unstopped. ⁶Then will the lame leap like a deer, and the mute tongue shout for joy. Water will gush forth in the wilderness and streams in the desert. ⁷The burning sand will become a pool, the thirsty ground bubbling springs. In the haunts where jackals once lay, grass and reeds

and papyrus will grow. ⁸And a highway will be there; it will be called the Way of Holiness. The unclean will not journey on it; it will be for those who walk in that Way; wicked fools will not go about on it. ⁹No lion will be there, nor will any ferocious beast get up on it; they will not be found there. But only the redeemed will walk there, ¹⁰and the ransomed of the LORD will return. They will enter Zion with singing; everlasting joy will crown their heads. Gladness and joy will overtake them, and sorrow and sighing will flee away.

Wow. That's the kind of vengeance and retribution we could live with. Notice what happens when God pours out His vengeance: the wilderness blossoms, feeble hands receive strength, unstable knees become steady, the blind see, the deaf hear, the lame walk, the dumb speak, the desert flows with streams of water, and so forth.

The above is good news, but how could that possibly be *vengeance*? Again, because vengeance was never intended to be aimed at people (John 3:16–17), and people were never intended to go to hell. Hell was prepared for the devil and his angels (Matthew 25:41), and people go there only if they choose to; Jesus paid an unimaginable price to make a way for us to *escape* hell (Romans 5:5), and He offers it to everyone for free (Romans 5:15–16). But He won't override our will in the matter; we can do a terminally foolish thing if we insist on it.

Now you still might be thinking, "How does that answer the question?" The question was "How could the sick being healed and the wilderness blooming and all that be considered *vengeance?*" Because of Jesus' purpose in coming to earth:

> I John 3:8b: For this purpose the Son of God was manifested, **that he might destroy the works of the devil.**

And when the sick are healed, and streams flow in the desert, and the wilderness blooms, and the captives are freed, He is destroying the works of the devil. And even though this chapter is primarily about Old Testament Scriptures, here is an example where Jesus fulfilled what Isaiah prophesied about above:

> Matthew 14:10–14 (NIV): and [**Herod**] **had John beheaded** in the prison. ¹¹His head was brought in on a platter and given to the girl, who carried it to her mother. ¹²John's disciples came and took his body and buried it. Then they went and told Jesus. ¹³**When Jesus heard what had happened, he withdrew by boat** privately to a solitary place. Hearing of this, the crowds followed him on foot from the towns. ¹⁴**When Jesus landed and saw a large crowd, he had compassion on them and healed their sick.**

Note the sequence of events here: 1) John—Jesus' cousin, friend, and partner in ministry—was beheaded by Herod, 2) Jesus goes out in the desert and crowds of people follow Him, and 3) He heals them. Note how, and upon whom, Jesus took vengeance. Not on Herod; he was just a clueless puppet in the hands of the devil. On the contrary, Jesus took vengeance on Satan himself by destroying his works (of sickness, disease, injury, and so forth) in the people He came to save.

So now it's easier to understand Mike Bickle's statement: "God's judgments are directed only at those things that interfere with His love."

Wounded for Our Transgressions

Isaiah 53 is a well known Messianic passage that foreshadows Jesus' crucifixion and resulting atonement. One verse in it states:

> Isaiah 53:4–5: Surely he hath borne our griefs, and carried our sorrows: yet we did esteem him stricken, smitten of God, and afflicted. ⁵But he was wounded for our transgressions, he was bruised for our iniquities: the chastisement of our peace was upon him; and **with his stripes we are healed.**

Now there is some discussion as to the meaning of the final phrase "with his stripes we are healed." The "stripes" here refer the whip-marks on Jesus' back; the long bloody trails left behind by the cat-o'-nine-tails as He was scourged; that is not debated. What *is* debated is the meaning of the word "healed." Does it actually mean physically healed? Or does it mean "healed from our sinfulness;" that is, forgiven? Many people say it does mean forgiven, and it is confirmed twice, earlier in that same verse when it mentions our "transgressions" and "iniquities." But I don't think so.

Now be assured that I'm not saying that Jesus' crucifixion did *not* take care of our sins; it most certainly did. I'm just saying that that *particular* phrase—the final one in v. 5—is indeed referring to physical healing, and not forgiveness of sins. Here is my reasoning.

You may have seen in Book 2 of the "Thoughts On" series, *Is It Possible to Stop Sinning?* (available from the sources noted on BibleAuthor.DaveArns.com) that I demonstrated that we can much more reliably understand what the Bible authors meant by certain words *if other Bible authors define those words*, as opposed to us defining the words millennia later, and typically very unfamiliar with the culture and the language in which the statements were made. In Book 2, the words whose meanings became much more accurately understood by using this method were the words "repent" and "grace." Here, we'll look at some of the words in the Isaiah passage quoted above.

In Isaiah 53:4, it says that Jesus has "borne our griefs." "Griefs" in this instance comes from the Hebrew word חֳלִי (*choliy*, H2483), whose definitions include "malady," "anxiety," and "calamity" as well as "disease," "grief," and "sickness." Because the definitions include "anxiety" and "grief," it's understandable that people unfamiliar or uncomfortable with supernatural physical healing gravitate toward those definitions; indeed, those *are* valid definitions.

Similarly, Isaiah 53:4 says that Jesus "carried our sorrows." "Sorrows" in this instance came from the Hebrew word מַכְאוֹב (*mak'ob*, H4341), whose definitions include "anguish," "grief," and "sorrow." But its definitions also include "affliction" and "pain." Again, based on your doctrinal persuasions, you might gravitate toward the emotional comfort (which I am *not* belittling in any way), or you might gravitate toward supernatural, miraculous physical healing.

The problem with trying to decide such a question is that we are millennia after the fact, and the average American Christian (which is the primary audience expected for this book) is rather unfamiliar with the linguistic nuances of the Hebrew language and the subtleties of the culture from all those millennia ago. Fortunately, we don't have to make assumptions about the meaning intended here, because the Bible itself clarifies what is meant.

In Matthew 8, after Jesus had finished the Sermon on the Mount, He came down from the mountain and He healed a leper (vv. 2–3). Then He healed the Centurion's paralyzed servant (vv. 5–13). Then He healed Peter's mother-in-law of the fever (vv. 14–15). Then He healed *crowds* of people:

> Matthew 8:16 (TEV): When evening came, people brought to Jesus many who had demons in them. **Jesus drove out the evil spirits with a word and healed *all* who were sick.**
>
> Mark 1:32–34 (TEV): After the sun had set and evening had come, people brought to Jesus all the sick and those who had demons. ³³**All the people of the town gathered** in front of the house. ³⁴**Jesus healed many who were sick with *all* kinds of diseases and drove out many demons.** He would not let the demons say anything, because they knew who he was.
>
> Luke 4:40–41 (TEV): After sunset all who had friends who were sick with various diseases brought them to Jesus; **he placed his hands on every one of them and healed them *all*.** ⁴¹Demons also went out from many people, screaming, "You are the Son of God!" Jesus gave the demons an order and would not let them speak, because they knew he was the Messiah.

So the same story is told by all three of the synoptic Gospels, and what can we see? Basically, the *everybody in town* showed up (Mark 1:33), and Jesus healed *everyone* who was sick (Matthew 8:16, Luke 4:40). So what does this have to do with the correct interpretation of Isaiah 53:4–5? Just this: Matthew says that the reason Jesus healed all these people *is to fulfill the Isaiah Scripture* we are discussing. The very next verse in Matthew's account says:

> Matthew 8:17 That it might be fulfilled which was spoken by Esaias the prophet, saying, Himself **took our infirmities,** and **bare our sicknesses.**

AMP: And thus He fulfilled what was spoken by the prophet Isaiah, He Himself took [in order to carry away] our **weaknesses and infirmities** and bore away our **diseases.**

CEB: This happened so that what Isaiah the prophet said would be fulfilled: He is the one who took our **illnesses and carried away our diseases.**

CEV: So God's promise came true, just as the prophet Isaiah had said, "He **healed our diseases** and **made us well.**"

GNT: He did this to make come true what the prophet Isaiah had said, "He himself **took our sickness** and carried away our diseases."

NIRV: He did it to make what the prophet Isaiah had said come true. He had said, "He suffered the things we should have suffered. He **took on himself the sicknesses that should have been ours.**"

NIV: This was to fulfill what was spoken through the prophet Isaiah: "He took up our **infirmities** and carried our **diseases.**"

TEV: He did this to make come true what the prophet Isaiah had said, "He himself **took our sickness** and **carried away our diseases.**"

WE: What the prophet Isaiah said came true. He said, 'He took away the things that made us weak. He **took away the things that made us sick.**'

It could hardly be more clear: the question of how to interpret those words in Isaiah becomes clear when the Holy Spirit writes through Matthew. (By the way, the name "Esaias" is the Greek form of the Hebrew name "Isaiah.") Isaiah's Messianic prophecy describing the atoning work of Christ on the cross *includes physical healing* because Matthew says it does.

One more (massively important) detail. We've seen that Matthew says that Jesus healed people to fulfill the Messianic prophecy in Isaiah, as we just mentioned above. But did you notice *how many* people He healed in order to fulfill the prophecy?

Matthew 8:16 (TEV): When evening came, people brought to Jesus many who had demons in them. Jesus drove out the evil spirits with a word and healed **all** who were sick.

> Luke 4:40 (TEV): After sunset all who had friends who were sick with various diseases brought them to Jesus; he placed his hands on every one of them and healed them **all**.

This is seriously good news: Jesus healed *all* who were sick, *so that* Isaiah's prophecy would be fulfilled; read again the various translations of Matthew 8:17, above. And is His Messiah-ship less effective nowadays than it was back then? Of course not. So what does that compel us to conclude?

By His Stripes We Are What?

Another nugget in this Isaiah Scripture, which reinforces Matthew's interpretation of it, is found in the word "healed," where it says, "with his stripes we are healed." It's interesting to note that the Hebrew word for "healed" is רָפָא (*rapha'*, H7495) and its definition is "to mend, to cure, cause to heal, repair, make whole."

Now of course, you can be spiritually and/or emotionally mended, cured, healed and repaired. People who have trouble believing in supernatural physical healing typically don't have a problem accepting that. But the next phrase—that pesky "made whole"—is problematic. Why? Because, as my wife so astutely observed decades ago, "You can't be whole with pieces missing." In other words, physical healing *must* be included, because if we leave it out, the phrase "make whole" would not be satisfied. Leaving out physical healing, even if other things are healed, does not result in wholeness, *because we left something out.* Therefore, physical healing *must* be included, or else the statement that "with His stripes we are healed" would be false, because we wouldn't have been made whole. Being "partially whole" is a self-contradiction.

And if that weren't enough, students of the Bible will recognize that the word *rapha'* is part of "Jehovah Rapha," one of the Jehovah Names with which God makes known to us His essence, His nature, His eternal identity. Here is that passage:

> Exodus 15:26: . . .I will put none of these diseases upon thee, which I have brought upon the Egyptians: for *I am the LORD that healeth thee.*

The word for "healed" that God uses in Isaiah, where He says, "with his stripes we are *healed*," is the *same word* He used in Exodus 15:26, where God identifies Himself as "Jehovah Rapha," which is translated "the LORD Who heals you." See the Jehovah Names section below for more detail on God's self-disclosing Names.

How Reliable Is It?

Let's look at the Isaiah 53 passage once again; there are still *more* riches in it:

> Isaiah 53:4–5: **Surely** he hath borne our griefs, and carried our sorrows: yet we did esteem him stricken, smitten of God, and afflicted. ⁵But he was wounded for our transgressions, he was bruised for our iniquities: the chastisement of our peace was upon him; and with his stripes we are healed.

How likely was it that Jesus would provide the forgiveness and healing in His atoning death on the cross? Notice how various translations render how the Holy Spirit inspired Isaiah to write it:

> AMP: **Surely** He has borne our griefs (sicknesses, weaknesses, and distresses)...
>
> CEB: It was **certainly** our sickness that he carried...
>
> CJB: **In fact**, it was our diseases he bore...
>
> DOUAY: **Surely** he hath borne our infirmities...
>
> ERV: **The fact is,** it was our suffering he took on himself...
>
> MSG: But **the fact is**, it was our pains he carried...
>
> NLV: **For sure** He took on Himself our troubles...
>
> NOG: He **certainly** has taken upon himself our suffering...
>
> WYC: **Verily** he suffered our sicknesses... (**Truly** he suffered our sicknesses...)

So we see that it is not merely "hopefully," "likely," or "probably" that He carried away our sins and our sicknesses, but "the fact is" Jesus "surely," "certainly," "in fact," "for sure," "verily" and "truly" took them. Praise be to God!

God's Preferred Fast

In Isaiah 58, God bluntly states that hypocrisy—an outward religious "show" without a corresponding humility of heart—is disgusting to Him, and He exhorts the children of Israel to basically do what He later summarizes in "Love God above all and love your neighbor as yourself" (Matthew 22:37–39):

> Isaiah 58:6–11 (NIV): Is not this the kind of fasting I have chosen: to loose the chains of injustice and untie the cords of the yoke, to set the oppressed free and break every yoke? ⁷Is it not to share your food with the hungry and to provide the poor wanderer with shelter—when you see the naked, to clothe him, and not to turn away from your own flesh and blood? ⁸Then your light will break forth like the dawn, and **your healing will quickly appear;** then your righteousness will go before you, and the glory of the LORD will be your rear guard. ⁹Then you will call, and the LORD will answer; you will cry for help, and he will say: Here am I. If you do away with the yoke of oppression, with the pointing finger and malicious talk, ¹⁰and if you spend yourselves in behalf of the hungry and satisfy the needs of the oppressed, then your light will rise in the darkness, and your night will become like the noonday. ¹¹The LORD will guide you always; he will satisfy your needs in a sun-scorched land and will strengthen your frame. You will be like a well-watered garden, like a spring whose waters never fail.

The section before this is the one where God says that doing actions—even "good" actions—without the appropriate heart attitude is disgusting. Then in the passage shown above, He says what He *does* desire. It may include all the same actions and behavior, but when it is done with God-directed motives, all sorts of cool things result, one of which is physical healing.

One more thing: After reading the promises of God, Who cannot lie (Titus 1:2)—all those promises in the Law, the Psalms, the Proverbs, and the Prophets—we need to understand this:

> Hebrews 8:6: But now hath he [Jesus] obtained a more excellent ministry, by how much also he is the mediator of **a better covenant, which was established upon better promises.**

If all those promises for healing were contained in the old covenant (the Old Testament), and Jesus obtained for us a *better* covenant (the New Testament), which was established on better promises, *of course* the New Testament would contain healing. Since it's better, it would have to contain everything good that the old covenant did, and then some. This will be shown in numerous examples in the next chapter, which shows what Jesus did.

It should be clear by now, after reading all the above Scriptures, that God's heart, His intent, His will includes physical healing. It is certainly not *limited* to physical healing, but equally certainly His will does *include* it.

The "Jehovah" Names

God ascribes various attributes or descriptors to Himself in many places in the Bible, and of course everywhere He does so, His statement is absolutely true. But there's one collection of attributes that seem to me to be, if it were possible, even *more* true: these are the "Jehovah Names" of God. Whereas a descriptor specifies an attribute, or something that is true *about* Him, these Jehovah Names, because they are used as part of His Name, describe His very *essence,* His eternal *identity,* His intrinsic *nature.*

Here are the Jehovah Names of God. In English Bibles, some of these are left as Hebrew (e.g., "Jehovahnissi"), while some others are translated into English, but all of them are Jehovah Names when looking at the original Hebrew.

- **Jehovah Elohim** (The Lord God; i.e., the Lord of Lords (Genesis 2:4): "These are the generations of the heavens and of the earth when they were created, in the day that the Lord God made the earth and the heavens."
- **Jehovah Jireh** (The Lord Will Provide, Genesis 22:14): "And Abraham called the name of that place *Jehovahjireh:* as it is said to this day, In the mount of the Lord it shall be seen."
- **Jehovah Rapha** (The Lord That Heals, Exodus 15:26): "And [Moses, quoting God] said, If thou wilt diligently hearken to

the voice of the LORD thy God, and wilt do that which is right in his sight, and wilt give ear to his commandments, and keep all his statutes, I will put none of these diseases upon thee, which I have brought upon the Egyptians: for *I am the LORD that healeth thee.*"

- **Jehovah Nissi** (The LORD My Banner, Exodus 17:15): "And Moses built an altar, and called the name of it *Jehovahnissi. . .*"
- **Jehovah Mekoddishkem** (The LORD Who Sanctifies You, Exodus 31:13): "Speak thou also unto the children of Israel, saying, Verily my sabbaths ye shall keep: for it is a sign between me and you throughout your generations; that ye may know that *I am the LORD that doth sanctify you.*"
- **Jehovah Shalom** (The LORD Is Peace, Judges 6:24): "Then Gideon built an altar there unto the LORD, and called it *Jehovahshalom:* unto this day it is yet in Ophrah of the Abiezrites."
- **Jehovah Sabaoth** (The LORD of Hosts, I Samuel 1:3): "And this man went up out of his city yearly to worship and to sacrifice unto *the LORD of hosts* in Shiloh. And the two sons of Eli, Hophni and Phinehas, the priests of the LORD, were there."
- **Jehovah Raah** (The LORD My Shepherd, Psalm 23:1): "*The LORD is my shepherd;* I shall not want."
- **Jehovah Tsidkenu** (The LORD Our Righteousness, Jeremiah 23:6): "In his days Judah shall be saved, and Israel shall dwell safely: and this is his name whereby he shall be called, *The LORD our Righteousness.*"
- **Jehovah Shammah** (The LORD Is There, Ezekiel 48:35): "It was round about eighteen thousand measures: and the name of the city from that day shall be, *The LORD is there.*"

These ten compound Jehovah-names of God describe very important attributes of His very nature, His essence. And, of course, it is pretty well established to any Bible-believing Christian that God does not change:

> Psalm 102:25–27 (NIV): In the beginning you laid the foundations of the earth, and the heavens are the work of your hands. ²⁶They will perish, **but you remain;** they will all wear out like a garment. Like clothing

you will change them and they will be discarded. ²⁷**But you remain the same, and your years will never end.**

Malachi 3:6: For I am the LORD, **I change not;** therefore ye sons of Jacob are not consumed.

Hebrews 1:10–12 (AMP): And [further], You, Lord, did lay the foundation of the earth in the beginning, and the heavens are the works of Your hands. ¹¹They will perish, but **You remain and continue permanently;** they will all grow old and wear out like a garment. ¹²Like a mantle [thrown about one's self] You will roll them up, and they will be changed and replaced by others. But **You remain the same, and Your years will never end nor come to failure.**

Hebrews 13:8: Jesus Christ **the same yesterday, and to day, and for ever.**

James 1:17: Every good gift and every perfect gift is from above, and cometh down from the Father of lights, with whom is **no variableness,** neither shadow of turning.

So the attributes of God, *especially* those noted in the Jehovah Names, are unchangeable. And here's my point: in Exodus 15:26 (which we partially addressed earlier) God describes His very nature, His essence, as "the God that heals you." *That is His Name,* and it doesn't change, based on our faith level, whether so-and-so has sinned recently, whether nothing apparently happened when we prayed for someone, or anything like that. Or anything *at all.*

How Fares Your Soul?

The Apostle John makes a statement in III John that is a source of inspiration, comfort, and faith to many:

III John 2: Beloved, I wish above all things that thou mayest prosper and **be in health,** even as thy soul prospereth.

AMP: Beloved, I pray that you may prosper in every way and [**that your body**] **may keep well,** even as [I know] your soul keeps well and prospers.

CEB: Dear friend, I'm praying that all is well with you and that **you enjoy good health** in the same way that you prosper spiritually.

CEV: . . .dear friend, and I pray that all goes well for you. I hope that you are **as strong in body, as I know you are in spirit.**

EXB: My dear friend [Beloved], I pray that you are doing well [prospering] in every way [all respects] and **that your health is good,** just as your soul is doing fine [it is well with your soul; your soul is prospering].

GWORD: Dear friend, I know that you are spiritually well. I pray that you're doing well in every other way **and that you're healthy.**

LEB: Dear friend, I pray you may prosper concerning everything and **be healthy,** just as your soul prospers.

NLT: Dear friend, I hope all is well with you and that you are **as healthy in body as you are strong in spirit.**

Since all Scripture is God-breathed, as shown above, we know that this sentiment is not just from John, but is from God.

Chapter 4:

Jesus' Examples

There are two things that we must acknowledge before Jesus' example of ministry to the sick becomes personally convicting. First, we must realize that Jesus represented God's will *perfectly* during His entire earthly ministry:

> Hebrews 1:2–3a: [God] Hath in these last days spoken unto us by his Son, whom he hath appointed heir of all things, by whom also he made the worlds; ³Who being the brightness of his glory, and **the express image of his person**, and upholding all things by the word of his power, when he had by himself purged our sins, sat down on the right hand of the Majesty on high. . .
>
> v. 3a, ASV: . . .who being the effulgence of his glory, and **the very image of his substance**. . .
>
> AMP: He is the sole expression of the glory of God [the Light-being, the out-raying or radiance of the divine], and **He is the perfect imprint and very image of [God's] nature**. . .
>
> CEV: God's Son has all the brightness of God's own glory and **is like him in every way.**

ERV: The Son shows the glory of God. **He is a perfect copy of God's nature.** . .

ESV: He is the radiance of the glory of God and **the exact imprint of his nature.** . .

EXB: The Son reflects [or radiates; shines forth] the glory of God and **shows exactly what God is like [is the exact representation/imprint/stamp of his being/essence/nature].**

GWORD: His Son is the reflection of God's glory and **the exact likeness of God's being.**

HCSB: The Son is the radiance of God's glory and **the exact expression of His nature.** . .

PHILLIPS: This Son, radiance of the glory of God, **flawless expression of the nature of God.** . .

MSG: **This Son perfectly mirrors God,** and is stamped with God's nature.

NCV: The Son reflects the glory of God and **shows exactly what God is like.**

NIV: The Son is the radiance of God's glory and **the exact representation of his being.** . .

NLV: The Son shines with the shining-greatness of the Father. **The Son is as God is in every way.**

NLT: The Son radiates God's own glory and **expresses the very character of God.** . .

WE: He shines as bright as God. **He is just like God himself.**

And the second thing is this:

John 14:12: Verily, verily, I say unto you, He that believeth on me, **the works that I do shall he do also; and greater works than these shall he do;** because I go unto my Father.

AMP: I assure you, most solemnly I tell you, if anyone steadfastly believes in Me, **he will himself be able to do the things that I do; and he will do even greater things than these,** because I go to the Father.

CEV: I tell you for certain that if you have faith in me, **you will do the same things that I am doing. You will do even greater things**, now that I am going back to the Father.

ERV: I can assure you that whoever believes in me **will do the same things I have done. And they will do even greater things than I have done,** because I am going to the Father.

GNT: I am telling you the truth: those who believe in me **will do what I do—yes, they will do even greater things**, because I am going to the Father.

PHILLIPS: I assure you that the man who believes in me **will do the same things that I have done, yes, and he will do even greater things than these,** for I am going away to the Father.

TLB: In solemn truth I tell you, anyone believing in me **shall do the same miracles I have done, and even greater ones,** because I am going to be with the Father.

NET: I tell you the solemn truth, the person who believes in me **will perform the miraculous deeds that I am doing, and will perform greater deeds than these,** because I am going to the Father.

So from these two Scriptures, we can see first that Jesus is the *exact representation* of the Father, so we know that whatever Jesus did was God's will. Second, we know that we are supposed to do the same kinds of things Jesus did when He was on earth, and even bigger miracles than that. Wow.

So let's look at what Jesus did when He was on earth, in the area of physical healing.

Examples of Jesus Healing Individuals

First, let's look at examples of where Jesus healed individuals, or very small groups. Many times, Jesus healed a single person, and an important point is that *every single person who came to Jesus for healing got healed.* I have not found a single case where someone came to Jesus for healing and *didn't* get it. If you, the Reader, find one, please let me know.

The Royal Official's Son

The first healing that Jesus performed was a "tele-miracle"—a long-distance miracle—healing the son of a royal government official.

> John 4:46–54 (NIV): Once more he visited Cana in Galilee, where he had turned the water into wine. And there was a certain royal official whose son lay sick at Capernaum. ⁴⁷When this man heard that Jesus had arrived in Galilee from Judea, he went to him and begged him to come and heal his son, who was close to death. ⁴⁸"Unless you people see miraculous signs and wonders," Jesus told him, "you will never believe." ⁴⁹The royal official said, "Sir, come down before my child dies." ⁵⁰Jesus replied, "You may go. Your son will live." The man took Jesus at his word and departed. ⁵¹While he was still on the way, his servants met him with the news that his boy was living. ⁵²When he inquired as to the time when his son got better, they said to him, "The fever left him yesterday at the seventh hour." ⁵³Then the father realized that this was the exact time at which Jesus had said to him, "Your son will live." So he and all his household believed. ⁵⁴This was the second miraculous sign that Jesus performed, having come from Judea to Galilee.

Demoniac in the Synagogue

Once (at least) when Jesus was in church, a demon who had apparently been successfully hiding in the man for some time, manifested. When God's holiness gets too near to demons, it becomes intolerable to them, and they can't help but show themselves:

> Luke 4:33–36 (TEV): In the synagogue was a man who had the spirit of an evil demon in him; he screamed out in a loud voice, ³⁴"Ah! What do you want with us, Jesus of Nazareth? Are you here to destroy us? I

know who you are: you are God's holy messenger!" ³⁵Jesus ordered the spirit, "Be quiet and come out of the man!" The demon threw the man down in front of them and went out of him without doing him any harm. ³⁶The people were all amazed and said to one another, "What kind of words are these? With authority and power this man gives orders to the evil spirits, and they come out!"

A sad commentary on this is that there was apparently not enough holiness in the regular attenders and leaders of the synagogue to make the demon uncomfortable. Kinda makes you think: If a demonized person came to *my* church, would the demon be comfortable enough to successfully hide, or would there be enough of the presence of God in people to force him to show himself? Interesting thought.

Peter's Mother-in-Law

The fisherman-disciple Simon Peter was married, and his mother-in-law apparently lived with him and his wife. She came down with a fever, and. . .

> Luke 4:38–39: And he [Jesus] arose out of the synagogue, and entered into Simon's house. And Simon's wife's mother was taken with a great fever; and they besought him for her. ³⁹And he stood over her, and rebuked the fever; and it left her: and immediately she arose and ministered unto them.

An interesting point here is that Jesus addressed the *fever*, as if it were a personality. But there is no indicator here that the fever was directly caused by demonic attack. Modern healing ministries that teach people to "speak to the condition" got the idea from Jesus' example in this passage.

The Leper

A leper came to Jesus and asked to be healed. Jesus' response, both physically and verbally, was significant:

> Matthew 8:2–3 (NIV): A man with leprosy came and knelt before him and said, "Lord, if you are willing, you can make me clean." ³Jesus reached out his hand and touched the man. **"I am willing," he said. "Be clean!" Immediately he was cured of his leprosy.**

And this wasn't just a "mild" case of leprosy (if there is such a thing); look at how Luke, the physician, describes him. . .

> Luke 5:12–13: And it came to pass, when he was in a certain city, behold a man **full of leprosy**: who seeing Jesus fell on his face, and besought him, saying, Lord, if thou wilt, thou canst make me clean. ¹³And he put forth his hand, and touched him, saying, I will: be thou clean. And immediately the leprosy departed from him.

> NIV: While Jesus was in one of the towns, a man came along who was **covered with leprosy.** When he saw Jesus, he fell with his face to the ground and begged him, "Lord, if you are willing, you can make me clean." ¹³Jesus reached out his hand and touched the man. "I am willing," he said. "Be clean!" And immediately the leprosy left him.

Jesus' physical response was shocking because, back in Old Testament days, anyone who touched a leper was made unclean. In the Old Testament, the emphasis was on the seriousness of sin, and leprosy was a symbol for sin because it is so destructive. In the New Testament, which Jesus was introducing, the emphasis is on the power/love/grace of God overcoming sin. So where in the Old Testament, a clean person touching a leper would be defiled and made unclean, in the New Testament, a leper being touched by a person moving with the glory of God was healed, as in this case.

Jesus' verbal response to the leper is also earth-shaking for people who need physical healing, because, in case all the other Scriptural proofs above are insufficient, this one shows Jesus' will and, because He was the *exact representation* of the Father, it also shows God the Father's will as it pertains to physical healing. "I am willing," Jesus said. And earlier in this book, we showed that one of God's essential attributes was that He is a healer ("Jehovah Rapha") and that He doesn't change.

Would God Do the Same for Me?

Another very relevant and important point is that God is not a respecter of persons; that is, He doesn't play favorites—He doesn't show favoritism or partiality—it would be sinful to do so. Therefore, any promise that is given to one person is available to anyone else:

> II Chronicles 19:7 (NIV): Now let the fear of the LORD be upon you. Judge carefully, for **with the LORD our God there is no injustice or partiality** or bribery.
>
> Proverbs 28:21a (NIV): To show partiality is not good. . .
>
> Acts 10:34 (NIV): Then Peter began to speak: "I now realize how true it is that **God does not show favoritism. . .**"
>
> Romans 2:11 (NIV): For **God does not show favoritism.**
>
> Ephesians 6:9 (NIV): And masters, treat your slaves in the same way. Do not threaten them, since you know that he who is both their Master and yours is in heaven, and **there is no favoritism with him.**
>
> James 2:9 (NIV): But **if you show favoritism, you sin** and are convicted by the law as lawbreakers.

Keep that fact in mind as you read the rest of this book. Every promise in the Book is yours!

The Paralytic with Four Good Friends

This paralytic had some really good friends. They brought him to Jesus to be healed, and because he was paralyzed, they had to carry him. Then, when they got to the place where Jesus was, the crowd was so thick, they couldn't even get inside the house to ask Jesus to heal their friend. So they used their imagination and. . .

> Luke 5:17–26 (NIV): One day as he was teaching, Pharisees and teachers of the law, who had come from every village of Galilee and from Judea and Jerusalem, were sitting there. And the power of the Lord was present for him to heal the sick. [18]Some men came carrying a paralytic on

a mat and tried to take him into the house to lay him before Jesus. ¹⁹When they could not find a way to do this because of the crowd, **they went up on the roof and lowered him on his mat through the tiles into the middle of the crowd,** right in front of Jesus. ²⁰When Jesus saw **their faith,** he said, "Friend, your sins are forgiven." ²¹The Pharisees and the teachers of the law began thinking to themselves, "Who is this fellow who speaks blasphemy? Who can forgive sins but God alone?" ²²Jesus knew what they were thinking and asked, "Why are you thinking these things in your hearts? ²³Which is easier: to say, 'Your sins are forgiven,' or to say, 'Get up and walk'? ²⁴But that you may know that the Son of Man has authority on earth to forgive sins. . ." He said to the paralyzed man, "I tell you, get up, take your mat and go home." ²⁵Immediately he stood up in front of them, took what he had been lying on and went home praising God. ²⁶Everyone was amazed and gave praise to God. They were filled with awe and said, "We have seen remarkable things today."

Interesting side note: Jesus responded when He saw *their* faith—the paralytic's *friends'* faith. The ambient level of faith, or the amount of faith in the people around, is important, and it can help, as in this case, or hinder, as when Jesus went back to Nazareth, His home town:

> Mark 6:5–6a (NIV): **He could not do any miracles there**, except lay his hands on a few sick people and heal them. ⁶And he was amazed at their lack of faith. . .

This is astonishing: Because of the *people's* unbelief, even Jesus was unable to do any miracles! Except heal a few sick people. But that, in itself, is still encouraging: even when there was rampant unbelief, to the point where He couldn't do any big miracles, *Jesus still healed people!*

The Lame Man at the Pool of Bethesda

The story of Jesus healing the lame man at the pool of Bethesda has been used by some to support their contention that sometimes it's not God's will to heal people:

> John 5:2–9: Now there is at Jerusalem by the sheep market a pool, which is called in the Hebrew tongue Bethesda, having five porches. ³In these lay a great multitude of impotent folk, of blind, halt, withered, waiting for the moving of the water. ⁴For an angel went down at a certain season into the pool, and troubled the water: whosoever then first after the troubling of the water stepped in was made whole of whatsoever disease he had. ⁵And a certain man was there, which had an infirmity thirty and eight years. ⁶When Jesus saw him lie, and knew that he had been now a long time in that case, he saith unto him, **Wilt thou be made whole?** ⁷The impotent man answered him, Sir, I have no man, when the water is troubled, to put me into the pool: but while I am coming, another steppeth down before me. ⁸Jesus saith unto him, **Rise, take up thy bed, and walk.** ⁹And **immediately the man was made whole,** and took up his bed, and walked: and on the same day was the sabbath.

According to the theory mentioned above, this story indicates that God doesn't always want to heal everyone, and the justification is that there is no indication that God/Jesus healed anyone except the one man who had been lame for 38 years. Is this valid logic? Actually, no. It's true that the Bible doesn't say God/Jesus healed anyone except the one, but neither does it say He *didn't*. So we actually don't know if the other people were healed, and the reasoning is that the Bible doesn't say, *either* way.

To say that God *didn't* heal everybody at the Pool of Bethesda, simply because the text talks only about one man who was healed, is like concluding that, since John was the only one called the "Beloved Apostle," that Jesus didn't love all the rest of them. That's obviously a silly conclusion, arising from flawed logic. Note that I'm not saying Jesus *did* heal anyone else at the Pool of Bethesda that day; again, *the Bible doesn't say either way.*

But even if he didn't heal everyone there, it doesn't prove that it wasn't His will. For example, does God want everyone to be saved from dying in their sin? Of course; there are numerous Scriptures saying that. Here is just one:

> I Timothy 2:1–4 (NIV): I urge, then, first of all, that requests, prayers, intercession and thanksgiving be made for everyone— ²for kings and all those in authority, that we may live peaceful and quiet lives in all godliness and holiness. ³This is good, and pleases **God our Savior, ⁴who wants all men to be saved and to come to a knowledge of the truth.**

So we know that God wants everyone to be saved. But does everyone get saved? No. Why? Because there are other factors involved: Our faith, other people's faith, whether intercessors are obedient to pray, rebellion, fear, and a host of other things could affect the outcome. And some people actually don't *want* to be healed; their whole identity is wrapped up in their affliction, and they wouldn't know what to do with themselves if they didn't have their affliction. That's why Jesus asked the man:

> John 6:5c: . . .he saith unto him, **Wilt thou be made whole?**
>> AMP: He said to him, **Do you want to become well? [Are you really in earnest about getting well?]**
>> CJB: Yeshua . . . said to him, **"Do you want to be healed?"**
>> ERV: So he asked him, **"Do you want to be well?"**
>> GWORD: So Jesus asked the man, **"Would you like to get well?"**
>> PHILLIPS: . . .he said to him, **"Do you want to get well again?"**
>> NABRE: . . .he said to him, **"Do you want to be well?"**
>> NLV: Jesus said to him, **"Would you like to be healed?"**

Instead of asking "Did Jesus heal everyone at the Pool of Bethesda?", a more important and relevant question might be, "Did Jesus ever deny healing to anyone who *asked Him* for healing?" I haven't found anywhere in the Bible where that happened, and I've been studying the Bible for some time now. . .

The Man with the Withered Hand

The hypocrisy of the Pharisees in this passage is amazing; read it out of all three synoptic Gospels:

Matthew 12:9–15 (NIV): Going on from that place, he went into their synagogue, ¹⁰and a man with a shriveled hand was there. Looking for a reason to accuse Jesus, they asked him, "Is it lawful to heal on the Sabbath?" ¹¹He said to them, "If any of you has a sheep and it falls into a pit on the Sabbath, will you not take hold of it and lift it out? ¹²How much more valuable is a man than a sheep! Therefore it is lawful to do good on the Sabbath." ¹³Then he said to the man, "Stretch out your hand." **So he stretched it out and it was completely restored, just as sound as the other.** ¹⁴But the Pharisees went out and plotted how they might kill Jesus. ¹⁵Aware of this, Jesus withdrew from that place. Many followed him, and he healed all their sick. . .

Mark 3:1–6 (NIV): Another time he went into the synagogue, and a man with a shriveled hand was there. ²Some of them were looking for a reason to accuse Jesus, so they watched him closely to see if he would heal him on the Sabbath. ³Jesus said to the man with the shriveled hand, "Stand up in front of everyone." ⁴Then Jesus asked them, "Which is lawful on the Sabbath: to do good or to do evil, to save life or to kill?" But they remained silent. ⁵He looked around at them in anger and, deeply distressed at their stubborn hearts, said to the man, "Stretch out your hand." **He stretched it out, and his hand was completely restored.** ⁶Then the Pharisees went out and began to plot with the Herodians how they might kill Jesus.

Luke 6:6–11 (NIV): On another Sabbath he went into the synagogue and was teaching, and a man was there whose right hand was shriveled. ⁷The Pharisees and the teachers of the law were looking for a reason to accuse Jesus, so they watched him closely to see if he would heal on the Sabbath. ⁸But Jesus knew what they were thinking and said to the man with the shriveled hand, **"Get up and stand in front of everyone."** So he got up and stood there. ⁹Then Jesus said to them, **"I ask you, which is lawful on the Sabbath: to do good or to do evil, to save life or to destroy it?"** ¹⁰He looked around at them all, and then said to the man, **"Stretch out your hand."** He did so, and **his hand was completely restored.** ¹¹But they were furious and began to discuss with one another what they might do to Jesus.

No wonder Jesus was angry (Mark 3:5): if the Pharisees actually cared about the guy with the withered hand, they'd undoubtedly had years during which they could have sought God and interceded for his healing. Or at the very least, they could have rejoiced with him when he *did* get healed...

The Centurion's Servant

Lest we think all Roman soldiers were bad guys, look at this story:

> Matthew 8:5–13 (NIV): When Jesus had entered Capernaum, a centurion came to him, asking for help. ⁶"Lord," he said, "my servant lies at home paralyzed and in terrible suffering." ⁷Jesus said to him, **"I will go and heal him."** ⁸The centurion replied, "Lord, I do not deserve to have you come under my roof. But just say the word, and my servant will be healed. ⁹For I myself am a man under authority, with soldiers under me. I tell this one, 'Go,' and he goes; and that one, 'Come,' and he comes. I say to my servant, 'Do this,' and he does it." ¹⁰When Jesus heard this, he was astonished and said to those following him, "I tell you the truth, I have not found anyone in Israel with such great faith." ¹³Then Jesus said to the centurion, "Go! It will be done just as you believed it would." **And his servant was healed at that very hour.**

This is quite a story, and not just because Jesus healed yet another person. This Roman centurion "astonished" Jesus with his faith (v. 10). The word "astonished" in the NIV or "marvelled" in the KJV comes from the Greek word θαυμάζω (*thaumazo*, G2296), and it means to wonder, admire, or marvel. Other translations render the word as Jesus being "impressed," "amazed," "surprised," "wondered," "stunned." It's staggering to think that a person's level of faith could "amaze" or "impress" God, but there it is. The level of faith in this centurion is something we should all strive for.

But there's something else in what the centurion said, that often escapes people when they read this story. I know it escaped me for decades. I read the centurion's statement as "I too am a man *in* authority... I tell this one 'Go,' and he goes..." But that's not what the centurion said. He actually said, "I too am a man *under* authority... I tell this one 'Go,' and he goes..."

The centurion knew that since he was *under* authority, he was acting under orders when he gave a command, and any subordinate who questioned his authority would have to go talk to *his* boss, which would be much less comfortable than talking to the centurion himself. And because of his understanding of the chain of command, the centurion understood that Jesus too was a man *under* authority, and therefore was acting under orders from His superior officer, God Himself. And no sickness, disease, or demon in hell could prevail against *that* kind of authority. Hence, he was absolutely confident when he told Jesus, "Just say the word, and my servant will be healed."

The Son of the Widow of Nain

In the following story, as in so many others, Jesus was moved with compassion. And in doing so, Jesus, the "exact representation" of the Father, revealed that the Father too has compassion on us. He rejoices with us when we rejoice, He weeps with us when we weep. But it goes farther than just "I feel sorry for you" or "I feel sorry with you." He is more willing than we realize to actually meet our needs:

> Luke 7:11–16: And it came to pass the day after, that he went into a city called Nain; and many of his disciples went with him, and much people. ¹²Now when he came nigh to the gate of the city, behold, **there was a dead man carried out**, the only son of his mother, and she was a widow: and much people of the city was with her. ¹³And when the Lord saw her, he had compassion on her, and said unto her, Weep not. ¹⁴And he came and touched the bier: and they that bare him stood still. And he said, Young man, I say unto thee, Arise. ¹⁵**And he that was dead sat up, and began to speak.** And he delivered him to his mother. ¹⁶And there came a fear on all: and they glorified God, saying, That a great prophet is risen up among us; and, That God hath visited his people.

When Jesus raised this man from the dead, everybody was amazed. Why are we amazed? God built our bodies in the first place; He can certainly repair them. What does it reveal about the state of our faith that we are so amazed when God raises someone from the dead? Jesus said we're *all* supposed to be doing that (John 14:12). This Scripture also shows that no sickness is beyond healing; not even fatal ones, and not even fatal ones that have already been fatal.

The Mute Demoniacs

What causes sickness and disease? Indirectly at least, Satan and his demons do, because of the fall of man, when Adam transferred his allegiance from God to the serpent, giving the enemy authority to beat us up. But some afflictions are caused *directly* by demonic forces, as in the following Scripture:

> Matthew 9:32–34 (TEV): As the men were leaving, some people brought to Jesus **a man who could not talk because he had a demon.** ³³But **as soon as the demon was driven out, the man started talking,** and everyone was amazed. "We have never seen anything like this in Israel!" they exclaimed. ³⁴But the Pharisees said, "It is the chief of the demons who gives Jesus the power to drive out demons."

So this guy was dumb—unable to speak—as a direct result of the demon. When Jesus cast out the demon, the hindrance went away, and he was able to speak once again. And the Pharisees, caring only that their power and popularity was being threatened by this One Who loved people and did something about it, immediately accused Jesus of casting out the demon by Satanic power, rather than by the power of God.

Later, in a separate incident, another demonized man, who was both dumb *and* blind, was brought to Jesus:

> Matthew 12:22 (TEV): Then some people brought to Jesus a man who was blind and could not talk because he had a demon. **Jesus healed the man,** so that he was able to talk and see.

So this guy was both blind and dumb as a direct result of the demon. When Jesus cast out the demon, the hindrance went away, as in the earlier case, and he was able to see and speak once again. Even though this particular verse doesn't say that Jesus healed him *by casting out the demon,* we know that's what happened, because two verses later, the Pharisees are (again) accusing Jesus of casting out the demon by the power of Beelzebub, the prince of demons, rather than by the power of God.

This is an important point: Sometimes when a person has afflicting symptoms, no physical reason can be found—everything "ought to" work. These cases may simply be a demon harassing the person, hindering normal nerve function or some such, and when the demon is cast out, the blockage is gone, and the body automatically starts functioning normally again. Of course not *all* deafness is caused by demonic activity; it could be actual damage to the auditory organs. See Healing the Deaf Mute below, where Jesus healed a deaf person, where no mention of demonic activity is made.

So is it appropriate to consider it a "healing"—as opposed to a "deliverance"—when a demon is cast out? I think so, and Luke apparently did as well, when he described Jesus in the following way:

> Acts 10:37–38 (NIV): You know what has happened throughout Judea, beginning in Galilee after the baptism that John preached— [38]how God anointed Jesus of Nazareth with the Holy Spirit and power, and how he went around doing good and **healing all who were under the power of the devil,** because God was with him.

So when Jesus delivered people from the direct, immediate power of the devil, the Bible considers that to be a healing. Therefore, we should too.

The Gadarene Demoniacs

One time, Jesus went to the region called Gadara (or Gerasa) where, next to the Sea of Galilee, was a graveyard, and two demonized Gadarene (or Gerasene) men who lived (if you can call it that) there. Mark's and Luke's versions of the story concentrate on Jesus' interactions with only one of the men, but we know from Matthew's account of the story (8:28–34) that there were actually two there.

> Mark 5:1–17 (NIV): They went across the lake to the region of the Gerasenes. ²When Jesus got out of the boat, a man with an evil spirit came from the tombs to meet him. ³This man lived in the tombs, and no one could bind him any more, not even with a chain. ⁴For he had often been chained hand and foot, but he tore the chains apart and broke the irons on his feet. No one was strong enough to subdue him. ⁵Night and day among the tombs and in the hills he would cry out and cut himself with stones. ⁶When he saw Jesus from a distance, he ran and fell on his knees in front of him. ⁷He shouted at the top of his voice, "What do you want with me, Jesus, Son of the Most High God? Swear to God that you won't torture me!" ⁸For Jesus had said to him, "Come out of this man, you evil spirit!" ⁹Then Jesus asked him, "What is your name?" "My name is Legion," he replied, "for we are many." ¹⁰And he begged Jesus again and again not to send them out of the area. ¹¹A large herd of pigs was feeding on the nearby hillside. ¹²The demons begged Jesus, "Send us among the pigs; allow us to go into them." ¹³He gave them permission, and the evil spirits came out and went into the pigs. The herd, about two thousand in number, rushed down the steep bank into the lake and were drowned. ¹⁴Those tending the pigs ran off and reported this in the town and countryside, and the people went out to see what had happened. ¹⁵When they came to Jesus, they saw the man who had been possessed by the legion of demons, sitting there, dressed and in his right mind; and they were afraid. ¹⁶Those who had seen it told the people what had happened to the demon-possessed man—and told about the pigs as well. ¹⁷Then the people began to plead with Jesus to leave their region.

There are several fascinating things to be realized from reading this story:

1. This heavily demonized man apparently knew, deep in his heart, that Jesus was his only hope of salvation, because of his response when Jesus showed up. Look at v. 6:

   Mark 5:6 (NIV): When he saw Jesus from a distance, **he ran and fell on his knees in front of him.**

   ASV: And when he saw Jesus from afar, **he ran and worshipped him. . .**

   AMP: And when from a distance he saw Jesus, **he ran and fell on his knees before Him in homage. . .**

   DOUAY: And seeing Jesus afar off, **he ran and adored him.**

   ERV: While Jesus was still far away, the man saw him. **He ran to Jesus and bowed down before him.**

   JUB: But when he saw Jesus afar off, **he ran and worshipped him.**

   MSG: When he saw Jesus a long way off, **he ran and bowed in worship before him. . .**

   NABRE: Catching sight of Jesus from a distance, **he ran up and prostrated himself before him. . .**

   NIRV: When he saw Jesus a long way off, **he ran to him. He fell on his knees in front of him.**

   NLT: When Jesus was still some distance away, the man saw him, **ran to meet him, and bowed low before him.**

   WE: Jesus was still far from him, but when he saw Jesus **he ran to him. He kneeled down in front of Jesus and worshipped him.**

   So even all these demons inside this man couldn't keep him from worshipping Jesus. Hmm. What's *our* excuse?

2. It's clear that this guy had *lots* of demons, but how many is that? He said his name was "Legion, for we are many." So what is a legion? It is a group of soldiers in the Roman army, the number of which (depending on which reference you check) ranges between 3,000 and 6,000 men. Regardless of which number you use, it's impressive. Let's use 6,000 as the size of a legion, for ease of subsequent math. When Jesus cast out the demons, He

let them go into a herd of 2,000 pigs. Demons are not omnipresent, so they can only be in one location at a time, and therefore they can only demonize one entity at a time. So the D:P ratio (the ratio of demons to pigs) was 3:1—three demons in every pig! No wonder they went nuts.

3. When v. 13 above says Jesus "gave them permission" to go into the pigs, it's even more impressive to read that particular verse out of Matthew:

Matthew 8:32: And **he said unto them, Go.** And when they were come out, they went into the herd of swine. . .

Wow. Jesus *really* knew the authority He had been given: 6,000 demons cast out with a single word! That shows how effective deliverance ministries can be; we should pray and intercede for those in such ministries that they would be as effective as Jesus was (keeping John 14:12 in mind).

4. The reaction of the townspeople would be humorous if it weren't so tragic. This man has been demonized for a long time (Luke 8:27), has been living among the tombs (Mark 5:3), running around naked (Luke 8:27), howling all day and all night (Mark 5:5), cutting himself with sharp stones (Mark 5:5), unsubdueable even with chains (Mark 5:4), and threatening everyone trying to pass by (Matthew 8:28). And apparently this is acceptable with the townspeople. Then Jesus comes along and delivers him, and when the townspeople see him sitting, and clothed, and in his right mind, *then* they were afraid, and asked Jesus to leave.

We, with the advantage of hindsight, can look back on these poor dumb townspeople and cluck condescendingly at their spiritual cluelessness. How could they have missed the point when God did such an amazing miracle *right there?* But how often do we do the same thing? God moves in our midst in a way that we've never seen, or that we're uncomfortable with, and we all too often dismiss, ridicule, or resist the moving of God, just like these townspeople did. (For much more detail on this concept of ridiculing what you don't understand, see Book 3 of the "Thoughts On" series: *Extra-Biblical Truth: A Valid Concept?*, available from the sources noted on BibleAuthor.DaveArns.com.)

Jairus' Daughter Raised from the Dead

Not all the religious leaders were as antagonistic toward Jesus as some of them were: Jairus was a ruler of the synagogue, and he, like the Pharisee Nicodemus, knew that God was with Jesus. So when Jairus had a need, he sought out Jesus as the only one Who could meet his need:

> Luke 8:41–42, 49–56: And, behold, there came a man named Jairus, and he was a ruler of the synagogue: and he fell down at Jesus' feet, and besought him that he would come into his house: ⁴²For he had one only daughter, about twelve years of age, and she lay a dying. But as he went the people thronged him. . . . ⁴⁹While he yet spake, there cometh one from the ruler of the synagogue's house, saying to him, Thy daughter is dead; trouble not the Master. ⁵⁰But when Jesus heard it, he answered him, saying, Fear not: believe only, and she shall be made whole. ⁵¹And when he came into the house, he suffered no man to go in, save Peter, and James, and John, and the father and the mother of the maiden. ⁵²And all wept, and bewailed her: but he said, Weep not; she is not dead, but sleepeth. ⁵³And they laughed him to scorn, knowing that she was dead. ⁵⁴And he put them all out, and took her by the hand, and called, saying, Maid, arise. ⁵⁵And her spirit came again, and she arose straightway: and he commanded to give her meat. ⁵⁶And her parents were astonished: but he charged them that they should tell no man what was done.

Many of us, like the other people from Jairus' household, even if we believe in divine healing, are not quite ready to believe that God could raise someone from the dead (v. 49). And the mourners were even worse: when someone says something in faith, such as Jesus saying "Weep not; she is not dead, but sleepeth," such people laugh out loud at the foolishness of the idea. Why? Because they "knew" she was dead. When God says something that seems to contradict what we can see with our own eyes, or seems to contradict "common sense," we have a choice about what we are going to choose to believe. There are many cases in the Bible about "facts" that God changed; usually, because someone had audacity enough to believe Him.

The Woman with the Issue of Blood

When Jesus was on His way to raise Jairus' daughter from the dead, He was being mobbed the whole way, people constantly bustling and swarming about Him. It was during this very crowded scene that a woman with an issue of blood touched the hem of His robe, and was instantly healed.

> Mark 5:25–34 (TEV): There was a woman who had suffered terribly from severe bleeding for twelve years, [26]even though she had been treated by many doctors. She had spent all her money, but instead of getting better she got worse all the time. [27]She had heard about Jesus, so she came in the crowd behind him, [28]saying to herself, "If I just touch his clothes, I will get well." [29]She touched his cloak, and her bleeding stopped at once; and she had the feeling inside herself that she was healed of her trouble. [30]At once Jesus knew that power had gone out of him, so he turned around in the crowd and asked, "Who touched my clothes?" [31]His disciples answered, "You see how the people are crowding you; why do you ask who touched you?" [32]But Jesus kept looking around to see who had done it. [33]The woman realized what had happened to her, so she came, trembling with fear, knelt at his feet, and told him the whole truth. [34]Jesus said to her, "My daughter, your faith has made you well. Go in peace, and be healed of your trouble."

This "issue of blood" that this woman had is much more serious than most modern Americans are aware today. Basically, her period never stopped for twelve years. What are the implications of this?

- First, according to the law of Moses, a woman having her period is unclean, both for the five to seven days *of* her period, and an additional seven days *after* her period:

> Leviticus 15:19, 25, 27 (TEV): When a woman has her monthly period, **she remains unclean for seven days.** Anyone who touches her is unclean until evening. [25]If a woman has a flow of blood for several days outside her monthly period or if her flow continues beyond her regular period, **she remains unclean as long as the flow continues,** just as she is during her monthly period. [28]**After her flow stops, she must wait seven days,** and then she will be ritually clean.

- So basically, this woman was ceremonially unclean for *twelve solid years*. As such, anything and anyone she touched was defiled and made unclean, so she was, in effect, a prisoner in her own home. No one would want to be around her, for fear of being made unclean and therefore being forbidden to go into the synagogue or the Temple. So for this woman to be in a bustling crowd, was to be making everyone around her unclean as soon as they bumped into her or vice versa. No wonder she didn't want to admit it.

- Having your period for twelve solid years is much more accurately called "hemorrhaging." She had been to many doctors, spending all her money on them, but only grew worse (v. 26). She must have been in very poor health, fatigued and emaciated from loss of blood. Plus, all her money was gone; she was indeed at the end of her rope. Jesus was her only remaining hope for being healed.

- Like the leper that Jesus healed by touching him, the contrast between the Old Testament and the New Testament was brought into stark contrast in the story of the woman with the issue of blood. In the Old Testament, the touch of a woman who was bleeding—having her period—caused a clean person to become unclean. In the New Testament that Jesus was introducing, the touch of a clean person empowered by the Holy Spirit would make the unclean person clean.

The Two Blind Men

The two blind men in this story had spiritual understanding: they called Jesus "Son of David." The phrase "Son of David," can refer to the obvious meaning of "David's immediate male offspring," as in:

> Proverbs 1:1 (NIV): The proverbs of **Solomon son of David**, king of Israel. . .

But in addition to that, it can mean "geneological descendent of David," as in Matthew 1:20, when the angel of the Lord appeared to Joseph, Mary's husband:

Matthew 1:20: But while he thought on these things, behold, the angel of the Lord appeared unto him in a dream, saying, **Joseph, thou son of David,** fear not to take unto thee Mary thy wife: for that which is conceived in her is of the Holy Ghost.

But most importantly, the phrase "Son of David" meant "Christ" or "Messiah," both of which mean "Anointed One." It was that meaning that many people employed when calling Jesus the "Son of David." Many people were sons of David in the sense of geneological descendents, but only One person was the Son of David in the sense of Messiah, the Savior, the miracle-worker:

Matthew 1:1 (NIV): A record of the genealogy of Jesus Christ **the son of David,** the son of Abraham. . .

Matthew 9:27 (NIV): As Jesus went on from there, two blind men followed him, calling out, "Have mercy on us, **Son of David!**"

Matthew 12:23 (NIV): All the people were astonished and said, "Could this be **the Son of David?**"

Matthew 15:22 (NIV): A Canaanite woman from that vicinity came to him, crying out, "**Lord, Son of David,** have mercy on me! My daughter is suffering terribly from demon-possession."

Matthew 20:30–31 (NIV): Two blind men were sitting by the roadside, and when they heard that Jesus was going by, they shouted, "**Lord, Son of David,** have mercy on us!" ³¹The crowd rebuked them and told them to be quiet, but they shouted all the louder, "**Lord, Son of David,** have mercy on us!"

Matthew 21:9 (NIV): The crowds that went ahead of him and those that followed shouted, "**Hosanna to the Son of David!**" "Blessed is he who comes in the name of the Lord!" "Hosanna in the highest!"

Matthew 21:15 (NIV): But when the chief priests and the teachers of the law saw the wonderful things he did and the children shouting in the temple area, "**Hosanna to the Son of David,**" they were indignant.

Matthew 22:42 (NIV): "What do you think about **the Christ?** Whose son is he?" "**The son of David,**" they replied.

Mark 12:35 (NIV): While Jesus was teaching in the temple courts, he asked, "How is it that the teachers of the law say that **the Christ is the son of David?**"

And there are more. But back to the two blind men, they knew that Jesus was the promised Messiah, the Savior, the One Who could work miracles, and so:

> Matthew 9:27–30a (NIV): As Jesus went on from there, two blind men followed him, calling out, "Have mercy on us, Son of David!" [28]When he had gone indoors, the blind men came to him, and he asked them, "Do you believe that I am able to do this?" "Yes, Lord," they replied. [29]Then he touched their eyes and said, "According to your faith will it be done to you;" [30]and their sight was restored.

Our faith does indeed play a major role in whether or not we get healed, as it was for these two blind men, as well in the healing of the woman with the issue of blood, the raising of Jairus' daughter from the dead, the healing of the centurion's servant, and others. Of course, our faith is not the *only* factor, but it is an important one. Therefore, when we need healing from God, that is *one* of the things we should address.

The Canaanite Woman's Daughter

This is a fascinating story because it shows the power of prayer and faith to actually move the hand of God in this way. The "this way" that I am talking about is to cause God to change His mind about the timing of something, based on the hunger and faith of someone. This happened several times in the Bible:

- **The Tabernacle of David.** David, the "man after God's own heart" (Acts 13:22) caught a glimpse of God's *real* goal in intimacy and fellowship, so even while technically under the Old Covenant, he set up the "Tabernacle of David." Even though the Tabernacle of Moses still existed, the ark hadn't been there since it was captured by the Philistines (I Samuel 4:10–11). Later, when David brought the ark back (II Samuel 6), he put it in a new tabernacle that he had set up (v. 17), and appointed worshippers to praise and worship God continually (I Chronicles 16:37). In David's Tabernacle, he did not include animal sacrifices, as the Law mandated, because he understood by God's Spirit that He didn't really want them (Psalm 40:6, 51:16–17), and they didn't work anyway (Hebrews 10:4). Although the Tabernacle of David did house the Ark of the Covenant, it was not hidden in a back room (the Holy of Holies), but was accessible for all to see. This new order of worship and open access to God for everybody was "scheduled" to be revealed at the crucifixion and resurrection of Christ (Mark 15:38), but David understood it centuries before, and "pulled" it by faith into his present time.

- **Jesus' First Miracle.** We know that Jesus did only what He saw the Father do (John 5:19). This would necessarily have to include His making the following statement to His mother at the wedding of Cana, when she told Him they had run out of wine, and expected Him to do something about it:

John 2:4 (NET): Jesus replied, "Woman, why are you saying this to me? My time has not yet come."

So Jesus, saying only what the Father told Him to say, stated plainly that it was not yet time for Him to start His public, supernaturally empowered ministry. But Mary, who had heard Gabriel's announcement (Luke 1:26–38), was impregnated by the Holy Spirit (v. 35), heard the shepherds talk about the heavenly host rejoicing at Jesus' birth, and pondered the implications (2:18–19), heard Simeon's Messianic prophecy over the three-month-old Jesus (2:33), saw him "talking shop" with the teachers in the temple when He was twelve (2:46–47), pondered that as well (v. 51), and saw Him grow up without sin, she knew He was destined for greatness beyond comprehension. So she told the servants, "Whatever He says to you, do it." (John 2:5). And then suddenly, it *was* time for Jesus to start His public, supernaturally empowered ministry and so, still doing only what the Father told Him to do, turned the water into wine. One sentence earlier it *wasn't* time, according to God the Father, but Mary's faith and hunger brought it into her "now."

- **The Woman at the Well and Other Samaritans.** At the beginning of Jesus' ministry He told His disciples *not* to go into any city of Samaria, but only to the "lost sheep of Israel" to preach (Matthew 10:5–8). Why did Jesus say this? Because the Father told Him to. But one day, while going from Judea to Galilee, they passed Sychar, a Samaritan city (John 4:3). It was about noon when they got there (v. 6), so Jesus sat down on the edge of Jacob's well (v. 6), while the disciples were off getting some food (v. 8). A woman came out of the city to draw water and Jesus asked her for a drink (v. 7). This was surprising to the woman (v. 9), but they talked, and Jesus saw that she was spiritually very hungry. He had a word of knowledge for her (vv. 17–18), and she realized He was sent from God (v. 19). The woman was so excited about meeting the Messiah that she left her waterpot, ran into the city to tell everyone Whom she had met (vv. 28–30). Many believed on Jesus because of the woman's testimony (v. 39). And suddenly, it *was* okay to go to a city of Samaria, so Jesus (still doing only what the Father told Him to), stayed there for a couple of days, preaching to them. As a result, many more believed Jesus was the Christ, the Savior of the world (vv. 41–42). So it *wasn't* yet time to preach to the Samaritans, but because of the hunger and faith of the Woman at the Well, suddenly it *was* time; she pulled the future into her "now."

Okay, so we've seen that faith and hunger does indeed move the hand of God, even to the point of bringing into existence early something God had planned for the future. And that's exactly what happened to the Canaanite woman with the demonized daughter:

> Matthew 15:21–28 (NIV) Leaving that place, Jesus withdrew to the region of Tyre and Sidon. [22]A Canaanite woman from that vicinity came to him, crying out, "Lord, Son of David, have mercy on me! My daughter is suffering terribly from demon-possession." [23]Jesus did not answer a word. So his disciples came to him and urged him, "Send her away, for she keeps crying out after us." [24]He answered, "I was sent only to the lost sheep of Israel." [25]The woman came and knelt before him. "Lord, help me!" she said. [26]He replied, "It is not right to take the children's bread and toss it to their dogs." [27]"Yes, Lord," she said, "but even the dogs eat the crumbs that fall from their masters' table." [28]Then Jesus answered, "Woman, you have great faith! Your request is granted." And her daughter was healed from that very hour.

When she initially came to Jesus, He didn't even respond. Why? We don't know specifically, although we know He was doing what the Father told Him to do. It could have been God/Jesus testing her resolve and her hunger to see if she was serious about seeking Him—we know He did that with other people (Exodus 20:20, Judges 3:1, Mark 6:48, Luke 24:28). But she was indeed serious, to the point of becoming annoying to the disciples (v. 23, above). Jesus' comment about taking the children's bread and giving it to the dogs was a reference to His ministry—He was the bread of life (John 6:35), and the Israelites were God's children (Exodus 4:22)—and it wasn't yet time to expand His ministry to the Gentiles. That is, until this woman had great faith, persistence, and hunger. Jesus acknowledged her faith, and healed her daughter (v. 28).

This woman received healing for her daughter even in a period of history when healing wasn't yet "supposed" to be available to the Gentiles. Now that healing *has* been made available to all people (that is the intent of this book, to show that that statement is true, both with the Scriptures above, and those to follow), we need to be all the more persistent to break through all the roadblocks the enemy would put in our way, in his attempts to keep us from being blessed by God.

And there's something else earth-shaking in the previous passage; did you notice it? Jesus considers healing to be "the children's bread" (v. 26)! And we already know how God responds when His children ask Him for bread:

> Matthew 7:9–11 (NIV): Which of you, if his son asks for bread, will give him a stone? ¹⁰Or if he asks for a fish, will give him a snake? ¹¹If you, then, though you are evil, know how to give good gifts to your children, **how much more** will your Father in heaven give good gifts to those who ask him!

So *of course* God will give His children bread—healing—when they ask Him!

Healing the Deaf Mute

In the following story, Jesus heals a man who is both deaf and dumb, but this is a different case than that described in The Mute Demoniacs above, because in this story, there is no implication of demonic activity; he was simply deaf for apparently physical reasons:

> Mark 7:32–35 (NIV): There some people brought to him a man who was deaf and could hardly talk, and they begged him to place his hand on the man. [33]After he took him aside, away from the crowd, Jesus put his fingers into the man's ears. Then he spit and touched the man's tongue. [34]He looked up to heaven and with a deep sigh said to him, "Ephphatha!" (which means, "Be opened!"). [35]At this, the man's ears were opened, his tongue was loosened and he began to speak plainly.

If this was a case of mere physical malformation to the ears, and was not demonic in origin, as the text implies, there is another miracle that must have taken place. Note that the man "could hardly talk" (v. 32), and that is very consistent with listening to deaf people today, when they try to talk. They can be shown all the right "shapes" to make with their mouths, tongues, jaws, lips, and so forth, but their deafness prevents them from hearing how it *sounds*, compared with how it's *supposed* to sound. The result is that it can be difficult to understand the hard of hearing.

This means, then, that when Jesus healed the man's ears, He also gave him the understanding, skills, and "instant experience" of language. Note that "he began to speak plainly" so, since he had apparently never heard anything, he had received an instant download of the parts of speech, vocabulary, grammar, inflection, suprasegmental phonemes, generative phonology, and all the other components of language we take for granted. Again, *wow*.

Healing the Blind Man

This story is the famous one in which Jesus spit on the blind man's eyes:

> Mark 8:22–25 (TEV): They came to Bethsaida, where some people brought a blind man to Jesus and begged him to touch him. ²³Jesus took the blind man by the hand and led him out of the village. After spitting on the man's eyes, Jesus placed his hands on him and asked him, "Can you see anything?" ²⁴The man looked up and said, "Yes, I can see people, but they look like trees walking around." ²⁵Jesus again placed his hands on the man's eyes. This time the man looked intently, his eyesight returned, and he saw everything clearly.

The above story has a nugget of truth in it that the more successful healing ministries have learned. Some people, after praying for healing, check with the person to see if the sickness or pain or injury is gone, and if it is not 100% gone, they consider the prayer to have failed and get discouraged.

But there is a much better approach: instead of asking whether the person is *completely healed,* ask if there has been *any improvement.* It is much more common that a partial healing will have been accomplished, rather than a full healing, by the time you first ask the prayee how he's doing. And an answer of "Yes, it's better" is much more encouraging and faith-building than "No, it's not done." Of course the *goal* is complete healing, but for those of us who are less aware of the authority God has granted us, His love for us, and our own sonship in Him, we often are slower at getting a healing fully manifested than Jesus was. Just keep at it, and it will get better and better as you realize the same Holy Spirit that empowered Jesus empowers you.

It is perfectly fine to check with the prayee as to his current level of pain or illness or injury before you lay hands on him and start praying (e.g., "On a scale of 0 to 10, what is your current pain level?"). Then you, as well as the prayee, will be more able to notice any improvement as you pray. Remember, Jesus did only what the Father told Him to, and He prayed twice for the same healing, and it came in two "installments." Note also that when you ask the prayee if he's doing better, that is not evidence of a lack of faith. We can learn from this that when it takes multiple "installments" of prayer to effect a full healing, we can't automatically assume we did anything wrong the first time(s) we prayed.

Minor historical detail: Why did the man say that people looked like trees walking around? Because their only fuel for cooking food was burning wood, and it was very common for people to walk around with large bundles of branches and twigs, balanced on their heads or shoulders, that they had gathered to take home for burning when fixing food. So in the minute or two before this man was fully healed, he likely saw some people walking by carrying such bundles of branches and sticks.

The Deaf Mute Epileptic Boy

Jesus' power and authority—and command to us—to heal the sick are not limited to physical problems; they also extend to healing mental problems, whether caused by demons or not, as the next account shows:

> Matthew 17:14–20 (NIV): When they came to the crowd, a man approached Jesus and knelt before him. [15]"Lord, have mercy on my son," he said. "He has seizures and is suffering greatly. He often falls into the fire or into the water. [16]I brought him to your disciples, but they could not heal him." [17]"O unbelieving and perverse generation," Jesus replied, "how long shall I stay with you? How long shall I put up with you? Bring the boy here to me." [18]Jesus rebuked the demon, and it came out of the boy, and he was healed from that moment. [19]Then the disciples came to Jesus in private and asked, "Why couldn't we drive it out?" [20]He replied, "Because you have so little faith. I tell you the truth, if you have faith as small as a mustard seed, you can say to this mountain, 'Move from here to there' and it will move. Nothing will be impossible for you."

Here is an example of the disciples being unable to heal someone. Of course, we can't conclude from this that it is not God's will to heal, because as soon as Jesus comes on the scene, He heals the boy. Not only that, but we can learn two very important points from Jesus' answer to the disciples' question of "Why couldn't we drive him out?". Look at Jesus' response, and the tone in which He gave it:

Matthew 17:17: Then Jesus answered and said, **O faithless and perverse generation, how long shall I be with you? how long shall I suffer you?** bring him hither to me.

AMP: And Jesus answered, **O you unbelieving (warped, wayward, rebellious) and thoroughly perverse generation! How long am I to remain with you? How long am I to bear with you?** Bring him here to Me.

CJB: Yeshua answered, "**Perverted people, without any trust! How long will I be with you? How long must I put up with you?** Bring him here to me!"

CEV: Jesus said, "**You people are too stubborn to have any faith! How much longer must I be with you? Why do I have to put up with you?** Bring the boy here."

ERV: Jesus answered, "**You people today have no faith. Your lives are so wrong! How long must I stay with you? How long must I continue to be patient with you?** Bring the boy here."

HCSB: Jesus replied, "**You unbelieving and rebellious generation! How long will I be with you? How long must I put up with you?** Bring him here to Me."

PHILLIPS: "**You really are an unbelieving and difficult people,**" Jesus returned. "**How long must I be with you, and how long must I put up with you?** Bring him here to me!"

TLB: Jesus replied, "**Oh, you stubborn, faithless people! How long shall I bear with you?** Bring him here to me."

MSG: Jesus said, "**What a generation! No sense of God! No focus to your lives! How many times do I have to go over these things? How much longer do I have to put up with this?** Bring the boy here."

NCV: Jesus answered, "**You people have no faith, and your lives are all wrong. How long must I put up with you? How long must I continue to be patient with you?** Bring the boy here."

WE: Jesus said, '**You people today do not believe. You have turned away from God. How long must I be with you? How long must I put up with you?** Bring the boy here to me.'

YLT: And Jesus answering said, '**O generation, unstedfast and perverse, till when shall I be with you? till when shall I bear you?** bring him to me hither;'

Wow. Look at the words Jesus used in describing the disciples: faithless, perverse, unbelieving, warped, wayward, rebellious, without trust, stubborn, wrong, difficult, insensible, unfocussed, and unstedfast. It sounds like Jesus was pretty irritated with the disciples, because they couldn't do something as trivial as cast out one measly demon. From Jesus' response, we can learn (at least) these three things about their situation:

- The miracle was prevented by the disciples' lack of faith.
- They *ought to* have had more faith, as we can see by Jesus' annoyance at their inability to cast the demon out.
- The limiting factor in the boy's deliverance was *not* the boy's faith or his father's faith. They had what they had, but when Jesus showed up, the boy was delivered.

And of course, we can also apply the same lessons to our own lives:

- When we pray for someone to be healed or delivered, and it doesn't happen, we *cannot* conclude it wasn't God's will for it to happen. We must look at our own faith first and, if it is insufficient, seek God for more love for people, because perfect love casts out fear (I John 4:18), and fear is just faith in failure—fear is a belief that the problem's severity or the devil's badness is too much for God to handle. We must also seek a greater revelation of God (Ephesians 1:17–19), because the more we get to know God, the more we realize just how big He is in comparison to any possible problem.
- Regardless of how much faith we think we have, it is safe to assume that we *ought* to have more (unless we have moved a mountain or at least a hill out of the way recently).
- When we pray for someone to be healed or delivered, and it apparently doesn't happen, we *cannot* conclude it was the prayee's lack of faith that prevented the miracle. In the passage above, the critical variable was the faith of the pray*er*, not of the pray*ee*.

At the end of the Matthew 17 passage above, the KJV adds:

Matthew 17:21: Howbeit **this kind goeth not out but by prayer and fasting**.

But if you read the story, you see that Jesus *didn't* start praying and fasting when the need arose. How then could He have cast it out? *Because He had already been praying and fasting.* Waiting until you're in the middle of an emergency or have an urgent need is not the best moment to start a fast; you don't have time. It's like waiting until suppertime and *then* planting the seeds, the harvest of which you want to eat for supper. It takes time to build faith through prayer and fasting, so don't wait until the emergency hits.

The silliness of waiting until the emergency arises to start fasting is illustrated in one of the sketches by the Christian comedian Mark Lowry. He tells a story about his childhood, when he did something for which he knew he would get in trouble. Sure enough, he soon hears his mother calling him in that tone of voice that confirmed he was indeed in big trouble. He says, "Immediately, I started praying and fasting," and of course the audience laughs. Why it is humorous? Because of the obvious foolishness of waiting until the urgent need arises to *start* praying and fasting. Being "all prayed up" is much preferable, and more effective.

In the case above, the epileptic seizures were caused by a demon, but of course, not all mental illness or problems are demonic. Ian Andrews, a British gentleman who has a worldwide healing ministry, really got a revelation of this truth, and ever since that time, he has had amazing results of people getting healed of dyslexia, ADD, ADHD, problems with memory and concentration, and more. And most of the healings of mental problems he sees are not demonically caused.

Mark's Account

When we read Mark's rendition of this story, there are some details he includes that Matthew did not include. Here it is:

> Mark 9:17–29 (NIV): A man in the crowd answered, "Teacher, I brought you my son, who is possessed by a spirit that has robbed him of speech. [18] Whenever it seizes him, it throws him to the ground. He foams at the mouth, gnashes his teeth and becomes rigid. I asked your disciples to drive out the spirit, but they could not." [19] "O unbelieving generation," Jesus replied, "how long shall I stay with you? How long shall I put up with you? Bring the boy to me." [20] So they brought him. When the spirit saw Jesus, it immediately threw the boy into a convulsion. He fell to the ground and rolled around, foaming at the mouth. [21] Jesus asked the boy's father, "How long has he been like this?" "From childhood," he answered. [22] "It has often thrown him into fire or water to kill him. **But if you can do anything,** take pity on us and help us." [23] "'If you can'?" said Jesus. "Everything is possible for him who believes." [24] Immediately the boy's father exclaimed, "I do believe; help me overcome my unbelief!" [25] When Jesus saw that a crowd was running to the scene, he rebuked the evil spirit. "You deaf and mute spirit," he said, "I command you, come out of him and never enter him again." [26] The spirit shrieked, convulsed him violently and came out. The boy looked so much like a corpse that many said, "He's dead." [27] But Jesus took him by the hand and lifted him to his feet, and he stood up. [28] After Jesus had gone indoors, his disciples asked him privately, "Why couldn't we drive it out?" [29] He replied, "This kind can come out only by prayer."

Several additional things we can glean from Mark's version:

- The boy wasn't a *little* boy anymore; he sounds like a young man, because when Jesus asked the father how long his son had been like that, the father replied, "From childhood."
- The father had no faith at all; notice that he said to Jesus in v. 22: "But *if* you can do anything. . ." Most people realize that God *can* heal us, but they don't know for sure whether He *wants* to or not. This father didn't even know if Jesus *could* heal his son; the needle of the Faith-o-Meter wouldn't have budged even a little. But Jesus healed the boy

anyway, which shows that our faith can overcome other people's lack of faith if they are willing.

- The father said in v. 24, "I do believe; help me overcome my unbelief!" No, he didn't believe; he already showed that in v. 22. But he was desperate, and Jesus had compassion, and the miracle came.
- The father apparently *had* had faith, because he brought his son to the disciples in the first place. But their failure in casting the demon out had destroyed his faith, as evidenced by his statement in v. 22. This is a sobering thought; we had better continue to seek God, so someone's failure to receive an instant healing or deliverance doesn't damage his faith, *or* our own. Of course, people should establish their beliefs and doctrines on God's Word, and not their own experiences, but unfortunately, many people do just that.
- The demon that caused convulsions was also causing deafness and dumbness (vv. 17, 25).

A lot of meat from one little story, no?

The Ten Lepers

In this story, all ten lepers approached Jesus (as much as they were allowed to, since they were lepers), and asked Him to heal them. They said, "Jesus," so they knew Who He was, then "Master," so they realized He was able to heal them, and finally "Have mercy on us," so they believed He could be entreated to intervene on their behalf:

> Luke 17:12–19: And as he entered into a certain village, there met him ten men that were lepers, which stood afar off: ¹³And they lifted up their voices, and said, Jesus, Master, have mercy on us. ¹⁴And when he saw them, he said unto them, Go shew yourselves unto the priests. And it came to pass, that, **as they went, they were cleansed.** ¹⁵And one of them, when he saw that he was healed, turned back, and with a loud voice glorified God, ¹⁶And fell down on his face at his feet, giving him thanks: and he was a Samaritan. ¹⁷And Jesus answering said, Were there not ten cleansed? but where are the nine? ¹⁸There are not found that returned to give glory to God, save this stranger. ¹⁹And he said unto him, Arise, go thy way: thy faith hath made thee whole.

God's creativity never ceases to amaze. In this situation, he doesn't lay hands on these lepers, like he did the single leper he healed earlier in this chapter (see The Leper, above). Here, He simply tells the lepers to go do something; in this case, to show themselves to the priests (in accordance with Leviticus 14), and *as they went*, they were healed.

God still uses this approach quite a lot today; I have heard many a testimony where God told someone to do something, and when they obeyed, they were blessed with the healing or other blessing they were seeking. Usually these actions God asks us to take are quite easily done, but they require a step of faith.

The typical scenario is that the command comes to you in the form of a thought and you immediately think, "Why should I do that?" If you recognize the still, small, voice of the Lord, you immediately answer yourself, "Because God told me to." And that is enough, so you obey, and then God does the miracle.

Here's another interesting thing about the priests' role in Leviticus 14's description of the procedure for being declared healed of leprosy. Israel didn't have doctors, per se, so the priests were the closest thing (humanly speaking), and they had to examine and make determinations as to the presence or absence of some diseases, like leprosy in this case.

So in modern vernacular, Jesus basically told the ten lepers to go to the doctor for an exam, so the healing of their leprosy could be confirmed by the medical professionals. *But they weren't healed yet!* However, as they stepped out in faith and obeyed Jesus' command, *then* they were healed, and in plenty of time for their medical exams. Once the priests declared them clean, they could re-enter normal society again without the stigma of leprosy preventing them from social interactions.

We can also learn from this example of what Jesus did, that it is *not* evidence of lack of faith to get a medical exam to confirm a supernatural miraculous healing.

The Man Born Blind

This story is interesting on several accounts; let's take a look:

John 9:1–7: And as Jesus passed by, he saw a man which was blind from his birth. ²And his disciples asked him, saying, Master, who did sin, this man, or his parents, that he was born blind? ³Jesus answered, Neither hath this man sinned, nor his parents: but that the works of God should be made manifest in him. ⁴I must work the works of him that sent me, while it is day: the night cometh, when no man can work. ⁵As long as I am in the world, I am the light of the world. ⁶When he had thus spoken, he spat on the ground, and made clay of the spittle, and he anointed the eyes of the blind man with the clay, ⁷And said unto him, Go, wash in the pool of Siloam, (which is by interpretation, Sent.) He went his way therefore, and washed, and came seeing.

As students of the Bible are aware, our English Bibles were translated from the original Hebrew and Greek languages, *which did not have punctuation;* the punctuation was put in during the translation process. As such, there may be a few misleading places in the Bible because of poorly chosen punctuation during translation, even though the original language did not contain the error (because the original language did not contain punctuation). I believe this passage may be one of those cases.

In v. 2, the disciples asked Jesus, "Did this man sin, or did his parents sin, that he was born blind?" And the KJV rendering of Jesus' answer is as follows. . .

John 9:3–4a: Jesus answered, Neither hath this man sinned, nor his parents: but that the works of God should be made manifest in him. ⁴I must work the works of him that sent me, while it is day. . .

But could it be that the punctuation that the translators inserted was wrong? Consider:

John 9:3–4a (proposed): Jesus answered, Neither hath this man sinned, nor his parents. But that the works of God should be made manifest in him, ⁴I must work the works of him that sent me, while it is day. . .

Do you see the difference? Because of the colon after the word "parents" and the period after "him," the original KJV implies he was born blind *so that* the works of God should be made manifest in him. In other words, God intentionally caused his blindness so he could show Himself magnanimous by later removing it. This has led to countless cases where people suffer through years of agony and disability, clinging to a thread of belief that "God wants me to suffer with this disease because eventually His works will be made manifest in me." This is a lie from the pit of hell.

We have seen from the multitudes of Scripture above, and which will be confirmed by even more Scriptures hereafter, God's original intent was health, God's immutable nature and name include health and healing, God has made many very plain promises that He offers healing, and then we have Jesus' numerous examples of healing *every one* who came to Him for healing.

So let's get back to the punctuation situation. Using exactly the same words, if we put a period after "parents" and a comma after "him," it comes across completely differently and, I might add, in a way that is much more in agreement with the rest of Scripture. And, after all, since the disciples had asked who had sinned, the man or his parents, a reply from Jesus saying "Neither this man sinned, nor his parents" answers the question, doesn't it? Well, doesn't it? Then Jesus goes on to say in the next sentence, "But that the works of God should be made manifest in him, I must work the works of him that sent me. . ." That fits together better also; see John 5:17, 36, 10:32, and 14:10 for confirmation.

Whether or not you agree with my theory that the punctuation inserted by the translators was inappropriate, if you just read the story, it is plain that God was not glorified until *after* the man was healed. It was the *healing* of the man, not his blindness, that glorified God.

And one more thing, concerning whether God made him blind in the first place, just so He could be revered when He removed the blindness later. Just consider such an action, if done by a human father: if a human father intentionally blinded his child for years because he knew people would be impressed when he later reversed the blindness, *he would be jailed for child abuse,* and rightly so. The cruelty of such a father would be almost unbelievable. And yet we attribute such actions to God, Whose very nature is love (I John 4:8).

This idea is reminiscent of that old joke, "I love to beat my head against a brick wall because it feels so good when I stop," except in this version, God is cast in the role of beating our heads against the brick wall so we'll thank Him when He stops. What a distorted and perverted view of God!

What does God say to such ideas?

> Matthew 7:7–11: Ask, and it shall be given you; seek, and ye shall find; knock, and it shall be opened unto you: ⁸For every one that asketh receiveth; and he that seeketh findeth; and to him that knocketh it shall be opened. ⁹Or what man is there of you, whom if his son ask bread, will he give him a stone? ¹⁰Or if he ask a fish, will he give him a serpent? **¹¹If ye then, being evil, know how to give good gifts unto your children, how much more shall your Father which is in heaven give good things to them that ask him?**

If you have your own kids, how would you feel if they told their friends that you gave them various diseases or injuries to "teach them something," or so you would look good later when you fixed the diseases or injuries? Would *you* appreciate being portrayed in such a light?

Raising Lazarus

John writes about how Jesus raised his friend Lazarus from the dead after he had been dead four days, embalmed, and already in the tomb. Lazarus was the brother of Mary and Martha, and Jesus loved them all (John 11:5). At one point, Lazarus got sick and died. Let's pick up the story at v. 3:

> John 11:3–7 (NIV): So the sisters sent word to Jesus, "Lord, the one you love is sick." ⁴When he heard this, Jesus said, "This sickness will not end in death. No, it is for God's glory so that God's Son may be glorified through it." ⁵Jesus loved Martha and her sister and Lazarus. ⁶Yet

when he heard that Lazarus was sick, he stayed where he was two more days. ⁷Then he said to his disciples, "Let us go back to Judea."

At this point, some people who have been taught that God makes people sick for His glory will pounce on v. 4 and say, "See? The sickness was for God's glory!" The problem is that we're talking about apples and oranges here; those two ideas are *very* different, even though the wording used to express them is similar. Here are the two different ideas, expressed in such a way that the difference can clearly be seen:

- "God causes sickness so He will get glory when He removes it." This idea, as I so delicately expressed it earlier, is a lie from the pit of hell.
- "God can use any situation in our lives to show His love, and He gets the glory through it." This idea is much more consistent with Scripture, and with God's character, and His role as a Father.

The enormous difference between these two ideas is that in the first, God *causes* the sickness, and in the second, God *doesn't* cause the sickness, but He'll gladly heal it. That is quite a difference. Satan is the one who causes sickness, because it is his character to "steal, kill, and destroy" (John 10:10). This concept is also shown in Genesis, when Joseph talks to his brothers, who had sold him into slavery many years earlier:

Joseph is a type (foreshadowing, prophetic figure) of Christ, and many things in his life were Messianic in their ultimate fulfillment. Here is just a partial list:

- Both Joseph and Jesus were first-born sons.
- Both were shepherds.
- Both were prophesied to become powerful rulers.
- Both had brothers who didn't believe in God's call on their lives.
- Both were falsely accused.
- Both were "gotten rid of" by their brethren (or so they thought).
- Joseph was sold as a slave, Jesus was betrayed for the price of a slave.

- Both went to Egypt.
- Both were with two others condemned to die, one of which was pardoned.

And there are many more. But the point here is how Joseph described the evil done to him:

> Genesis 50:20 (TEV): You plotted evil against me, **but God turned it into good**, in order to preserve the lives of many people who are alive today because of what happened.

In the same way, when Satan comes against us, directly or indirectly, to steal from, kill, and destroy us, God will happily turn it into good if we seek Him, and believe in His goodness and love toward us. So when we are sick, we are authorized and encouraged to pray that God will heal us, because He wants to do so. But that is a far cry from God *causing* the sickness in the first place, just so He can remove it later.

So, getting back to the raising of Lazarus from the dead, let's continue the story in v. 11:

> John 11:11–15 (TEV): Jesus said this and then added, "Our friend Lazarus has fallen asleep, but I will go and wake him up." [12]The disciples answered, "If he is asleep, Lord, he will get well." [13]Jesus meant that Lazarus had died, but they thought he meant natural sleep. [14]So Jesus told them plainly, "Lazarus is dead, [15]but for your sake I am glad that I was not with him, so that you will believe. Let us go to him."

That's odd. Why did Jesus say that He was glad He wasn't with Lazarus? Because He knew that humans tend to see death as more permanent than sickness, and even though the disciples had already seen Him overcome both sickness and death in people, He knew that it was more faith-building to see another resurrection, than a mere healing.

> John 11:17–32 (TEV): When Jesus arrived, he found that Lazarus had been buried four days before. [18]Bethany was less than two miles from Jerusalem, [19]and many Judeans had come to see Martha and Mary to comfort them about their brother's death. [20]When Martha heard that Jesus was coming, she went out to meet him, but Mary stayed in the house. [21]Martha said to Jesus, "If you had been here, Lord, my brother would not have died! [22]But I know that even now God will give you

whatever you ask him for." ²³"Your brother will rise to life," Jesus told her. ²⁴"I know," she replied, "that he will rise to life on the last day." ²⁵Jesus said to her, "I am the resurrection and the life. Those who believe in me will live, even though they die; ²⁶and those who live and believe in me will never die. Do you believe this?" ²⁷"Yes, Lord!" she answered. "I do believe that you are the Messiah, the Son of God, who was to come into the world." ²⁸After Martha said this, she went back and called her sister Mary privately. "The Teacher is here," she told her, "and is asking for you." ²⁹When Mary heard this, she got up and hurried out to meet him. ³⁰(Jesus had not yet arrived in the village, but was still in the place where Martha had met him.) ³¹The people who were in the house with Mary comforting her followed her when they saw her get up and hurry out. They thought that she was going to the grave to weep there. ³²Mary arrived where Jesus was, and as soon as she saw him, she fell at his feet. "Lord," she said, "if you had been here, my brother would not have died!"

Almost as if "on cue," to confirm the statement Jesus made in v. 15, both Martha and Mary realize that Jesus could have *prevented* Lazarus' death (v. 21 and v. 32, respectively), but don't seem to understand that He could *reverse* Lazarus' death—even after physical death, it's not too late as far as God is concerned. Martha says some things that indicate a glimmer of hope in that direction (vv. 22, 27), but can't seem to bring herself to actually say it out loud.

So, in tears, Mary arrives where Jesus was waiting for her:

John 11:33–37 (TEV): Jesus saw her weeping, and he saw how the people with her were weeping also; his heart was touched, and he was deeply moved. ³⁴"Where have you buried him?" he asked them. "Come and see, Lord," they answered. ³⁵Jesus wept. ³⁶"See how much he loved him!" the people said. ³⁷But some of them said, "He gave sight to the blind man, didn't he? Could he not have kept Lazarus from dying?"

Just like the disciples in v. 15, Martha in v. 21, and Mary in v. 32, here are people in the crowd saying the same thing. In v. 37, they're basically saying, "If He'd been here in time, He could've healed Lazarus, but now he's dead, so Jesus is too late." Jesus was about to show otherwise.

John 11:38–45 (TEV): Deeply moved once more, Jesus went to the tomb, which was a cave with a stone placed at the entrance. [39]"Take the stone away!" Jesus ordered. Martha, the dead man's sister, answered, "There will be a bad smell, Lord. He has been buried four days!" [40]Jesus said to her, "Didn't I tell you that you would see God's glory if you believed?" [41]They took the stone away. Jesus looked up and said, "I thank you, Father, that you listen to me. [42]I know that you always listen to me, but I say this for the sake of the people here, so that they will believe that you sent me." [43]After he had said this, he called out in a loud voice, "Lazarus, come out!" [44]He came out, his hands and feet wrapped in grave cloths, and with a cloth around his face. "Untie him," Jesus told them, "and let him go." [45]Many of the people who had come to visit Mary saw what Jesus did, and they believed in him.

This whole scenario was orchestrated by God (surprise, surprise). Look at the strategic sequence in which the strategic events happened:

1. Jesus was absent when Lazarus died.

2. Just for good measure, Jesus stayed away a few more days after Lazarus died, removing any possibility of people thinking, "He must have still been alive when they buried him, and he recovered enough to come out when Jesus called."

3. Jesus finally did show up, even though He didn't need to. He could have raised Lazarus from the dead from wherever He had been before going back to Bethany, similar to when He remotely healed the centurion's servant. But then the people wouldn't have known it was Him Who did the miracle, and therefore wouldn't have believed in Him. (Such belief was for their benefit, of course; God doesn't need His ego stroked.)

4. Jesus required the people to act in faith: He told *them* to take away the stone. Again, He didn't need to ask them to do it, He could have had an angel do it, like He would do at His own resurrection; it would have been easier and faster that way. But He had the *people* do it.

5. Jesus prayed "for show," in other words, *for the benefit of anyone listening,* as opposed to being just directed at God. And the fact that He did it shows that there is nothing intrinsically wrong

with doing so. (Of course, you shouldn't pray *solely* for the benefit of onlookers, lest you become like the Pharisee in Luke 18:10–14.) Look at v. 42, where Jesus said, "I know that you always listen to me, but **I say this for the sake of the people here, so that they will believe that you sent me.**" He prayed out loud *for the benefit of the people nearby,* so they could hear it, realize what was going on, and believe in Him.

6. Jesus did the part that only He could do—raising Lazarus from the dead—and then had the people get involved (again) in what they could do. Consider this: When Lazarus was wrapped in his graveclothes, his arms and legs were tied together as they wrapped him up into a bundle in preparation for burial; they didn't expect him to be going anywhere. Which means *he didn't walk* to the door of the grave; he must have floated there (as Jesus would do in Acts 1:9), or something equally amazing. And even had his legs been free, he couldn't see where he was going because the cloth was still around his face (v. 44). But the fact remains that Lazarus was still tied up when he arrived at the door of the grave, which is why Jesus told the people to "Untie him and let him go."

And when all of the above steps were accomplished, "many people. . . believed in him." Good choice.

The Woman with the Spirit of Infirmity

The attitude of some people regarding physical healing is, "Well, God knows my address. If He wants to heal me, He knows where to find me." And this actually works, *on rare occasion.* But in the vast majority of the time, God is a rewarder of them who *diligently* seek Him, and there are many Scriptures to that effect. But once in a while, God will just sovereignly do something for reasons we'll probably understand only in eternity. The woman below is an example:

> Luke 13:10–17 (NIV): On a Sabbath Jesus was teaching in one of the synagogues, [11]and a woman was there who had been crippled by a spirit for eighteen years. She was bent over and could not straighten up at all. [12]When Jesus saw her, he called her forward and said to her, "Woman, you are set free from your infirmity." [13]Then he put his

hands on her, and immediately she straightened up and praised God. ¹⁴Indignant because Jesus had healed on the Sabbath, the synagogue ruler said to the people, "There are six days for work. So come and be healed on those days, not on the Sabbath." ¹⁵The Lord answered him, "You hypocrites! Doesn't each of you on the Sabbath untie his ox or donkey from the stall and lead it out to give it water? ¹⁶Then should not this woman, a daughter of Abraham, whom Satan has kept bound for eighteen long years, be set free on the Sabbath day from what bound her?" ¹⁷When he said this, all his opponents were humiliated, but the people were delighted with all the wonderful things he was doing.

Note that in this case *Jesus* called *her* forward. There is no indication that she was seeking a healing from Him, and He didn't ask her if she wanted to be healed, as He sometimes did (e.g., John 5:6). It looks like in this case, Jesus was trying to make a point: the hypocrisy of leading your animals to water on the Sabbath being acceptable, but healing someone on the Sabbath *not* being acceptable. So this lady was simply "in the right place at the right time." (You'd agree with that statement if you believe in coincidence or luck; personally, I don't have enough faith for that.) Or perhaps God simply wanted to show yet again His goodness and love for people.

Here again, a physical limitation—severe reduction in range of spinal motion—was directly caused by a demon, the "spirit of infirmity" referred to in v. 11. Note that in this case, Jesus didn't directly address the demon, nor even refer to it, as He sometimes did. He simply exercised the authority with which He was imbued when He was baptized in the Holy Spirit (Luke 3:22), and which we also have (John 20:21).

The Man with Dropsy

"Dropsy" is an archaic word that is synonymous with the more modern term "edema," which means excessive swelling caused by water retention. So this man's arms and legs, and probably face, hands, and other parts as well, were severely swollen.

Again, Jesus seems to want to make a point to the Pharisees about how it is never inappropriate to do good:

> Luke 14:1–6 (NIV): One Sabbath, when Jesus went to eat in the house of a prominent Pharisee, he was being carefully watched. ²There in front of him was a man suffering from dropsy. ³Jesus asked the Pharisees and experts in the law, "Is it lawful to heal on the Sabbath or not?" ⁴But they remained silent. So taking hold of the man, he healed him and sent him away. ⁵Then he asked them, "If one of you has a son or an ox that falls into a well on the Sabbath day, will you not immediately pull him out?" ⁶And they had nothing to say.

Because this man was "in the house" of the Pharisee, it seems more likely he was there for the specific purpose of getting his healing, although the text doesn't say. The implication is there, though, because the synagogue (where the woman with the spirit of infirmity was, in the previous section) is a public place that was regularly attended by most Jews, it is entirely possible she was there simply to go to the synagogue, with no specific goal of getting healed. Here, with the man with dropsy, because they were in the Pharisee's private residence (v. 1), it seems unlikely the man would have been there had it not been for Jesus' presence.

The hypocrisy of the Pharisees is quite evident here: Jesus was being "carefully watched" by them (v. 1), they "remained silent" and didn't answer Jesus' first question because it would have exposed their hypocritical attitudes (v. 4), and they "had nothing to say" to Jesus' second question because it again would have exposed their hypocritical attitudes yet more (v. 6). The attitude and goals of the Pharisees were clearly to retain their power and control over the people, not to bless them and accurately represent God to them. Let us ever be watchful, lest we start emulating the Pharisees.

Blind Bartimaeus and Friend

The story of blind Bartimaeus is a well known one, and most tellings of the story include only Bartimaeus, even though both he and his friend, also blind, were healed at the same time. All three synoptic Gospels tell this story, so let's look at it from each viewpoint, because each Gospel includes some details of the story that the others don't.

Matthew's Account

First, let's read the story from Matthew:

> Matthew 20:29–34 (NIV): As Jesus and his disciples were leaving Jericho, a large crowd followed him. ³⁰Two blind men were sitting by the roadside, and when they heard that Jesus was going by, they shouted, "Lord, Son of David, have mercy on us!" ³¹The crowd rebuked them and told them to be quiet, but they shouted all the louder, "Lord, Son of David, have mercy on us!" ³²Jesus stopped and called them. "What do you want me to do for you?" he asked. ³³"Lord," they answered, "we want our sight." ³⁴Jesus had compassion on them and touched their eyes. Immediately they received their sight and followed him.

In Matthew's account of the story, as Jesus and the disciples were leaving Jericho, there were two blind men sitting by the road. Because there was a "large crowd" following him, they could hear that something was going on, but they didn't know what. So they asked whomever happened to be close enough to respond, and they were told that Jesus was passing by. This was wonderful news to them because they had heard of His miracles of healing on other people, and they were convinced that Jesus was the long-awaited Messiah.

How do we know that? Because they called Jesus "Son of David," similar to the other two blind men that Jesus healed (see that section, above, for more details on the equivalence of "Messiah" and "Son of David.") By the way, those two blind men mentioned earlier in this chapter are not the same as the two blind men we are currently discussing: the previous two were much earlier in Jesus' ministry than the current two, and the previous two were healed indoors, while the two currently under discussion were healed outdoors.

Once Jesus asked the two men what they wanted, and they respond "our sight," Jesus touched their eyes. Matthew's is the only Gospel where it is mentioned that Jesus touched their eyes to heal them.

Mark's Account

Now let's look at the Mark's account of the story. Mark's account, like Luke's account, concentrates on Jesus' interaction with only one of the blind men, and Mark names him: "Bartimaeus." Bible scholars have suggested that it is likely that Mark personally knew Bartimaeus, which was why he mentioned him by name. And this is very plausible: if I were telling a story about a couple guys who received a miraculous touch from God, but I knew only one of them, I think it is very likely that I would be more excited for—and give much more detail on—the guy I knew.

> Mark 10:46–52 (NIV): Then they came to Jericho. As Jesus and his disciples, together with a large crowd, were leaving the city, a blind man, Bartimaeus (that is, the Son of Timaeus), was sitting by the roadside begging. [47]When he heard that it was Jesus of Nazareth, he began to shout, "Jesus, Son of David, have mercy on me!" [48]Many rebuked him and told him to be quiet, but he shouted all the more, "Son of David, have mercy on me!" [49]Jesus stopped and said, "Call him." So they called to the blind man, "Cheer up! On your feet! He's calling you." [50]Throwing his cloak aside, he jumped to his feet and came to Jesus. [51]"What do you want me to do for you?" Jesus asked him. The blind man said, "Rabbi, I want to see." [52]"Go," said Jesus, "your faith has healed you." Immediately he received his sight and followed Jesus along the road.

Mark also points out that Bartimaeus was not about to lose this opportunity to get a touch from God: he made himself heard, even to the point of being obnoxious (at least in some people's eyes), because lots of people told him to basically sit down and shut up (v. 48). But he would not be denied; he shouted all the more for Jesus to have mercy on him. And it worked; Jesus heard Bartimaeus and asked people to bring him to Him. Then all of a sudden, everybody's all supportive of Bartimaeus: "Cheer up! He's calling you!"

Randy Clark, of Global Awakening, notes that this passage is an excellent illustration of how the work of knowledge works (I Corinthians 12:8). Note that it is an *illustration*, not an example; Jesus' ministry has many *examples* of words of knowledge, but this passage is an explanatory illustration.

Here, in a nutshell, is why it is an illustration. It is very common in modern-day meetings where the Holy Spirit is allowed to move, that someone will be hoping, praying, believing for a miraculous healing or some other desperately needed blessing. Soon, someone else has a word a knowledge—God communicates to someone in one of several different ways—that someone present needs that exact blessing the first person is seeking. That builds faith, and the person stands up and says, "That's me!" and the healing or blessing is given.

Now notice the parallels to the story of Bartimaeus:

Bartimaeus	Modern Meeting
There is an environment where the power of God is moving mightily: Jesus and the disciples were going from town to town ministering miraculously.	God calls one or more well known healing ministers to go to some location and host a conference or series of meetings.
Word spreads, and Jesus has a "large crowd" around Him (v. 46).	Word spreads, and the person overhears people talking about the conference, or gets an email, or sees an ad, and comes to the meeting.
Desperate for a touch from God, Bartimaeus calls out to Jesus, "Have mercy on me!" (v. 47).	Desperate for a touch from God, the person prays, "God, please answer my prayer!"
Those who are uncaring for Bartimaeus' situation and need tell him to shut up; there's no hope anyway (v. 48).	The enemy, the accuser of the brethren, tells the person all the reasons he's unworthy to receive anything from God, so why bother?
Undeterred, Bartimaeus disregards the discouraging advice and calls out even more passionately (v. 48).	The person recognizes the voice of the enemy, and prays even more passionately for his healing or other blessing.
Jesus hears Bartimaeus' call, and tells someone who is willing to be obedient to tell him that he has gotten Jesus' attention.	God hears the prayer of the person in need, and gives a word of knowledge to someone who is willing to be obedient, and who states the particular problem, showing the person that he has gotten God's attention.
The people who had known about Bartimaeus' need hear Jesus' call to him, get excited for him, and encourage him to take advantage of the offer (v. 49).	The people who know about the person's need and/or prayer request hear the word of knowledge being announced, and they get excited for him, and encourage him to take advantage of the offer.
Faith arises, and Bartimaeus realizes his time for blessing has come, so he throws his cloak aside and comes to Jesus (v. 50), and Jesus lays hands on him and heals him (Matthew 20:34).	Faith arises, and the person realizes his time for blessing has come, so stands up out of his chair and comes forward to the front of the gathering, where hands are laid on him and Jesus heals him.

Notice how Bartimaeus responded when he realized he had gotten Jesus' attention: *he throws his cloak aside.* This is not just an irrelevant detail. Even in those days, there were scam artists, and a slothful, dishonest person could conceivably *pretend* to be blind, and just leech off the compassion of others; it's easier than working for a living.

To avoid such unethical behavior, anyone who was truly blind had to go to the priests, who would examine his eyes and confirm that he was indeed blind, and was therefore "authorized" to beg for alms from passersby. As a publicly recognizable indicator of that authorization from the priests—in effect, his "license" to beg—he was given a certain kind of cloak (presumably difficult to counterfeit) that showed people he was indeed blind and was worthy of receiving their alms.

It was that kind of cloak that Bartimaeus cast aside. Once he had Jesus' attention, there was no doubt in his mind that he would be healed within moments. And indeed he was. Similarly, when someone calls out a word of knowledge that matches what you have been praying for, that too causes a great increase in faith that God will answer your prayer within moments.

Luke's Account

And now let's read Luke's account of the story:

> Luke 18:35–43 (NIV): As Jesus approached Jericho, a blind man was sitting by the roadside begging. [36]When he heard the crowd going by, he asked what was happening. [37]They told him, "Jesus of Nazareth is passing by." [38]He called out, "Jesus, Son of David, have mercy on me!" [39]Those who led the way rebuked him and told him to be quiet, but he shouted all the more, "Son of David, have mercy on me!" [40]Jesus stopped and ordered the man to be brought to him. When he came near, Jesus asked him, [41]"What do you want me to do for you?" "Lord, I want to see," he replied. [42]Jesus said to him, "Receive your sight; your faith has healed you." [43]Immediately he received his sight and followed Jesus, praising God. When all the people saw it, they also praised God.

Now if you were paying attention, you might have noticed an apparent discrepancy between Matthew's account and Luke's account of the story. (You might have noticed the same apparent discrepancy between Matthew's account and Mark's account, but I decided to discuss it here, so the section on Mark's account wouldn't get overly long. . .)

So what is the discrepancy? Matthew's account states that this miracle happened when Jesus and the disciples were *leaving* Jericho, but Mark's and Luke's accounts state that it happened when they were *approaching* Jericho. Skeptics who are unfamiliar with the region where Jesus ministered often pounce on this as "proof" that the Bible couldn't have been inspired by God, is wrong and untrustworthy, doesn't merit putting your faith in, and so forth. So what's the answer?

When you hear the name "Denver," what do you think of? Probably the city in Colorado, right? But there's also a Denver in Pennsylvania, and a Denver in North Carolina. Or when you hear the name "Houston," what do you think of? Probably the city in Texas, right? But there's also a Houston in Alaska, and Massachusetts, and Missouri. And there are many, many other such examples.

And that is exactly the situation that occurred in the Holy Land in Jesus' day: there were two different towns named Jericho at the same time. The first one is the one most people know about, where "Joshua Fit de Battle," and the walls fell down. That city, while mostly in ruins, still existed as a village in Jesus' day, and was still populated. But also, about two miles southwest of there, was the new Jericho built by Herod the Great. If Jesus healed Bartimaeus and his friend between these two towns, on His way from to the other, both accounts would have been true.

Since the old Jericho and the new Jericho were only about two miles apart, *and* since they were both on one of the roads to Jerusalem, it's not at all a stretch to think that Jesus was on the road between them, probably quite a few times. Indeed, it would be a stretch to think that it *didn't* happen at least sometimes. And since Jesus was healing people pretty much every day, it's very reasonable that Jesus did *many* miracles while He was leaving—and simultaneously approaching—Jericho.

Malchus' Ear

The following is an amazing story, not simply because Jesus healed someone supernaturally, but also because of the context in which it happened. Shortly before his betrayal, Jesus and the disciples were in the Garden of Gethsemane, and Jesus was praying while the disciples were sawing logs:

> Luke 22:45–53 (NIV): When he rose from prayer and went back to the disciples, he found them asleep, exhausted from sorrow. [46]"Why are you sleeping?" he asked them. "Get up and pray so that you will not fall into temptation." [47]While he was still speaking a crowd came up, and the man who was called Judas, one of the Twelve, was leading them. He approached Jesus to kiss him, [48]but Jesus asked him, "Judas, are you betraying the Son of Man with a kiss?" [49]When Jesus' followers saw what was going to happen, they said, "Lord, should we strike with our swords?" [50]And one of them struck the servant of the high priest, cutting off his right ear. [51]But Jesus answered, "No more of this!" And he touched the man's ear and healed him. [52]Then Jesus said to the chief priests, the officers of the temple guard, and the elders, who had come for him, "Am I leading a rebellion, that you have come with swords and clubs? [53]Every day I was with you in the temple courts, and you did not lay a hand on me. But this is your hour—when darkness reigns."

Here comes a mob to arrest Jesus, and one of the disciples (namely, Peter; see John 18:10), in a desperate attempt to protect Jesus from the mob, draws his sword and cuts off the ear of Malchus, the servant of the high priest (his name also is specified in John 18:10). As many people have speculated, Peter was probably not aiming for his ear, but rather trying to cut Malchus' head off, and only quick reflexes on Malchus' part saved him from beheading. I think this is very plausible, but again, it is only speculation.

Regardless of Peter's actual intent, Jesus' restraint was truly amazing. He *really* understood His purpose. As He had said the week before, on

"Palm Sunday," when everyone was praising Him, He still knew that the time for unimaginable pain and burden was imminent:

> John 12:27 (NIV): "Now my heart is troubled, and what shall I say? 'Father, save me from this hour'? No, **it was for this very reason I came to this hour.**"

But He also knew it was the Father's will, and He wouldn't stay dead:

> John 10:17–18: Therefore doth my Father love me, because I lay down my life, that I might take it again. ¹⁸**No man taketh it from me, but I lay it down of myself.** I have power to lay it down, and I have power to take it again. This commandment have I received of my Father.

And what *really* makes Jesus' restraint amazing is that He didn't have to go through with it. If He had actually wanted protection, look what was at His disposal:

> Matthew 26:52–53 (NIV): "Put your sword back in its place," Jesus said to him, "for all who draw the sword will die by the sword. ⁵³Do you think I cannot call on my Father, and he will at once put at my disposal more than twelve legions of angels?"

We saw above that a Legion was 6,000 soldiers, so twelve legions of angels is 72,000 angels. Angels are not to be trifled with; they are certainly not the chubby little babies shooting arrows of love into the palpitating hearts of swooning paramours. Angels are more than a little intimidating, which is why when they're not disguising themselves as people (Hebrews 13:2), their most common greeting is "Fear not" (Matthew 28:5, Luke 1:13, 1:30, 2:10, etc.).

So here is Jesus saying that He could have more than 72,000 angels fighting for Him instantly, should He so choose. And when you realize that it only takes *one* angel to lock Satan up in the bottomless pit for a thousand years (Revelation 20:1–3), you suddenly have a much more healthy respect for what angels are like, and *especially* for what Jesus voluntarily went through for us.

Your Faith has Made You Well

Did you notice how many times Jesus said something to the effect of "Your faith has made you well," or otherwise indicated that the faith people had was instrumental in causing/allowing His miracle-working power to heal the people? It happened in at least The Paralytic With Four Good Friends, The Centurion's Servant, The Woman with the Issue of Blood, The Two Blind Men, The Canaanite Woman's Daughter, The Ten Lepers, Blind Bartimaeus and Friend. And in the place where the disciples *failed* to heal The Deaf Mute Epileptic Boy by casting the demon out, Jesus said it was a *lack* of faith.

What can we learn from all the above accounts where Jesus indicated it was their faith that made them well? *You can't have faith that God will heal you if you think He sometimes doesn't want to heal.* After all, how could you know that you'd be one of the "lucky" ones? You couldn't. Which means there would always be an awareness that you might not be one of the lucky ones, so the confidence, the faith, the conviction, would never arise.

Do you see the upshot of this? If you do not believe in healing, it is like the proverbial self-fulfilling prophecy: You don't have faith God will heal you, so the healing doesn't come, so it reinforces your idea that God doesn't always want to heal, so you don't have faith God will heal you, so the healing doesn't come, so it reinforces your idea that God doesn't always want to heal, so you don't have faith God will heal you, so the healing doesn't come, so it reinforces your idea that God doesn't always want to heal, and on and on, in a vicious, faith-killing cycle.

On the other hand, we have these people who *do* have faith that Jesus will heal them, and—surprise, surprise—He does. Note that in the Scriptures above, *100%* of the people who came to Jesus for healing got healed.

And healing is still going on every day, in places all over the world where the Spirit of God is free to move, and there is a hunger for His presence. By the thousands, people are being healed in amazing, dramatic, undeniable, and medically confirmable ways every day, and you can read their stories, hear their testimonies, and even participate in the events, if you get your news from the proper sources.

What Is Faith, Anyway?

Many people who have believed for years that God doesn't heal the sick, are usually reinforced in their belief by the fact that, in their experience, God hasn't healed anybody, as mentioned above. They can often "prove" that God doesn't heal people nowadays because they have prayed for a healing for themselves or someone else, or have heard about someone else doing so, and nothing happened. How do they know? Because they haven't seen any change.

What's wrong with this picture? Do you see the problem? When someone says, "I know God doesn't answer prayers like that because *I don't see* any change," it is clear that he doesn't understand what faith is:

> Hebrews 11:1 (TEV): To have faith is to be sure of the things we hope for, to be certain of the things **we cannot see.**

The very definition of faith is to be sure of things "we cannot see," so *of course* there will be a period of time where we don't see the answer. If you *could* see it, you wouldn't need to have faith for it anymore. So if we have faith in some promise of God, but we don't see it yet, what should we do? Keep believing, and confirm with our mouths what we believe in our hearts:

> II Corinthians 4:13: We having the same spirit of faith, according as it is written, I believed, and therefore have I spoken; **we also believe, and therefore speak. . .**

This is exactly what the skeptics use to "prove" that Christians who believe God wants to heal them are crazy, or unrealistic, or in denial, or whatever: "They say they're healed, but they're obviously not, anyone can see that!" (This statement is someone like saying, "You claim that Japan is real, but I've never seen it, so that proves it doesn't exist!") Yet, believing in something God has said, even though you don't yet see it, is what God calls faith. And, at some point, that faith bears fruit in the form of the answer we were believing for: Our faith will have made us well, just like all those people to whom Jesus said, "Your faith has made you well." They had faith that they would be healed *before* they were able to actually see the manifestation of the healing in their bodies. Just like today.

Let's look at some examples out of the "Hall of Faith" in Hebrews 11. First, what was God's response to these people having faith in Him and what He promised, even though they hadn't seen it yet (giving the skeptics ample opportunity to mock them)?

Hebrews 11:2: For by it [faith] the elders **obtained a good report.**

AMP: For by [faith—trust and holy fervor born of faith] the men of old **had divine testimony borne to them** and obtained a good report.

CEV: It was their faith that made our ancestors **pleasing to God.**

ERV: **God was pleased** with the people who lived a long time ago because they had faith like this.

GWORD: **God accepted** our ancestors because of their faith.

GNT: It was by their faith that people of ancient times **won God's approval.**

NOG: **God accepted** our ancestors because of their faith.

NET: For by it the people of old **received God's commendation.**

NLV: **God was pleased** with the men who had faith who lived long ago.

RSV: For by it the men of old **received divine approval.**

WE: There were people long ago believed God. **He said they were good** because they believed him.

So here we have people who believed what God had said—*even though circumstances didn't look like what God said was true*—and because of that, these people "obtained a good report," "won God's approval," "received God's commendation" and "divine approval," were "pleasing to God," "accepted" by God, and were called "good" by God.

Just a few of the people commended this way are:

- **Noah** had faith for a *hundred years* in God's statement that the Flood would come (Genesis 5:32, 7:6).
- **Abraham** had faith for twenty-five years in God's statement that he and Sarah would have a son (Genesis 12:4, 21:5).
- **Joseph** *never* did see in his lifetime, what he was having faith for (the children of Israel leaving Egypt).

So some of these people waited decades, or even the rest of their lives, for the manifestation of what they were believing for, and because of that *they kept believing God,* and God commended, accepted, and approved of them.

But what about all these people who are believing for healing, but it hasn't shown up yet? *Keep believing.* You know God's Word promises it; we've seen huge amounts of Scripture above that make it very clear. And concerning the people who think you're foolish to believe such a thing, because it "obviously" didn't happen, pray for them, that they would understand what faith is:

> I Corinthians 2:14 (NIV): The man without the Spirit does not accept the things that come from the Spirit of God, for they are foolishness to him, and **he cannot understand them, because they are spiritually discerned.**

Is faith really that important? Yes, enormously so:

> Hebrews 11:6 (NIV): And **without faith it is impossible to please God,** because anyone who comes to him must believe that he exists and that he rewards those who **earnestly** seek him.

It says "earnestly" seek Him, not just "seek Him when it's convenient," or "seek Him until you're tired of doing so," or "seek Him until someone makes fun of you." *Earnestly* seek Him, and He will reward you.

Jesus Healing Large Crowds

The above major section shows the cases where Jesus healed individuals or small groups. Although He certainly did that, God did not limit Jesus to healing only individuals or small groups. It didn't take long for Jesus' fame to spread, and then He was regularly swarmed by people; it was not uncommon for Him to be surrounded by crowds numbering in the tens of thousands (Matthew 14:21, 15:38). So let's take a look at the cases where Jesus healed multitudes. Again, we're trying to ascertain, by looking at what Jesus did in His earthly ministry, what God's heart is on the subject of divine healing.

Before the Sermon on the Mount

With Jesus healing everyone who came to Him, right from the get-go, it didn't take long for huge crowds to gather. He had many disciples following Him, even before He picked out The Twelve from among them. Jesus goes up into a mountain to pray and stayed there, praying all night:

> Luke 6:13: And when it was day, he called unto him his disciples: and **of them he chose twelve,** whom also he named apostles. . .

So at this point, He chose The Twelve out of a large number of disciples. Immediately after choosing the official twelve disciples:

> Luke 6:17–19: And he came down with them, and stood in the plain, and the company of his disciples, and **a great multitude of people** out of all Judaea and Jerusalem, and from the sea coast of Tyre and Sidon, which came to hear him, and to be healed of their diseases; [18]And they that were vexed with unclean spirits: and **they were healed.** [19]And the whole multitude sought to touch him: for **there went virtue out of him, and healed them all.**

So, Luke's account has Jesus healing *everybody* who came to Him. And this was not just everybody in a small clump of people, this was everybody in a "great multitude" of people. And Matthew's gospel confirms both these ideas: that of the "great multitude" (Matthew says "all those who were sick" from the "whole country of Syria"), and that He healed them all (Matthew says "Jesus healed them all").

> Matthew 4:23–24 (TEV): Jesus went all over Galilee, teaching in the synagogues, preaching the Good News about the Kingdom, and **healing people who had all kinds of disease and sickness.** ²⁴The news about him spread through the whole country of Syria, so that **people brought to him all those who were sick, suffering from all kinds of diseases and disorders: people with demons, and epileptics, and paralytics—and Jesus healed them all.**

And immediately after healing all these people, he definitely had their attention, so they were open to hearing His ideas on things. And that's when He preached the Sermon on the Mount. Evangelism is *so* much easier when people can see that God is actually real, and that He is good!

In the Evening

In the evening of the day when Jesus healed the centurion's servant and Peter's mother-in-law, massive crowds were around Him:

> Matthew 8:16–17 (TEV): When evening came, people brought to Jesus many who had demons in them. **Jesus drove out the evil spirits with a word and healed all who were sick.** ¹⁷He did this to make come true what the prophet Isaiah had said, "He himself took our sickness and carried away our diseases."

> Mark 1:32–34 (TEV): After the sun had set and evening had come, people brought to Jesus all the sick and those who had demons. ³³All the people of the town gathered in front of the house. ³⁴**Jesus healed many who were sick with all kinds of diseases and drove out many demons.** He would not let the demons say anything, because they knew who he was.

> Luke 4:40–41 (TEV): After sunset all who had friends who were sick with various diseases brought them to Jesus; **he placed his hands on every one of them and healed them all.** ⁴¹Demons also went out from many people, screaming, "You are the Son of God!" Jesus gave the demons an order and would not let them speak, because they knew he was the Messiah.

Mark's version above uses a particular word that is often misunderstood in English, because of the difference between its *denotation* and its *connotation*. If you're unfamiliar with those words, *denotation* means "the explicit or direct meaning of a word or expression." In other words, a word's denotation is what the word or expressions really means. On the other hand, *connotation* means "an associated meaning of a word or expression." In other words, a connotation is an idea that is not really what the word means, but people often associate it with the word anyway.

In modern English, the denotation or the word "many"—what it actually means—is "constituting a large number" or "numerous." But in many modern American speakers' usage, it has also taken on the connotation of "a majority but not all." Now this additional, associated meaning may indeed be warranted, depending on the context, as in, "I bought a carton of eggs, but many of them were broken." The implication indeed is that a disappointingly large fraction of them were broken, but not all of them.

The problem arises when we make the "but not all" meaning part of the *denotation* of the word and apply it in every case, instead of realizing it is merely a connotation, and even then, in only a subset of cases. I have seen this passage from Mark's account of the story, where it says Jesus healed "many" people and drove out "many" demons, used to support the contention that sometimes God doesn't want to heal some people. The reasoning goes, "See? It says that Jesus healed 'many' people, but it doesn't say He healed them *all*. And He cast out 'many' demons, but it doesn't say He cast out *all* of them. So that proves that sometimes God chooses not to heal some people."

There are some obvious problems with that line of reasoning, the first of which is that the "but not all" connotation is a modern addition to the denotation, and which isn't included in the word's definition. For example, if "many" people came to Jesus and He healed them all, how many did He heal? The answer is "many"—that's the number of people who came to Him for healing. There is no valid reason for adding the connotation to the denotation unless the Bible actually indicates that He healed fewer than the number of people who came to Him for healing.

And secondly, the Bible itself refutes that contention that Jesus healed fewer than came to Him. Indeed, if we look at the accounts in Matthew and Luke, the Bible explicitly says that Jesus healed them *all*. So we can see from these parallel accounts of the same story that the Bible does *not* include in the word "many" the connotation of "but not all" along with the denotation of "a great number."

See also the earlier section Wounded for Our Transgressions for a detailed discussion on how Matthew's account of the story clarifies what Isaiah meant in one of his Messianic prophecies about the Atonement, and what is included in it.

After Healing the Mute Demoniac

After the first of the mute demoniacs was healed (see The Mute Demoniacs above), and the Pharisees accused Jesus of casting out demons by the power of the devil, He again went around the countryside, healing *every* sickness and *every* disease:

> Matthew 9:35: And Jesus went about all the cities and villages, teaching in their synagogues, and preaching the gospel of the kingdom, and **healing every sickness and every disease** among the people.

He healed *every* sickness and *every* disease. And where did He do this? In *all* the cities and *all* the villages. Wow!

After Healing the Man with the Withered Hand

After Jesus healed the man with the withered hand (see The Man with the Withered Hand above), the Pharisees were infuriated with Jesus: He was pointing out their hypocrisy, He was doing good on the Sabbath day, He was eroding their control over the people, and more.

So they got together, trying to figure out how they could do away with Him. How did Jesus respond?

> Matthew 12:15: But when Jesus knew it, he withdrew himself from thence: and **great multitudes** followed him, and **he healed them all**. . .

"Great multitudes" followed Him, and He "healed them all. . ."

Peter's Sermon to Cornelius

You may remember—after Jesus' death, resurrection, and ascension, as well as after Pentecost and the conversion of Saul of Tarsus—when Peter had the vision of the great sheet with clean and unclean animals in it, and Cornelius' vision of the angel telling him to go see Peter. This was the first large-scale revelation that God was also accepting Gentiles into His Kingdom. When Peter starts talking to Cornelius and his family and friends, he refers to Jesus' ministry:

> Acts 10:34–38 (NIV): Then Peter began to speak: "I now realize how true it is that God does not show favoritism [35]but accepts men from every nation who fear him and do what is right. [36]You know the message God sent to the people of Israel, telling the good news of peace through Jesus Christ, who is Lord of all. [37]You know what has happened throughout Judea, beginning in Galilee after the baptism that John preached— [38]how God anointed **Jesus of Nazareth** with the Holy Spirit and power, and how he went around doing good and **healing all who were under the power of the devil, because God was with him**."

Note that Peter said that Jesus healed *all* who were oppressed by, or under the power of, the devil.

It's beginning to look like there's a pattern here. In every case I've been able to find, whenever people came to Jesus for healing, be that individually, in a small group, or in a great multitude, Jesus healed them all. *In every case.*

Why Did Jesus Heal?

We just read Acts 10, where Peter is talking to Cornelius and his household and he described how Jesus healed *all* who were oppressed of the devil. Now let's look at another nugget in v. 38, where Peter is talking about. . .

> Acts 10:38: How God anointed Jesus of Nazareth with the Holy Ghost and with power: who went about doing good, and healing all that were oppressed of the devil; **for** God was with him.

Have you ever wonder what the "for" is for? Jesus went around "healing all that were oppressed of the devil *for* God was with him." That little connecting word "for"—what does it mean? Let's look in some other translations and see if they can shed any light on the subject:

> CEB: . . .Jesus traveled around doing good and healing everyone oppressed by the devil **because** God was with him.
>
> DARBY: . . .healing all that were under the power of the devil, **because** God was with him.
>
> ERV: . . .Jesus went everywhere doing good for people. He healed those who were ruled by the devil, **showing that** God was with him.
>
> GWORD: Jesus did these things **because** God was with him.
>
> ISV: . . .**because** God was with him, he went around doing good and healing everyone who was oppressed by the Devil.

Many other translations agree with the few that are listed above: Jesus healed *because* God was with Him, or *showing that* God was with Him. Again, the healings were evidence—corroborating proof—that God the Father was backing up Jesus' verbal claims, and it is consistent with His statement in Matthew 9:6, where He offered physical healing as the *proof* that He was authorized to forgive sins (see Forgiveness and Healing Together below for details). As mentioned in that section, do *we* offer physical healing as proof that our message of Jesus' forgiveness is true? Jesus (and therefore God) thought it was appropriate, fitting, and proper to do so; how could we conclude otherwise?

If It Be Thy Will

Chapter 5:

Are *All* Christians Supposed to Heal the Sick?

Now we're getting into the area where the proverbial rubber meets the road. People can talk all day about what God intended when He created everything millennia ago, or what Jesus' intent and goals were during His earthly ministry millennia ago, but when it gets to the point of having to decide "How does this affect my day-to-day Christian life?", people tend to get nervous. This nervousness (i.e., fear) often manifests itself as defensiveness, as in, "Don't tell *me* I have to go heal people!"

Now why would people be so quick to backpedal in terror at the prospect of blessing someone and seeing Jesus exalted? We haven't even mentioned any Scriptures that imply we should. Except, of course, that perfect health was God's will in the first place. And that one of His identities—His "Jehovah Names"—is Healer. And the many promises in the Old Testament that He will do so. And Jesus' actions during His earthly ministry, and the fact that He is to be our example; we are supposed to do the same things that He did, and even greater ones. But other than those, are there any Biblical commands where *we*—regular people—are to heal the sick?

Glad you asked.

The Disciples

Let's take a look at what Jesus empowered the disciples to do when He sent them out to do the Father's will:

> Matthew 10:1 And when he had called unto him his twelve disciples, **he gave them power** against unclean spirits, to cast them out, and **to heal all manner of sickness and all manner of disease.**
>
> Mark 3:14–15: And **he ordained twelve,** that they should be with him, and that he might send them forth to preach, ¹⁵And **to have power to heal sicknesses, and to cast out devils...**
>
> Luke 9:1: Then he called his twelve disciples together, and **gave them power and authority over all devils, and to cure diseases.**

So in all three synoptic Gospels, Jesus gives the disciples power to heal all kinds of sickness and disease, and to cast out all demons. From this we can very reasonably surmise that He gave them that power *so they would use it*. And indeed, that is the case; let's continue the Matthew and Luke passages begun above:

> Matthew 10:5–8: These twelve Jesus sent forth, and commanded them, saying, Go not into the way of the Gentiles, and into any city of the Samaritans enter ye not: ⁶But go rather to the lost sheep of the house of Israel. ⁷And as ye go, preach, saying, The kingdom of heaven is at hand. ⁸**Heal the sick, cleanse the lepers, raise the dead, cast out devils:** freely ye have received, freely give.
>
> Luke 9:2, 6: And **he sent them** to preach the kingdom of God, and **to heal the sick...** ⁶And **they departed,** and went through the towns, **preaching the gospel, and healing every where.**

At this point in the conversation, some people reply (I have heard them), "But that was Jesus telling the *disciples* to do that. He doesn't mean for *us* to do that!" This line of thought—the idea that what Jesus said to the disciples "back in Bible days" doesn't necessarily apply to us nowadays—is *exceedingly* dangerous. Why? Because *everything* Jesus said in the Bible was spoken to people "back in Bible days." And if that means we don't need to abide by it, then:

- We don't need to let our light shine (Matthew 5:16), because that was spoken to the people back in Bible days.
- We don't need to be reconciled to our brothers (Matthew 4:23–24), because that was spoken to the people back in Bible days.
- We don't need to avoid lust (Matthew 5:27–30), because that was spoken to the people back in Bible days.
- We don't need to turn the other cheek (Matthew 5:38–39), because that was spoken to the people back in Bible days.
- We don't need to love our enemies (Matthew 5:44–48), because that was spoken to the people back in Bible days.
- We don't need to lay up treasures in heaven (Matthew 6:20–21), because that was spoken to the people back in Bible days.
- We don't need to seek first the Kingdom of God (Matthew 6:33), because that was spoken to the people back in Bible days.
- We don't need to deny ourselves and take up our cross (Matthew 16:24), because that was spoken to the people back in Bible days.
- We don't need to forgive our brothers (Matthew 18:21–22), because that was spoken to the people back in Bible days.
- We don't need to serve each other (Matthew 20:26–27), because that was spoken to the people back in Bible days.

. . .and there are hundreds, if not thousands, of other examples which—if you actually believe they do not apply to modern-day people—render the whole Bible pointless. Presumably, since you are reading this book, you realize that Jesus' commands to His disciples apply to us in the twenty-first century as well as to those people in "Bible times." In other words, we are *still* in "Bible times," because the Bible hasn't gone out of date, nor has it become obsolete.

Now that that is settled, we still need to deal with the fact that Jesus tells His disciples to "heal the sick, cleanse the lepers, raise the dead, cast out devils." And we will do so, shortly.

The Seventy-Two

After Jesus sent the twelve disciples into the surrounding villages to—among other things—heal the sick, He sent seventy-two others to do the same:

> Luke 10:1, 8–9, 16–17 (NIV): After this the Lord appointed seventy-two others and sent them two by two ahead of him to every town and place where he was about to go. . . . ⁸"When you enter a town and are welcomed, eat what is set before you. ⁹Heal the sick who are there and tell them, 'The kingdom of God is near you.' . . . ¹⁶He who listens to you listens to me; he who rejects you rejects me; but he who rejects me rejects him who sent me.'" ¹⁷The seventy-two returned with joy and said, "Lord, even the demons submit to us in your name."

Lest anybody even during "Bible days" think that Jesus' commands applied only to The Twelve, He sent out this other, bigger batch of disciples to do the same thing He assigned The Twelve to do.

And, lest anybody think that the Twelve plus the Seventy-Two were the only ones who were authorized to do miraculous signs and wonders, there were others who apparently knew that God was not a respecter of persons, and just realized, "Hey, this stuff works! I want to serve God that way too!" as this man did:

> Mark 9:38–40 (TEV): John said to him, "Teacher, we saw a man who was driving out demons in your name, and we told him to stop, because he doesn't belong to our group." ³⁹"Do not try to stop him," Jesus told them, "because no one who performs a miracle in my name will be able soon afterward to say evil things about me. ⁴⁰For whoever is not against us is for us."

We can learn from this you don't need an open-eyed vision of God's Throne Room accompanied by choirs of angels to authorize/endorse/

entitle you to heal the sick. The mere fact that He commands it in His Word should be enough for us.

The Great Commission

What is the "Great Commission?" It is Jesus' command as to how to do evangelism after He ascended back to heaven after the resurrection. Here's what He said:

> Matthew 28:16–20 (NIV): Then the eleven disciples went to Galilee, to the mountain where Jesus had told them to go. [17]When they saw him, they worshiped him; but some doubted. [18]Then Jesus came to them and said, "All authority in heaven and on earth has been given to me. [19]Therefore **go and make disciples of all nations**, baptizing them in the name of the Father and of the Son and of the Holy Spirit, [20]and **teaching them to obey everything I have commanded you.** And surely I am with you always, to the very end of the age."

It's that pesky little phrase Jesus said in v. 20 that often trips up modern-day people. That little phrase that says they were to teach all the new disciples "to obey *everything* I have commanded you." Notice that He said "*everything,*" not just "those things you're comfortable with" or "those things you can do whether God shows up or not." That would necessarily include those places where Jesus commanded His disciples to "heal the sick, cleanse the lepers, raise the dead, cast out devils."

And it's just possible that someone who's *really* nervous about the prospect of praying for the sick, might glimpse a potential loophole here. Jesus told His disciples to teach their disciples to obey everything that he had said, but he didn't tell those *new* disciples, in turn, to pass it on to the third generation, did He? Bzzzzt!—I'm sorry, wrong answer.

Jesus told His disciples to teach the new disciples to obey *everything* He had commanded them. That would have to include the command to teach the new disciples to obey everything He had commanded them. In other words, "everything" Jesus commanded would have to include the command to propagate it to the new disciples. So no, the teach-the-new-disciples command did not stop after the first generation of disciples after Jesus. *Every* generation of disciples is to do what Jesus told His original twelve disciples to do, including passing it on to subsequent generations of disciples.

Being Christlike

One of our responsibilities as Christians is to become as much like Christ as possible. Jesus said:

> John 14:12: Verily, verily, I say unto you, **He that believeth on me, the works that I do shall he do also; and greater works than these shall he do;** because I go unto my Father.

That's an amazing statement: the same works that Jesus did, we should do. But who's the "we" here? The "we" refers to those that believe on Jesus—*all believers*. Wow.

Chuck Parry, Associate Director of the Healing Rooms at Bethel Church in Redding, California, tells of a Bible study he did many years ago. In his book *Free Falling*, he describes (on p. 61) the time when he first saw the verse where Jesus said "If you love me, keep my commandments" (John 14:15). He wanted with all of his heart to keep Jesus' commandments, but he didn't know what they were, so he methodically looked through the four Gospels to see every place where Jesus said something in the imperative; i.e., gave someone a command, and he counted the number of times each type of command was given.

Chuck discovered, to his surprise, these facts about what Jesus commanded:

- The *third* most common command that Jesus gave was "fear not" or some equivalent (e.g., "be not afraid," etc.).
- The *second* most common command that Jesus gave was "believe" or some equivalent (e.g., "have faith," "doubt not," etc.).
- The *most common* command that Jesus gave was "be healed" or some equivalent (e.g., "be whole," etc.).

So doesn't it make sense that if we are to keep His commandments, we would need to have as a major part of our ministries, common acts of supernatural healing? As mentioned above, evangelism is *so* much easier when people realize that Jesus is not just a philosophy, or your opinion, or merely a historical figure, but a living, powerful, loving God who knows them and cares for them!

"So Send I You"

After the resurrection, Jesus appeared to the disciples. He literally did: they were in a locked room for fear of their own potential crucifixions, and *poof!*—He suddenly appeared in the middle of the group.

> John 20:19–21 (NIV): On the evening of that first day of the week, when the disciples were together, with the doors locked for fear of the Jews, Jesus came and stood among them and said, "Peace be with you!" ²⁰After he said this, he showed them his hands and side. The disciples were overjoyed when they saw the Lord. ²¹Again Jesus said, "Peace be with you! **As the Father has sent me, I am sending you.**"

Note that last phrase: "As the Father has sent me, I am sending you." What does "as" mean? It means "in the same way." So how did the Father send Jesus? With all the resources of heaven behind Him, and brought into play through the Holy Spirit. Which means, that is how Jesus is sending us: With all the resources of heaven behind us, and brought into play through the Holy Spirit.

If It Be Thy Will

Chapter 6:

Post-Ascension Examples of Healing

We already saw in the previous chapter where the disciples, both the Twelve and the Seventy-Two, went out and healed people as part of preaching the Gospel. Are there other Biblical examples besides these? Jesus was still on earth when the Twelve and the Seventy-Two were sent out; does His command still apply now that He's no longer on earth?

The Apostles at Solomon's Porch

Note the emphasized words in the following passage; every one has far-reaching consequences:

> Acts 5:12, 15–16 (TEV): **Many miracles and wonders** were being performed among the people by the apostles. All the believers met together in Solomon's Porch. . . . [15]As a result of what the apostles were doing, sick people were carried out into the streets and placed on beds and mats **so that at least Peter's shadow might fall on some of them** as he passed by. [16]And **crowds of people came in** from the towns

around Jerusalem, bringing those who were sick or who had evil spirits in them; and **they were all healed.**

You've probably heard that it wasn't Peter's shadow that healed the people, and that is true. A shadow, in itself, has no substance, and in fact, it is an *absence* of something: light. The point here is that if the people got close enough to Peter that his shadow fell on them, they were close enough to the anointing—the manifest presence, power, and glory of God—that they would be healed. This still happens today in meetings all over the world where the Holy Spirit is allowed to flow, and it is often called an "atmosphere" of healing. In such a situation, just getting *close* to the person God is using will result in God's blessing being poured out, whether anyone prays for a specific need or not.

While this particular usage of the word "atmosphere" to describe the ambient spiritual condition is somewhat new, the concept is very Biblical, both in the Old Testament and the New. The Scriptures below show some of these situations: in the first two, there was an atmosphere of prophecy, and people just started prophesying whether they were specifically seeking the Lord for it or not, and the third example describes an atmosphere of healing.

First, let's look at when Moses and the seventy elders of Israel gathered around the tabernacle to meet God:

> Numbers 11:25: And the LORD came down in a cloud, and spake unto him, and took of the spirit that was upon him, and gave it unto the seventy elders: and it came to pass, that, **when the spirit rested upon them, they prophesied, and did not cease.**

Next is a story of when King Saul was trying to capture and kill David. Saul sends a garrison of men to capture David, while he was hanging around the prophet Samuel. God "takes them out of commission," so to speak, as well and the next two garrisons of men that Saul sends:

> I Samuel 19:19–24 (NIV): Word came to Saul: "David is in Naioth at Ramah"; [20]so he sent men to capture him. But when they saw a group of prophets prophesying, with Samuel standing there as their leader,

the **Spirit of God came upon Saul's men and they also prophesied.** ²¹Saul was told about it, and **he sent more men, and they prophesied too.** Saul sent men a third time, and **they also prophesied.**

So these three detachments of soldiers couldn't perform their duty for Saul—capturing David—because they were so busy prophesying! So finally Saul, apparently thinking, "If you want something done right, do it yourself. . .", goes there himself to capture David:

> ²²Finally, he himself left for Ramah and went to the great cistern at Secu. And he asked, "Where are Samuel and David?" "Over in Naioth at Ramah," they said. ²³So Saul went to Naioth at Ramah. But **the Spirit of God came even upon him, and he walked along prophesying** until he came to Naioth. ²⁴**He stripped off his robes and also prophesied in Samuel's presence.** He lay that way all that day and night. This is why people say, "Is Saul also among the prophets?"

So the same thing happens to Saul himself. That must have been quite a prophetic atmosphere! Below, notice the wording used to describe what we now call an "atmosphere of healing:"

> Luke 5:17 (NIV): One day as he was teaching, Pharisees and teachers of the law, who had come from every village of Galilee and from Judea and Jerusalem, were sitting there. And **the power of the Lord was present for him to heal the sick.**

As shown in an earlier chapter, Jesus healed *everyone* who came to Him for healing, so the power to heal the sick was never lacking, but here, Luke clearly points out that "the *power was present*. . . to heal the sick." This is a perfect description of an "atmosphere" of healing, and it was a very similar thing that happened with Peter, when anyone within a shadow-length away from him got healed, just because of the intensity of the presence of God on him.

You may also have heard about the "atmosphere of repentance" or "atmosphere of salvation" that hovered around Smith Wigglesworth, Dwight L. Moody, and other powerful evangelists. People just getting on the same train car with Wigglesworth, or walking within a block or two of Moody's meetings, would be overcome with an awareness of their own sinfulness, cry out to God for mercy, and get gloriously saved. Boy, do we need a resurgence of this kind of atmosphere! And thankfully, it is again on the rise all over the world, where God is free to move and His Spirit is not quenched.

Philip in Samaria

The Philip referred to here was not the Philip who was one of the original twelve disciples; this Philip was a *waiter;* basically a server in a restaurant:

> Acts 6:1–6 (NIV): In those days when the number of disciples was increasing, the Grecian Jews among them complained against the Hebraic Jews because their widows were being overlooked in the daily distribution of food. ²So the Twelve gathered all the disciples together and said, "It would not be right for us to neglect the ministry of the word of God in order to wait on tables. ³Brothers, choose seven men from among you who are known to be **full of the Spirit and wisdom.** We will turn this responsibility over to them ⁴and will give our attention to prayer and the ministry of the word." ⁵This proposal pleased the whole group. They chose Stephen, a man full of faith and of the Holy Spirit; also **Philip,** Procorus, Nicanor, Timon, Parmenas, and Nicolas from Antioch, a convert to Judaism. ⁶They presented these men to the apostles, who prayed and laid their hands on them.

Here's a classic example of how there is no Biblical distinction between "sacred" and "secular." Here's a food server whom God used mightily to further His Kingdom:

> Acts 8:5–7 (NIV): Philip went down to a city in Samaria and proclaimed the Christ there. ⁶When the crowds heard Philip and saw the miraculous signs he did, they all paid close attention to what he said. ⁷With shrieks, **evil spirits came out of many, and many paralytics and cripples were healed.**

To see again how the Bible does not associate the connotation "but not all" to the word "many," as modern English speakers often do, see the section In the Evening above.

Peter Meets Aeneas at Lydda

When Peter went to Lydda, he ran across a man with what the KJV refers to as "palsy"—paralysis, usually accompanied by tremors. Here's what happened:

> Acts 9:32–35 (NIV): As Peter traveled about the country, he went to visit the saints in Lydda. ³³There he found a man named Aeneas, a paralytic who had been bedridden for eight years. ³⁴"Aeneas," Peter said to him, "Jesus Christ heals you. Get up and take care of your mat." Immediately Aeneas got up. ³⁵**All those who lived in Lydda and Sharon saw him and turned to the Lord.**

Look at the result of this one man's miraculous healing! *"All those who lived in Lydda and Sharon saw him and turned to the Lord."* (v. 35). Yet again, we see that evangelism is made incomparably easier and more effective by the inclusion of signs and wonders. No evangelist should attempt to preach the Gospel *without* signs and wonders, especially since they're available to *all* of us, and we have *all* been commanded to do them. And as we'll see below, *the Gospel is not even complete* without signs and wonders.

Peter Meets Tabitha at Joppa

The signs and wonders that happened after Jesus' ascension didn't include only healing; they raised the dead too, almost as if they believed John 14:12:

> Acts 9:36–42 (NIV): In Joppa there was a disciple named Tabitha (which, when translated, is Dorcas), who was always doing good and helping the poor. ³⁷About that time **she became sick and died,** and her body was washed and placed in an upstairs room. ³⁸Lydda was near Joppa; so when the disciples heard that Peter was in Lydda, they sent two men to him and urged him, "Please come at once!" ³⁹Peter went with them, and when he arrived he was taken upstairs to the room. All the widows stood around him, crying and showing him the robes and other clothing that Dorcas had made while she was still with them. ⁴⁰Peter sent them all out of the room; then he got down on his knees and prayed. **Turning toward the dead woman, he said, "Tabitha, get up."** She

opened her eyes, and seeing Peter she sat up. ⁴¹He took her by the hand and helped her to her feet. Then he called the believers and the widows and presented her to them alive. ⁴²This became known all over Joppa, and many people believed in the Lord.

Think about the time involved here. First, Tabitha dies, and her body is washed and prepared for burial. Then, the news of Peter's being in Lydda reaches the disciples in Joppa (about ten miles away). Then, there is undoubtedly some discussion as to what, if anything, they should do since Peter is there. Once they decide, the send word to Peter in Lydda. Now back in these days, they couldn't just call Peter's cell phone, and have him hop in his car and be there in fifteen minutes (although there is an occasional reference to the disciples all being in one Accord), so it probably took the better part of a day to walk there. Then, after they had talked to Peter and he had agreed to come, they had to walk back. So, all told, Tabitha had probably been dead for a duration comparable to that of Lazarus when Jesus raised him: about four days.

And yet again, note the evangelical fallout of this one miracle, impressive though it was: "many people believed in the Lord." The more you see the positive results of signs and wonders on the spiritual receptivity of people, the more it becomes totally ludicrous to contemplate evangelism without them.

The Apostle Paul

Years ago, I heard a theory that said the Apostle Paul did very few, if any, miracles. This was quite surprising to me, because I had never gotten that impression, and I had been a student of the Bible for quite some time. But it was presented to me as A Well Known Fact™ as if *everyone* ought to know that. So, as is my wont, I checked the statement against the Scriptures to see if it were true. What I found made me wonder just where they had gotten that idea, because I'm pretty sure it wasn't the Bible.

> Acts 13:9–11 (TEV): Then Saul—also known as Paul—was filled with the Holy Spirit; he looked straight at the magician ¹⁰and said, "You son

of the Devil! You are the enemy of everything that is good. You are full of all kinds of evil tricks, and you always keep trying to turn the Lord's truths into lies! ¹¹The Lord's hand will come down on you now; **you will be blind** and will not see the light of day for a time." At once **Elymas felt a dark mist cover his eyes, and he walked around trying to find someone to lead him by the hand.**

Acts 14:3 (NIV): So Paul and Barnabas spent considerable time there [at Iconium], speaking boldly for the Lord, who confirmed the message of his grace by enabling them to do **miraculous signs and wonders.**

Acts 14:8–10 (NIV): In Lystra there sat **a man crippled in his feet, who was lame from birth and had never walked.** ⁹He listened to Paul as he was speaking. Paul looked directly at him, saw that he had faith to be healed ¹⁰and called out, "Stand up on your feet!" At that, **the man jumped up and began to walk.**

Acts 15:12 (NIV): The whole assembly became silent as they listened to Barnabas and Paul telling about the **miraculous signs and wonders God had done among the Gentiles through them.**

Acts 16:16–18 (NIV): Once when we were going to the place of prayer, we were met by a slave girl who had a spirit by which she predicted the future. She earned a great deal of money for her owners by fortune-telling. ¹⁷This girl followed Paul and the rest of us, shouting, "These men are servants of the Most High God, who are telling you the way to be saved." ¹⁸She kept this up for many days. Finally **Paul became so troubled that he turned around and said to the spirit, "In the name of Jesus Christ I command you to come out of her!" At that moment the spirit left her.**

Acts 19:11–12 (NIV): God did **extraordinary miracles through Paul,** ¹²so that even handkerchiefs and aprons that had touched him were taken to the sick, and their illnesses were cured and the evil spirits left them.

Acts 20:9–12 (NIV): Seated in a window was a young man named Eutychus, who was sinking into a deep sleep as Paul talked on and on. When he was sound asleep, **he fell to the ground from the third story and was picked up dead.** ¹⁰Paul went down, threw himself on the young man and put his arms around him. "Don't be alarmed," he said. "He's alive!" ¹¹Then he went upstairs again and broke bread and ate. After talking until daylight, he left. ¹²The **people took the young man home alive** and were greatly comforted.

Acts 28:3–5 (NIV): Paul gathered a pile of brushwood and, as he put it on the fire, a viper, driven out by the heat, fastened itself on his hand. ⁴When the islanders saw the snake hanging from his hand, they said to each other, "This man must be a murderer; for though he escaped from the sea, Justice has not allowed him to live." ⁵**But Paul shook the snake off into the fire and suffered no ill effects.**

Acts 28:7–9 (TEV): Not far from that place were some fields that belonged to Publius, the chief of the island. He welcomed us kindly and for three days we were his guests. ⁸Publius' father was in bed, sick with fever and dysentery. **Paul went into his room, prayed, placed his hands on him, and healed him.** ⁹When this happened, **all the other sick people on the island came and were healed.**

I Corinthians 2:4 (NIV): **My message and my preaching were** not with wise and persuasive words, but **with a demonstration of the Spirit's power. . .**

As you can see from the plethora of Scriptures above, it is silly to say that Paul did few miracles or no miracles. And of all the miracles whose types are described at all, the vast majority are healings.

And indeed, signs and wonders and miracles are the *proof* of an apostle; his proof of apostleship:

II Corinthians 12:11–12: I am become a fool in glorying; ye have compelled me: for I ought to have been commended of you: for in nothing am I behind the very chiefest apostles, though I be nothing. ¹²Truly **the signs of an apostle** were wrought among you in all patience, in **signs, and wonders, and mighty deeds.**

12:12, AMP: Indeed, **the signs that indicate a [genuine] apostle** were performed among you fully and most patiently in **miracles and wonders and mighty works.**

CJB: The **things that prove I am an emissary—signs, wonders and miracles**—were done in your presence, despite what I had to endure.

CEV: When I was with you, I was patient and worked **all the powerful miracles and signs and wonders of a true apostle.**

ERV: When I was with you, I patiently did **the things that prove I am an apostle—signs, wonders, and miracles.**

ESV: The **signs of a true apostle** were performed among you with utmost patience, with **signs and wonders and mighty works.**

EXB: When I was with you, I patiently did **the things that prove I am an apostle** [The signs of an apostle were performed among you, with all patience/perseverance]—**signs, wonders, and miracles** [powerful deeds].

GWORD: While I was among you **I patiently did the signs, wonders, and miracles which prove that I'm an apostle.**

GNT: The **many miracles and wonders that prove that I am an apostle** were performed among you with much patience.

PHILLIPS: You have had an exhaustive demonstration of the **power God gives to a genuine messenger of his in the miracles, signs and works of spiritual power** that you saw with your own eyes.

TLB: When I was there **I certainly gave you every proof that I was truly an apostle,** sent to you by God himself, for **I patiently did many wonders and signs and mighty works** among you.

MSG: All the signs that mark a true apostle were in evidence while I was with you through both good times and bad: **signs of portent, signs of wonder, signs of power.**

NOG: While I was among you **I patiently did the signs, wonders, and miracles which prove that I'm an apostle.**

NCV: When I was with you, **I patiently did the things that prove I am an apostle—signs, wonders, and miracles.**

NIRV: You can recognize apostles by the signs, wonders and miracles they do. Those things were faithfully done among you no matter what happened.

NIV: I persevered in demonstrating among you **the marks of a true apostle, including signs, wonders and miracles.**

NLV: When I was with you, **I proved to you that I was a true missionary. I did powerful works** and there were special things to see. These things were done in the strength and power from God.

NLT: When I was with you, I certainly gave you **proof that I am an apostle.** For **I patiently did many signs and wonders and miracles** among you.

VOICE: **Miracles, wonders, and signs** were all performed right before your eyes, **proving I am who I say, a true emissary of Jesus.**

So if the performing of signs, wonders, and miracles is the *proof* of an apostle (which the Bible confirms very clearly above), Paul *better* have had them in his ministry, or else he was not the apostle we think he was.

Indeed, even *the Gospel itself* is proven and validated and confirmed by signs, wonders, and miracles. In other words, if someone's ministry does not include signs, wonders, and miracles, he is missing an essential part of the Gospel, and his fruit will be much less than it could be. Basically, he is attempting to do an enormously big job, but not using the power tools God makes available and tells us to use. Look what Paul says:

> Romans 15:18–19: For I will not dare to speak of any of those things which Christ hath not wrought by me, to make the Gentiles obedient, by word and deed, [19]**Through mighty signs and wonders,** by the power of the Spirit of God; so that from Jerusalem, and round about unto Illyricum, **I have fully preached the gospel of Christ.**

Do you see what Paul said here? He *fully* preached the Gospel *through mighty signs and wonders!* In other words, you can't *fully* preach the Gospel while omitting mighty signs and wonders. So the proof that the gospel is valid is the fact that God confirms it by the signs, wonders, and miracles that humans, in and of themselves, can't possibly do.

Talk is cheap; *anyone* can preach a doctrine and say it's true. So why should people believe us Christians when we say that the Bible is true, and that Jesus loves them? We'd better have some kind of miraculous proof, or else there's no reason for them to believe us. And God is happy to confirm His word when we are obedient even in doing the faith-stretching things He commanded:

> Mark 16:20 (TEV): The disciples went and preached everywhere, and the Lord worked with them and **proved that their preaching was true by the miracles that were performed.**

Acts 14:3 (NIV): So Paul and Barnabas spent considerable time there [in Iconium], speaking boldly for the Lord, **who confirmed the message of his grace by enabling them to do miraculous signs and wonders.**

And Jesus even goes one step farther than that. He not only is happy to confirm His word with signs following (as in the two Scriptures above), but *Jesus Himself* told people they didn't need to believe Him unless He did miracles to back it up.

John 10:37: If I do not the works of my Father, **believe me not.**

Wow. That's rather blunt, isn't it? This will be a surprise many people in the modern church, but Jesus said it, right there. Are we willing to say that to people when *we* are preaching the Gospel? If we followed Jesus' lead and told people not to believe us unless we back it up by performing signs and wonders, we would quickly have to come to grips with where we stand with God. *That's* somewhat sobering, isn't it?

So in this last section we have been talking more generically about "signs wonders, and miracles" and not healing specifically, but if we follow Jesus' lead, most of those miraculous events *will* be healing. Bodily health is very important to people, and if they find out for certain that Jesus is real (because He just healed them), that will go a long way toward convincing them that the rest of the Gospel is true as well.

If It Be Thy Will

Chapter 7:

Hindrances to Healing

I have believed in divine healing for decades now, and have spent quite a bit of time with Christians who didn't believe in it, or didn't want to pray for it, either for themselves or someone else. Why would this happen? Why *wouldn't* Christians want to increase their effectiveness in fulfilling their calling? Why *wouldn't* they want to show God's love to people in an undeniable way? Why *wouldn't* they want to dramatically increase the effectiveness of their evangelistic efforts? There are many reasons why Christians don't pray for miraculous healings, and this chapter will cover the more common ones.

There are, unsurprisingly, many hindrances to supernatural, miraculous, divine healing. There are many proverbial "monkey wrenches" that can get into the process to hinder healing. But one thing is certain: of all the problems that potentially could hinder a healing from being manifested, *the problems are never on God's end.*

So let's look at some of the things that could hinder, reduce, or delay a supernatural healing.

What If It Doesn't Work?

There are several aspects to be objection of "What if it doesn't work?" The first one I can think of is: how do you *know* it didn't work?

How Do You *Know* It Didn't Work?

For example, in a Bible Study that I lead twice a month on Saturdays, we prayed for a man who had chronic chest pain. Nothing visible happened when we prayed for him, or for the rest of the day. But the following Wednesday evening, he felt the Spirit of the Lord come over his chest like a warm blanket, and he hasn't had any chest pain since. So, did the prayer work?

If we had gotten discouraged and concluded by the absence of instant results that the prayer did not work, we could have nullified our prayers by putting more trust in the strength of the enemy to make him sick, than in the strength of God to make him well. I have heard many stories like this, where the answer to prayer comes a while *after* the prayer is finished. Oftentimes, this happens in order to reinforce to both the pray*er* and the pray*ee* that *God* is the source of the healing, not the person praying. This happens to people in every level of ministry, from beginners like myself all the way up to the big names in worldwide healing ministries. Of course, we would all *like* instantaneous answers to our prayers, but we walk by faith, not by sight (II Corinthians 5:7).

Here's another scenario: I have heard several testimonies about people who were prayed for, who had incurable and fatal diseases, and apparently "nothing happened." But then the pray*er* hears, *years* later, that the person is still alive, when doctors (years before) had given the person only a few months to live. It was like the disease just stopped, although its effects weren't yet reversed. So did such a prayer really fail? No, it was a partial healing, and the fact that something *did* happen should provoke us to continue (or resume) praying for the complete manifestation of the healing.

Of course, the *goal* is to have instantaneous healings like Jesus did. But until we're there, healings that take a little bit longer are still precious gifts from God, and should be received with gratitude and faith.

Why Would God Delay a Healing Like That?

You might think it's odd that God might choose to delay a healing until a while after the person was prayed for—a few minutes, hours, or even days. Well, assuming it *is* God Who is delaying it (and we don't know that for sure), it could be, as mentioned above, that He wants to make sure that the pray*ee* realizes that the source of the healing is God, and not the pray*er*; sometimes, people put other people up on a pedestal. Or, it could be that God wants to make sure that the pray*er* doesn't get puffed up by a large number of dramatic healings, so He delays the manifestation of the healing until after the prayer time is over for a while. Or both.

But the previous paragraph assumes that the delay was God's doing, which may or may not be the case. It could be that the healing came instantly, when some other aspect of the pray*ee*'s life got resolved, and that could have happened a while after the prayer was prayed.

Did Something Else Get Healed?

Sometimes we pray for Problem A, and we're disappointed when Problem A is apparently not healed. But then later, we find out that Problem B got healed. This can be quite a surprise, especially when we didn't even know that Problem B existed.

Randy Clark tells a story like this: he prayed for a man with a bad case of toenail fungus, and the next day the man was rejoicing because he got healed of high blood pressure.

I haven't had exactly the same experience in my own life, but I have had similar ones. It's not uncommon to for people to have a variety of things wrong with them—six or eight or even more—and they want prayer for all of them. I have found myself praying primarily for one or two things, and when *they* don't show a noticeable improvement, I have found myself getting disappointed or even discouraged. Then I find out that some other thing that someone else prayed for, or that I had completely forgotten about, *was* healed, and I'm thankful that I stayed at it long enough to find that out, rather than go with first appearances, and giving up.

Is It In Process?

Because healings often happen more slowly for us than for Jesus, we often think that because the healing wasn't *completed* before our eyes, that it didn't even start. But this is often very wrong. Sometimes we can lead ourselves into discouragement simply because we ask the wrong questions. For example, rather than ask the person if the pain is *gone,* ask him if it is *less.* Another words, have the person notice not only *whether* pain is present or not—a binary, yes-or-no answer—but at what the *level* of pain is, on the scale of 0 to 10. This way, any improvement is a faith-builder, leading to more prayer and even more improvement.

Consider the following two scenarios:

1. Someone comes to you for prayer for severe pain. You ask him, "Hurts pretty bad, does it?" He replies, "Sure does." So you pray, and then ask him if it still hurts, and he says yes. You turn away, tail dragging, feeling convinced by the enemy that your prayer "didn't work," and you are even more resistant to praying for someone else later. What you don't realize is that the pain *was* reduced; it just didn't go away completely.

2. Someone comes to you for prayer for severe pain. You ask him, "How much pain do you have, on a scale of 0 to 10?" He replies, "Six." So you pray, and then after a few minutes ask him, "How much pain do you have now, using the same scale?" and he replies, "Four." You both rejoice, and get encouraged, and keep praying. Pretty soon, the pain is at level 2, then 1, then 0, and you are both ecstatic.

I've seen the second scenario many times in my own experience of praying for people, and I've heard about it happening to many other people also. When a little bit of improvement is noticed, it increases your faith to pray more, so more happens, which is more faith-building, which leads you to pray more, and pretty soon, the pain (or whatever the initial problem was) is completely gone. But with the first approach above, because you asked the wrong question, you're likely to abort the prayer—*and* the resultant healing—before it fully manifests.

Is That Really the Issue?

One reason people say "What if it doesn't work?" is that they're trying to deflect attention away from the fact the they're afraid of what people might think of them if they do something "radical" like pray for someone's healing. I know that some people do that because I have done it myself. But after the fear of the moment is over, and I thought about it honestly, I realized that I cared more about my "image" in other people's minds than I did about their getting delivered of whatever problem I was afraid to pray for.

That was a pretty disgusting realization. I was so selfish that I would rather protect my perceived image in their minds, than take a risk that could deliver them from a years-long health problem.

What If It *Actually* Doesn't Work?

Suppose for a moment that you could know with absolute certainly that the prayer you just prayed would have no effect at all. (And keep in the mind the above reasons why you couldn't actually know that.) But just suppose for a moment that you could know for sure. What harm would it have done for you to pray?

I have prayed for many people and nothing *apparently* happened—I say "apparently" because I can't actually know that nothing *did* happen. What were the results? In the vast majority of cases, even those in which no perceptible change happened, the person was very blessed by the fact that I was willing to show that I cared, that I noticed them, and that I considered them to be worth my time. And that can be *such* a blessing and encouragement to people. I mean, think about it: you're showing God's love to people—how bad could it *be?* Keep I Corinthians 13 in mind: ". . .and the greatest of these is love."

And if you think about it, discontinuing praying because you didn't get the results you wanted is rather like the baby who is just taking his first steps into toddlerhood. He hangs on to the couch tightly, and then lets go to take a wavering step toward the chair, then—*whump!*—he falls on his behind. After two or three such incidents, if the baby had the attitude of many adults, he'd think, "Walking doesn't work; I've tried it. Some other people may have that gift, but *I* sure don't. I'll leave walking to the people who have that gift."

The baby may be able to get away with that attitude for a few months, but pretty soon, the people who did *not* give up their attempts to walk, and therefore are now walking as a normal part of everyday life, notice the baby's lack of walking. They notice the baby's stunted development, and soon get concerned: "Why isn't the baby walking? Is something wrong with him?"

The people who regularly pray for people to be healed often look that way at Christians who don't. Their concern is sincere and their motives are honorable, but they often don't say anything because Christians who don't pray for the miraculous often get very offended if anyone implies that they could be doing something they're not.

And this is not meant to be condemning; why did Jesus command us to do *anything*? All of His commands to us are for one overarching reason: *for our benefit and blessing.* But it takes humility and teachability to receive advice from others; it tends to make us realize that we may not know everything. The people who have experienced God's power flowing through them and have seen illnesses and injuries be healed before their eyes, *want* other Christians to experience that unspeakably thrilling blessing as well.

So if you're a little nervous about starting to pray for people's healing, that's okay, just remain faithful to obey Jesus' Great Commission, even if you don't feel confident, and God will honor your obedience. And if you think about it, you will never grow in *any* area of your life *if you're unwilling to start doing things you've never done before.* Said another way, growth in any area *requires* that we start doing things we haven't done before. Here are a few Scriptures that have spurred me on over the years:

> Galatians 6:9–10: And **let us not be weary in well doing: for in due season we shall reap, if we faint not.** [10]As we have therefore opportunity, let us do good unto all men, especially unto them who are of the household of faith.

I think you'd agree that praying for someone's healing is an example of "doing good." Even if "nothing happens," you at least got a chance to show God's love. And that is *not* trivial in value.

Proverbs 24:10: If thou faint in the day of adversity, **thy strength is small.**

Hmm. Solomon doesn't pull any punches, does he?

And one more thing. I've heard testimonies like this: a person who knows God wants to heal people asks a sick person if he can pray for him. The sick person replies, "What if it doesn't work?" To which the pray*er* replies, "What if it *does?*" The sick person acknowledges that it couldn't hurt, and so agrees to being prayed for, and there is often a significant improvement, if not a complete healing. We could ask ourselves a similar question, whether we're considering praying for someone else, or being prayed for ourselves: "Why *not* pray?"

Insufficient Faith in the Pray*ee*

You may remember in the chapter above called Jesus' Examples that Jesus often said to the people He just healed, "Your faith has made you well." So we can tell that faith on the part of the one desiring the healing is a good thing to have. But is it indispensable?

As we saw in Mark's account of the deaf and dumb epileptic boy above, the boy's father had no faith left at all after the disciples failed to heal and/or deliver the boy. But Jesus healed him anyway. Why? Because the faith of the pray*er* is more important than that of the pray*ee*. So if you're praying for someone's healing and nothing seems to happen, *never* tell him it was because he didn't have enough faith, even if you think it's true. Jesus' faith overcame the epileptic's father's absence of faith, and He healed his son in spite of it.

So, when we pray for someone and he's healed before our eyes, of course that is faith-building, and of course that's desirable. But how about when we pray for someone, and nothing perceptible happens?

That should tell us that we need to seek God, in our own prayer closet, for:

- More love for people (I Timothy 6:11b), because this will motivate us toward compassion, which is a Godly trait;
- More wisdom and revelation (Ephesians 1:17–18), because this will allow us to understand what hindrances to healing might be present, and how to deal with them;
- More favor with God, because we, like Jesus, need to grow in favor with God (Luke 2:52), resulting in more of His power flowing through us.

And actually, when you think about it, if you believe that God will *not* heal you, it is pretty much guaranteed that it will be a self-fulfilling prophecy. Jesus said so many times "Your faith has made you well," that we know it's important. It's not the *only* thing that's important, though, which is why I said above that it's "pretty much" guaranteed—it's not *absolutely* guaranteed because the pray*er*'s faith can override the pray*ee*'s lack of faith sometimes. As mentioned, Jesus demonstrated this in the story of the The Deaf Mute Epileptic Boy, above. And sometimes, God just sovereignly heals someone in spite of the fact that both the pray*er* and the pray*ee* are expecting it *not* to happen. Ian Andrews has many stories of this sort, from the early days of his ministry.

As Steve Thompson (founder of NU World Ministries and author of *You May All Prophesy*) says, "Generally, God will meet us at our level of hunger. If we feel like we can live without something, we probably will." A very sobering thought, that.

Bill Johnson, Senior Pastor of Bethel Church in Redding, California, says it this way: "[Jesus] illustrated a lifestyle that is within reach but must be reached for. It will not come to us. Much of what we *need* in life will be brought to us, but most of what we *want* we will have to go get. It's just the way of the Kingdom."

It's actually a good thing that the person receiving the healing doesn't have to have faith in *every* case. If it were otherwise, it would be difficult to raise people from the dead, because they wouldn't have enough faith!

The above few paragraphs assume the person has heard about healing and is willing to be prayed for, but can't honestly say that he has faith that God will heal him. That's the way it often is, but there is another possibility as well: Maybe the person doesn't have faith to be healed because he's never heard that God *can* heal him. This is much more common in the unchurched, because you can't read the Bible for very long before you run across a story about God or Jesus healing someone—it does happen an awful lot. But if you were raised in a Christian group that never talked about healing, pro *or* con, or if you've not yet met Jesus, it is entirely possible that the possibility of supernatural healing had never crossed your mind.

In the context of evangelism, healing is a wonderful tool to get people saved, because it shows undeniably that Jesus is real and that He cares for them; see Sin In The Prayee's Life below for more discussion on that topic. Here, let's discuss the Christian who has never been taught about physical healing, and who hasn't read the Bible enough to run across it. He would likely not have faith to be healed, if he have never looked into it enough to read what God says about it. Here is a classic case of "what you don't know *can indeed* hurt you," as Hosea points out:

> Hosea 4:6: **My people are destroyed for lack of knowledge:** because thou hast rejected knowledge, I will also reject thee, that thou shalt be no priest to me: seeing thou hast forgotten the law of thy God, I will also forget thy children.
>
> > GNT: **My people are doomed because they do not acknowledge me.** You priests have refused to acknowledge me and have rejected my teaching, and so I reject you and will not acknowledge your sons as my priests.
> >
> > ISV: **My people are destroyed because they lack knowledge of me.** Because you rejected that knowledge, I will reject you as a priest for me. Since you forget the Law of your God, I will also forget your children.

MSG: **My people are ruined because they don't know what's right or true.** Because you've turned your back on knowledge, I've turned my back on you priests. Because you refuse to recognize the revelation of God, I'm no longer recognizing your children.

NLV: **My people are destroyed because they have not learned. You were not willing to learn.** So I am not willing to have you be My religious leader. Since you have forgotten the Law of your God, I also will forget your children.

NLT: **My people are being destroyed because they don't know me.** Since you priests refuse to know me, I refuse to recognize you as my priests. Since you have forgotten the laws of your God, I will forget to bless your children.

Notice that it's *God's people* here who are being destroyed, doomed, ruined. And why is this the case? Because we lack knowledge, we do not acknowledge Him, we don't know what's right and true, we have not learned (because we were unwilling)—in short, *we don't know Him*. The more we learn about Him, His love, and His nature, the more we'll realize that He has given us *everything* that pertains to life and godliness (II Peter 1:3).

"God Wants Me Sick to Teach Me Something"

The question of whether God actually *wants* us to be sick "for His glory" was covered in great detail above in the section The Man Born Blind. That section, plus pretty much every other Scripture in this whole book, show us rather compellingly that He does *not* want us to be sick. But there are two ideas related to this one closely enough that I'll put them here.

But before we continue, let's look at one more aspect of the belief that "God wants me sick to teach me something." For the people who believe that, there is naturally an aversion to having people pray for them for healing; that is tantamount to asking God for something that they believe is against His will. So of course they wouldn't have faith that He will answer by healing them. But that would also mean, if they *really* believed that God wants them sick to teach them something, that they should not seek any kind of medical expertise, assistance, treatments, surgery, or medications either, because "God wants them sick."

If you find yourself in this situation—avoiding prayer for healing because you say that God wants you sick to teach you something—but yet you are taking medications or receiving medical treatment of whatever kind to ameliorate or overcome the illness for which you have refused prayer, be advised that you are contradicting your own words. You are basically asking people in the medical field to assist you in disobeying God. Is that something you want on your conscience? And if you find your actions and your words contradicting each other like this, it is a classic case of double-mindedness. What does the Bible say about praying when you're double-minded?

> James 1:6–8 (NIV): But when he asks, **he must believe and not doubt**, because he who doubts is like a wave of the sea, blown and tossed by the wind. ⁷**That man should not think he will receive anything from the Lord;** ⁸**he is a double-minded man,** unstable in all he does.

"God Used My Sickness For His Glory"

Although this is an entirely different question, if the difference is ignored, it leads to the "God wants me sick to teach me something" idea. And that difference *is* so often ignored, many people don't even notice the difference until it is pointed out to them.

The difference is that in the "God wants me sick to teach me something" idea, it is God's *perfect will* that some people be sick. Mounds of Scriptures above have shown this to be utterly false. However, can God *use* someone's sickness for His glory? Of course He can. As we saw in the Raising Lazarus section above, Jacob's son Joseph told his brothers—the very ones who had sold him into slavery—that even though they meant their whole plan for evil, *God turned it to good.*

Now some will say at this point, "But Joseph *had* to get sold into slavery and all that so he would be in Egypt when Pharaoh had the dream!" No, not at all. That's how God orchestrated it, given Joseph's brothers' actions, but God could have delivered all those people from starvation in any number of other ways (Jeremiah 32:27), had Joseph's brothers actually acted civilly toward him. As Mordecai told his cousin, Queen Esther:

> Esther 4:14 (WEB): For **if you altogether hold your peace at this time, then will relief and deliverance arise to the Jews from another place,** but you and your father's house will perish: and who knows whether you haven't come to the kingdom for such a time as this?

Note that although God chose to use Queen Esther to deliver the Jews from the evil machinations of Haman, it's not like the whole plan of Redemption would have fallen apart, had Esther refused to participate. God is infinitely resourceful, and though He wants to bless us by using us for His purposes, if we refuse, His ultimate goals will not be derailed.

So back to the subject of healing, can God use someone's sickness for His glory? In other words, can God receive glory through someone's sickness? Of course. But he would receive even more glory through the person's healing. See again the section The Man Born Blind above.

Couldn't I Have a Sickness for a Greater Good?

The answer to this is *very qualified* yes, *if* we refuse to cooperate with Him in the first place. In other words, yes, it could be a distant second; a far less desirable "Plan B." For example, Paul scolds the church in Corinth because they were not dealing with sin in the congregation as they should. In particular, a man in the church was having sex with his stepmother, and not only did he refuse to repent, but the church didn't even try to address it either:

> I Corinthians 5:3 (WEB): For I most assuredly, as being absent in body but present in spirit, have already, as though I were present, judged him who has done this thing. ⁴In the name of our Lord Jesus Christ, you being gathered together, and my spirit, with the power of our Lord Jesus Christ, ⁵are to **deliver such a one to Satan for the destruction of the flesh, that the spirit may be saved in the day of the Lord Jesus.**

Could the "destruction of the flesh" include physical illnesses? Very likely yes. But notice *why* this whole scenario happened: *the guy was openly sinning and didn't even pretend to repent.* It's not like God was capriciously and arbitrarily wanting to make this guy sick—if that is indeed what happened—God's perfect will was that the guy would repent of his sin. But since he didn't, he basically "forced" God into getting his attention with the proverbial two-by-four. Note the motivation for the destruction of the flesh: *that the spirit may be saved.*

But here's another thought: what does "flesh" mean in the Bible? It certainly can mean the physical body, as in:

> I Peter 4:1: Forasmuch then as Christ hath suffered for us **in the flesh**, arm yourselves likewise with the same mind: for he that hath suffered **in the flesh** hath ceased from sin. . .

But "flesh" can also mean the sinful nature, as in:

> Romans 8:8–9: So then they that are **in the flesh** cannot please God. ⁹But ye are not **in the flesh,** but in the Spirit, if so be that the Spirit of God dwell in you. Now if any man have not the Spirit of Christ, he is none of his.

So which meaning is appropriate for interpreting the phrase "the destruction of the flesh?" Are they different Greek words? No, they are both translated from the Greek word σάρξ (*sarx*, G4561). So "destruction of the flesh" may mean the guy had left himself wide open to illness until he repented. Or, it may mean the guy would be subject to reaping catastrophe in many areas of his life, from what he was sowing in this one unrepentant sin, so eventually his sinful nature would realize that the momentary pleasure of sin isn't worth the unpleasant consequences. That is the way some versions of the Bible translate that verse. But the whole situation could have been moot—the whole question of the interpretation of *sarx* in this verse could have been rendered academic—had he just repented of his sin.

Insufficient Faith in the Pray*er*

We saw above, in the section The Deaf Mute Epileptic Boy, that the disciples couldn't cast the demon out of the boy. When they asked Jesus why they couldn't, we saw Jesus answer them in no uncertain terms, because they didn't have any (or enough) faith. So we understand that our own lack of faith when we pray for someone to be healed, can indeed be a hindrance. But what could cause our own lack of faith?

One thing that could greatly hinder our own faith that God would heal the sick is teaching and training that we've heard for years, but which contradicts the Bible. For example, there is a doctrine that states that God predestines people to heaven or hell; that is, regardless of their actions, attitudes, desires, or choices, some people will go to heaven for eternity, and others to hell for eternity. Some proponents of this doctrine even claim that free-will choices don't even exist—that there is no such thing.

If you have sat under this teaching for years, where God arbitrarily and unchangeably chooses to send some people to torment in hell for *eternity* and there's nothing they can do about it, it's obvious that He would certainly have no problem deliberately causing painful and debilitating illnesses for the short lifetimes that people live on earth. So obviously, this doctrine would seriously damage anyone's faith that God would want to heal them.

It's obvious that I don't believe this predestination doctrine; it's way too inconsistent with God's Word, as well as God's character (for a great deal more detail, see Book 6 of the "THOUGHTS ON" series: *Free to Choose?*, available from the sources noted on BibleAuthor.DaveArns.com). But if you have been exposed to it for years, you'll need to read the Scriptures for a while with the constant question in your mind, "Does this Scripture lead me to believe that I can *choose* to obey God? Or that I have *no* choice that could alter the outcome? If my fate is already irrevocably determined, why even bother?"

Another doctrine that could completely shut down one's faith that God would heal people today is called "cessationism." In a nutshell, it is the belief that God ceased doing anything miraculous around the end of the first century. Basically, it is a religious version of only the first half of that motivational poster often seen in businesses large and small: "Those who say the task is impossible are usually interrupted by those who are doing it." Those who believe the cessationist doctrine will say the miracles are impossible, in spite of what all the Scriptures shown above say.

Fortunately, this doctrine is much easier to overcome if you put yourself in a position to learn. It's amazing how years—*decades*—of wrong teaching can be overturned by one single miraculous encounter with God. If you don't believe in divine healing, participate in some missions trips with ministries that see healings every day. You'll see firsthand how God is indeed doing miracles, by the thousands, every day, all over the world.

Sin in the Pray*ee*'s Life

As mentioned above, this could be a factor, especially if the person being prayed for is in open, blatant sin, and he is unrepentant about it. By "blatant sin," I mean actions that are clearly declared by the Bible to be sinful, such as fornication, adultery, stealing, and so forth. But the pray*er* should keep in mind that the "sinfulness status" of many actions is not as cut-and-dried as those just mentioned. For more detail, see "What Is Sin?", "Disputable Matters", and "I'm Doing Pretty Well" in Book 2 of the "Thoughts On" series: *Is It Possible to Stop Sinning?*, available from the sources noted on BibleAuthor.DaveArns.com.

So yes, sin in the person being prayed for *could* be a factor, but in my opinion, it is not that big of a factor in God's eyes. Now before you go and misunderstand me, note that I am *not* saying "Sin is unimportant to God." What I *am* saying is "Sin in the pray*ee* is usually not a factor in preventing healing from manifesting."

Why would I say that? Simply because of Jesus' approach to evangelism, as well as that of the apostles, after Jesus ascended. What was that approach?

Luke 10:9 (TEV): . . .heal the sick in that town, and say to the people there, 'The Kingdom of God has come near you.'

Note how Jesus instructs the disciples to evangelize: first He says, "heal the sick. . ." and then He says ". . .and say to the people there, 'The Kingdom of God has come near you.'" It is things such as healings and other miracles that show people there actually *is* a God Who loves them, and He is backing you up in what you're saying about Him. Once they realize this fact, they usually climb all over each other trying to get to Him.

Do you see the point? Because Jesus used healing to show that He was really the Messiah, so people would repent and turn to God, their sin couldn't have prevented the healings from taking place. Why? *Because people are sinners before they get saved.* To say that "healing is a form of evangelism" while also maintaining "sin in those you are praying for will prevent healings from happening" is self-defeating and self-contradictory, similar to the statement "No one can respond to God until he is saved." Well, if that were true, no one could *ever* get saved, because salvation happens when we respond to God's wooing us:

John 6:44a: No man can come to me, except the Father which hath sent me draw him. . .

So the very fact that Jesus used healing as a major tool—if not *the* major tool—in evangelism, shows that he is not averse to healing people who are still sinning. In fact, to withhold healing from sinners would have a two-fold negative effect:

- It would prevent them from coming in contact with the very power they need in their lives to *remove* their sins. The same Atonement that provides forgiveness also provides healing.
- Withholding healing from people until they stopped sinning would turn the healing into a *reward* instead of a *gift*.

Physical and/or mental healing corresponds to its spiritual counterpart of forgiveness; hence, leprosy being a symbol for sin in the Bible, and healing from leprosy being a symbol of forgiveness. (For more detail, see the section "Cleansing From Leprosy" in Book 4 of the

"Thoughts On" series: *Gold Dust, Jewels, and More: Manifestations of God?*, available from the sources noted on BibleAuthor.DaveArns.com.) Indeed, the physical act of healing is symbolic of the spiritual act of forgiveness. And again, withholding either from people until they got their acts together would turn it into a *works-based reward* instead of a *grace-based gift*.

Another thing about using healing as an evangelistic tool, as Jesus and the early church did, and people are rediscovering now: It puts into practice a verse in Proverbs:

> Proverbs 16:6: **By mercy and truth iniquity is purged:** and by the fear of the LORD men depart from evil.

Physical healing is certainly a very tangible way of demonstrating the truthfulness of God's mercy, as well as His love, His power, His goodness, His kindness, His compassion, and so forth. Paul reiterated this idea:

> Romans 2:4 (NIV): Or do you show contempt for the riches of his kindness, tolerance and patience, not realizing that **God's kindness leads you toward repentance?**

When people see that God is real, He has power, and that He loves them enough to heal them of bodily infirmities, they are much more likely to realize that God has their best interests in mind. Healing is *extremely* effective in bringing people to repentance and a saving knowledge of God.

A Spiritual Hindrance

This is a generalization of the concept of Sin in the Pray*ee*'s Life above, because sin in the pray*ee*'s life can indeed be a hindrance. But there are other possible hindrances that don't involve explicit, deliberate sin.

For example, it is possible that the enemy has caused something in us, or subtly talked us into accepting, something from him that will hinder our fellowship with God. This is entirely possible, which is why Paul tells us to "examine ourselves" before taking communion, so we can get such things resolved before they become even larger problems:

> I Corinthians 11:27–28 (TEV): It follows that if one of you eats the Lord's bread or drinks from his cup in a way that dishonors him, you are guilty of sin against the Lord's body and blood. ²⁸So then, **you should each examine yourself first, and then eat the bread and drink from the cup.**

Now, in case you're thinking that Paul is getting overly worked up about something that is not that big a deal, let's read the next few verses:

> I Corinthians 11:29–31 (TEV): For if you do not recognize the meaning of the Lord's body when you eat the bread and drink from the cup, you bring judgment on yourself as you eat and drink. ³⁰**That is why many of you are sick and weak, and several have died.** ³¹If we would examine ourselves first, we would not come under God's judgment.

Wow! Look at v. 30: "*That is why many of you are sick and weak, and several have died.*" So apparently, taking communion with a flippant attitude, or with unrepentant sin in our lives, or anything else that dishonors God, can prevent healing from happening. Corinth was a church that was very familiar with the supernatural gifts of the Spirit, undoubtedly they prayed for each other when they got sick; this explains why some of them didn't get the healings for which they were praying. It is worth noting that it was fatal in some cases.

Fear

Fear is a more serious thing than most people realize. Now before we go on, let me make sure we're talking about the same thing. I am *not* talking about the fear of the Lord, which is a good thing:

> Ecclesiastes 12:13: Let us hear the conclusion of the whole matter: **Fear God**, and keep his commandments: for this is the whole duty of man.
>
> I Peter 2:17: Honour all men. Love the brotherhood. **Fear God.** Honour the king.

Also, I am not talking about a more experienced believer seeing the potential danger of a less experienced believer's situation, and wanting him to reconsider his intended course of action. Paul illustrates this:

> II Corinthians 11:3: But **I fear**, lest by any means, as the serpent beguiled Eve through his subtilty, so your minds should be corrupted from the simplicity that is in Christ.
>
> II Corinthians 12:20 (NIV): For **I am afraid** that when I come I may not find you as I want you to be, and you may not find me as you want me to be. **I fear** that there may be quarreling, jealousy, outbursts of anger, factions, slander, gossip, arrogance and disorder.

On the contrary, I am talking about the fear that tries to tell us that the strength of the problem is greater than the strength of God's power to fix it. Think about when God or an angel shows up: they often say "Fear not" or something equivalent:

> Matthew 14:27 (TEV): But immediately Jesus spoke to them, saying "Cheer up! I AM! **Don't be afraid.**"
>
> Matthew 17:7 (NIV): But Jesus came and touched them. "Get up," he said. "**Don't be afraid.**"
>
> Matthew 28:5: And the angel answered and said unto the women, **Fear not ye:** for I know that ye seek Jesus, which was crucified.
>
> Matthew 28:10 (NIV): Then Jesus said to them, "**Do not be afraid.** Go and tell my brothers to go to Galilee; there they will see me."

Luke 1:13 (WEB): But the angel said to him, "**Don't be afraid**, Zacharias, because your request has been heard, and your wife, Elizabeth, will bear you a son, and you shall call his name John."

Luke 1:30 (DOUAY): And the angel said to her: **Fear not**, Mary, for thou hast found grace with God.

Luke 2:10 (TEV): but the angel said to them, "**Don't be afraid!** I am here with good news for you, which will bring great joy to all the people."

Luke 5:9–10 (NIV): For he and all his companions were astonished at the catch of fish they had taken, ¹⁰and so were James and John, the sons of Zebedee, Simon's partners. Then Jesus said to Simon, "**Don't be afraid;** from now on you will catch men."

John 6:20 (TEV): "**Don't be afraid,**" Jesus told them, "it is I!"

And there are many more. But what we need to realize is that Jesus, or the angel, when saying, "Fear not," is not giving us a wimpy "there, there" pat on the back. They are giving us a command, which we can choose to obey or not: "*Don't* be afraid." Why is this important? Because, as noted above, *fear is actually faith in an evil outcome.* Fear is faith that the devil is stronger than God, the problem is bigger than the solution, evil is stronger than good, sin is stronger than grace, and so forth. And, in the context of this book: fear is faith that sickness is stronger than healing.

This may have been what actually opened the door to the attacks on Job, and caused God to allow Satan to attack him; he was apparently very fearful of losing his stuff, his kids, and his health. Look what he says:

Job 3:25: For the thing which **I greatly feared** is come upon me, and that which **I was afraid of** is come unto me.

Indeed, fear can be an actual demonic spirit. And such a spirit does not come from God, so guess who it comes from?

II Timothy 1:7: For **God hath not given us the spirit of fear**; but of power, and of love, and of a sound mind.

> AMP: For **God did not give us a spirit of timidity (of cowardice, of craven and cringing and fawning fear)**, but [He has given us a spirit] of power and of love and of calm and well-balanced mind and discipline and self-control.
>
> DARBY: For **God has not given us a spirit of cowardice**, but of power, and of love, and of wise discretion.
>
> YLT: for **God did not give us a spirit of fear**, but of power, and of love, and of a sound mind;

So, when we succumb to a spirit of fear (or cowardice or timidity), it is actually akin to what Adam did in the Garden of Eden: believing the word of the devil more than the Word of God. And that is serious; it is apparently enough to keep a person out of heaven:

> Revelation 21:8: But **the fearful**, and unbelieving, and the abominable, and murderers, and whoremongers, and sorcerers, and idolaters, and all liars, shall have their part in the lake which burneth with fire and brimstone: which is the second death.

So how do we combat fear? We fall in love with Jesus more and more. When we love Him, we'll spend time with Him. When we spend time with Him, we'll realize how big He is in comparison to Satan. And when we realize how big Jesus is and how perfectly He loves us, we'll realize how ludicrous it is to be afraid of the devil. The apostle John says it well:

> I John 4:18 (TEV): There is no fear in love; **perfect love drives out all fear.** So then, love has not been made perfect in anyone who is afraid, because fear has to do with punishment.

Therefore, if you find yourself fearful when someone prays for you for healing, that you won't actually get healed, the best course of action is to seek God until you actually *know* His heart on the matter, and how unspeakably much He loves you. When you really see that He wants good things for His kids even more than the best earthly parents want good things for theirs, fear goes away.

Giving Satan an Opportunity

The reason Satan had no authority over Jesus is because Jesus hadn't let Satan into His life; not even a little bit. Look how Jesus states it:

> John 14:30b: . . .the prince of this world cometh, and **hath nothing in me.**
>
> > AMP: . . .the prince (evil genius, ruler) of the world is coming. And **he has no claim on Me. [He has nothing in common with Me; there is nothing in Me that belongs to him, and he has no power over Me.]**
> >
> > BBE: . . .the ruler of this world comes: and **he has no power over me.** . .
> >
> > CJB: . . .the ruler of this world is coming. **He has no claim on me.** . .
> >
> > NIV: . . .the prince of this world is coming. **He has no hold on me.** . .
> >
> > EXB: . . .the ruler [prince] of this world [Satan] is coming. **He has no power [no claim/hold; nothing] over me.** . .
> >
> > MSG: . . .the chief of this godless world is about to attack. But don't worry—**he has nothing on me, no claim on me.**

Why did Satan have no hold/claim/power over Jesus? Because Jesus never gave him an opportunity to do so; Jesus followed the principle Paul would later describe as:

> Ephesians 4:27: Neither give place to the devil.
>
> > CEB: Don't provide an opportunity for the devil.
> >
> > CEV: and don't give the devil a chance.
> >
> > ERV: Don't give the devil a way to defeat you.
> >
> > ESV: and give no opportunity to the devil.
> >
> > GWORD: Don't give the devil any opportunity to work.
> >
> > NIV: and do not give the devil a foothold.
> >
> > NRSV: and do not make room for the devil.
> >
> > WE: Do not let the devil control you.

And remember, God does not command us to do *anything* without giving us the ability to obey Him. Convicting, no?

One of the most common ways we give the devil an opportunity in our lives is unforgiveness and its ilk. Start hanging around people who often pray for the sick, and you'll hear *lots* of testimonies about how people got healed, but only after repenting of anger, bitterness, unforgiveness, resentment, and so forth. It's worth checking. . .

God is Sovereign

Here is a very common hindrance to healing, and is a major motivation for the "disclaimer" or the "condition" posed in the title of this book, which we often append to our prayers for healing: ". . .if it be Thy will." The sovereignty argument goes like this: "God is sovereign, and if He wants me to be healed, He'll heal me, and if He doesn't, praying won't do any good." So this view of sovereignty portrays God as unmoved by compassion (because He doesn't feel our pain), unmoved by faith (because His mind is made up), and a respecter of persons (because he chooses to heal some but not others). Let's see what the Bible says about these ideas, keeping in mind that Jesus is the "*exact* representation of the Father" (John 14:9b, Colossians 1:15, Hebrews 1:3):

- Jesus is very moved with compassion (Matthew 9:36, 14:14, 15:32, 20:34, Mark 1:41, 5:19, 6:34, 8:2, 9:22–25, Luke 7:13, etc.).
- Jesus is very responsive to faith (Matthew 8:10, 8:26, 9:2, 9:29, 15:28, 17:20, 21:21, Mark 2:5, 5:34, 10:52, Luke 5:20, 7:9, 7:50, 8:48, 17:6, 17:19, 18:8, 18:42, etc.).
- God is not a respecter of persons (II Samuel 14:14, II Chronicles 19:7, Acts 10:34, Romans 2:11, Ephesians 6:9, Colossians 3:25, and I Peter 1:17).

So, keeping in mind that Jesus *is* moved with compassion, and *is* moved by faith, and is *not* a respecter of persons, let's look at a familiar story, that of the woman with the issue of blood. We read this story in a previous chapter, but it can teach us still more:

> Luke 8:43–48 (NIV): And a woman was there who had been subject to bleeding for twelve years, but no one could heal her. ^{44}She came up behind him and touched the edge of his cloak, and immediately her

bleeding stopped. ⁴⁵"Who touched me?" Jesus asked. When they all denied it, Peter said, "Master, the people are crowding and pressing against you." ⁴⁶But Jesus said, "Someone touched me; I know that power has gone out from me." ⁴⁷Then the woman, seeing that she could not go unnoticed, came trembling and fell at his feet. In the presence of all the people, she told why she had touched him and how she had been instantly healed. ⁴⁸Then he said to her, "Daughter, your faith has healed you. Go in peace."

This story is as significant for what it *doesn't* say, as it is for what it *does* say. Specifically, let's look at the story from the woman's point of view: suppose the woman had stayed at home that day that Jesus was in her town. Suppose she had had the mindset of, "Well, God knows I've got this problem, and Jesus listens to Him. So if God wants to heal me, He knows where I live." Do you think the woman would have gotten healed with that kind of a mindset? God knew about her issue of blood for the entire twelve years she had it (not to mention eternity past). If God had wanted her healed, He could have done it at any time during those twelve years. But He didn't, so does that prove that it wasn't His will to heal her? Obviously not; He *did* heal her, but not until this point in time. So what changed?

Before we answer that, let's also look at this story from Jesus' point of view. Whatever He chose to do, He only did it because it was what the Father wanted Him to do (John 5:19, et al), and He always chose to obey the Father. Was Jesus walking through town looking for the woman with the issue of blood? Did He send out His disciples to search for her, because He knew that it was her time to be healed? No; He didn't even know she was in the crowd that was swarming around Him.

So, from God the Father's point of view, He knew all along that the woman needed healing. And from Jesus' point of view, He didn't even know that the woman existed. At least, until she touched Him. The woman, defying social customs about appearing in public while unclean (see the section The Woman with the Issue of Blood above for more detail), pushed her way through the crowd, very non-passively, and plowed her way to Jesus, specifically to be healed. She knew that all she had to do was to touch his clothes and she would be healed (Mark 5:28).

How did she know that? What gave her the faith, the belief, the confidence that she would be healed, just from touching His clothes? Because *everybody* who came to Him for healing was being healed. If Jesus had *ever* sent anyone away unhealed, it would have opened the door to an credible justification—a plausible reason—for people to believe that God sometimes doesn't want to heal people. But I've never seen anywhere in the Bible where Jesus *didn't* heal someone who came to Him for healing. I encourage you, the reader, to search it out yourself, and if you find a place where Jesus *didn't* heal someone who came to Him for healing, please let me know. (For contact information, see the end of the book.)

So why did the woman get healed when she touched Jesus' robe? Jesus gives us the answer in v. 48: "Daughter, your faith has healed you." So in answer to the "What changed?" question posed above, the answer is this: Jesus was the *point of contact* between the woman and God—a point at which to release her faith. God had the power to heal, Jesus consistently, repeatedly, and constantly demonstrated God's heart on the matter, and that gave the woman the confidence that she too would be healed. After all, everybody else who came to Jesus for healing was being healed; why shouldn't she be healed as well? But it required her to *seek God* for her healing; it seems very unlikely that she would have been healed if she had just stayed home that day, saying "If God wants to heal me, He knows my address. . ."

Co-Laboring With Christ

Another aspect of the sovereignty question is this: "If God is everywhere and knows everything, why does He need me to do *anything?*" Of course, God *could* heal the sick very well by Himself; He *could* preach the gospel very well by Himself; He *could* cast out demons very well by Himself. In fact, He could do a better job than we could. So why does He want us to get involved if He could do the job better without us?

Because He loves us. What? "Because He loves us?" How does that answer the question?

He loves us, and therefore He wants to bless us, and He knows that the more we get to know Him, the more we will be blessed. And what is the best way to get to know people? Hang around with them and do stuff together. And that is exactly what God wants to do with us: He wants to hang around with us and do stuff together, and as we find out what He's like, the more we become like Him, which is His goal. So God wants to bless the people of this world, but He wants to do it *though us*. He likes to be around us—He not only loves us, He *likes* us.

And this is nothing new; it's been this way since the Garden of Eden, before sin entered the world:

> Genesis 2:19–20 (TEV): So he took some soil from the ground and formed all the animals and all the birds. Then he brought them to the man **to see what he would name them;** and that is how they all got their names. ²⁰**So the man named all the birds and all the animals;** but not one of them was a suitable companion to help him.

Couldn't God have named all the animals by Himself? Of course, *but He chose to let Adam get involved in the process.* Working together on stuff; that's what families *do*. This co-laboring idea carries through the entire Old Testament with everyone who chose to obey God, whatever He commanded them to do.

Couldn't God have communicated with Pharaoh or the children of Israel or the Canaanites or anyone else, or done their tasks, *better* than the humans He chose to use? Of course, but He chose to let His children, His servants, get involved in the process. Working together on stuff; that's what families *do*. And it carries through to Jesus' ministry:

> John 5:17: But Jesus answered them, **My Father worketh hitherto, and I work.**
>
> AMP: But Jesus answered them, **My Father has worked [even] until now, [He has never ceased working; He is still working] and I, too, must be at [divine] work.**

CEV: But Jesus said, "**My Father has never stopped working, and that is why I keep on working.**"

ERV: But he said to them, "**My Father never stops working, and so I work too.**"

EXB: But Jesus said to [answered] them, "**My Father never stops [is always; is still] working [even on the Sabbath], and so I keep working, too.**"

PHILLIPS: But Jesus' answer to them was this, "**My Father is still at work and therefore I work as well.**"

TLB: But Jesus replied, "**My Father constantly does good, and I'm following his example.**"

Acts 2:22 (TEV): Listen to these words, fellow Israelites! Jesus of Nazareth was a man whose **divine authority was clearly proven to you by all the miracles and wonders which God performed through him.** You yourselves know this, for it happened here among you.

Above, the co-laboring is shown in the Father and Jesus working together to accomplish God's will. And below, we see the same thing in Jesus working with the disciples during His earthly ministry, as well as after the resurrection:

Matthew 10:1, 5, 7–8: And when he had called unto him his twelve disciples, he gave them power against unclean spirits, to cast them out, and to heal all manner of sickness and all manner of disease. . . . ⁵These twelve Jesus sent forth, and commanded them, saying, . . . ⁷as ye go, preach, saying, The kingdom of heaven is at hand. ⁸Heal the sick, cleanse the lepers, raise the dead, cast out devils: freely ye have received, freely give.

Couldn't Jesus have done all this preaching, healing, delivering, cleansing, and raising by Himself, even better than the disciples? Of course He could, and He did, in order to show us how. And now He chooses to use us, both for His glory and for our blessing. Then after Jesus' death, resurrection, and ascension, Jesus carries on the tradition of working with and through us, co-laboring with His disciples, even though He could do the job better by himself:

Mark 16:20 (TEV): The disciples went and preached everywhere, and **the Lord worked with them and proved that their preaching was true by the miracles** that were performed.

Acts 14:3 (NASB): Therefore they spent a long time there *[in Iconium]* speaking boldly with reliance upon **the Lord, who was bearing witness to the word of His grace, granting that signs and wonders be done by their hands.**

Hebrews 2:3–4 (NIV): How shall we escape if we ignore such a great salvation? This salvation, which was first announced by the Lord, was confirmed to us by those who heard him. ⁴**God also testified to it by signs, wonders and various miracles, and gifts of the Holy Spirit distributed according to his will.**

When the disciples did this, they were doing what the apostle Paul would later describe like this:

I Corinthians 3:9: For **we are labourers together with God:** ye are God's husbandry, ye are God's building.

ASV: For **we are God's fellow-workers:** ye are God's husbandry, God's building.

AMP: For **we are fellow workmen (joint promoters, laborers together) with and for God;** you are God's garden and vineyard and field under cultivation, [you are] God's building.

CEB: **We are God's coworkers,** and you are God's field, God's building.

ERV: **We are workers together for God,** and you are like a farm that belongs to God. And you are a house that belongs to God.

PHILLIPS: In this work, **we work with God,** and that means that you are a field under God's cultivation, or, if you like, a house being built to his plan.

NIRV: **We work together with God.** You are like God's field. You are like his building.

VOICE: **We are gardeners and field workers laboring with God.** You are the vineyard, the garden, the house where God dwells.

Paul tells the Colossians a similar thing:

Colossians 1:29: Whereunto I also labour, striving **according to his working, which worketh in me mightily.**

    AMP: For this I labor [unto weariness], striving **with all the superhuman energy which He so mightily enkindles and works within me.**

    DARBY: Whereunto also I toil, combating according to **his working, which works in me in power.**

    DOUAY: Wherein also I labour, striving according to **his working which he worketh in me in power.**

    ESV: For this I toil, struggling with all **his energy that he powerfully works within me.**

    GNV: Whereunto I also labor and strive, according to **his working which worketh in me mightily.**

    HCSB: I labor for this, striving with **His strength that works powerfully in me.**

    NABRE: For this I labor and struggle, in accord with **the exercise of his power working within me.**

    NRSV: For this I toil and struggle with all **the energy that he powerfully inspires within me.**

    VOICE: This is why I continue to toil and struggle—because **His amazing power and energy surge within me.**

    YLT: for which also I labour, striving according to **his working that is working in me in power.**

These Scriptures point out that we are labouring *with* God, co-workers *working with Him* in the glorious Gospel. In fact, for the past decade or two, there seems to be a growing awareness of this concept in the Body of Christ as we grow in Him. This is wonderful, as can be seen by the good fruit in so many ministries that are doing the same works that Jesus did, and even greater ones (John 14:12).

So yes, God is sovereign, but that doesn't mean that we can sit back and do nothing and expect Him to do everything. He doesn't simply *prefer* us to co-labor with Him, He *requires* it. He commands and *expects* us to obey Him, even in those places where He tells us to "heal the sick, cleanse the lepers, raise the dead, and cast out demons." We are responsible to obey Him, and He will provide the raw power needed to make it happen.

One last thing: Astute readers will have noticed that I said above (where I mentioned Ian Andrews) that sometimes God chooses to heal people sovereignly. But then I turn around say that God does *not* sovereignly choose to *deny* healing from anyone. Am I being inconsistent about God's sovereignty? Am I using a double standard? That's a very good question, and the answer is no. The reason that answer is no is because *we know what God's will is,* on the topic of healing. He made it very plain when He identified Himself as "Jehovah Rapha" ("The Lord Who Heals You"), and when He said to the centurion about his sick servant, "I will. . . heal him," and when He said to the leper, "I am willing, be clean," and. . . well, pretty much every other Scripture referenced in this book.

The Fellowship of Christ's Suffering

Another hindrance to healing is a mistaken idea that we are to share in Christ's suffering, and sickness causes people to suffer, so therefore God will sometimes not heal people, because He wants us to suffer. Now here is an excellent opportunity to misconstrue what I am saying, and some people will do so, immediately be offended, and stop reading before they get far enough to realize what I am saying.

So let me be quick to elaborate on what I am trying to communicate, so you can hear my heart. I am *not* saying that it is a mistaken idea to think we should share in Christ's suffering. What I am saying is mistaken is the idea that *all* suffering is *Christ's* suffering. Let me explain, because if you buy into the idea that *all* suffering is Christ's suffering, you could "validly" come to the conclusion that we can serve God best by burning in hell forever. After all, what more intense suffering could there be?

This supposedly valid, albeit ridiculous, conclusion goes away once we look at the Scriptures related to suffering, and specifically examine what the Word has to say about what *Christ's* sufferings were.

Good Suffering

So let's take a look at some relevant Scriptures:

II Corinthians 1:5 (TEV): Just as **we have a share in Christ's many sufferings,** so also through Christ we share in God's great help.

Philippians 3:10 (TEV): All I want is to know Christ and to experience the power of his resurrection, **to share in his sufferings** and become like him in his death. . .

Colossians 1:24 (NIV): Now I rejoice in what was suffered for you, and **I fill up in my flesh what is still lacking in regard to Christ's afflictions,** for the sake of his body, which is the church.

I Peter 2:21–23: For even hereunto were ye called: because **Christ also suffered for us, leaving us an example, that ye should follow his steps:** [22]Who did no sin, neither was guile found in his mouth: [23]Who, when he was reviled, reviled not again; when he suffered, he threatened not; but committed himself to him that judgeth righteously. . .

I Peter 4:13 (NIV): But rejoice that **you participate in the sufferings of Christ,** so that you may be overjoyed when his glory is revealed.

These Scriptures and others like them clearly indicate that we are indeed called to share in the sufferings of Christ. That is not in question. But what we need to find out, in order to obey these Scriptures, is *what the sufferings of Christ are.*

Bad Suffering

Something we soon discover, when researching the Bible on the concept of suffering, is that *not all suffering is good,* or beneficial, or in God's will:

I Peter 2:20 (WYC): For **what grace is it, if ye sin, and be buffeted, and suffer?** But if ye do well, and suffer patiently, this is grace with God.

I Peter 4:15 (TEV): **If you suffer, it must not be because you are a murderer or a thief or a criminal or a meddler in other people's affairs.**

Jude 7 (NIV): In a similar way, Sodom and Gomorrah and the surrounding towns gave themselves up to sexual immorality and perversion. **They serve as an example of those who suffer the punishment of eternal fire.**

From these Scriptures and others like them, we see that not all suffering is beneficial. Indeed, suffering because of sin or foolishness is completely unnecessary. Why? Because sin and foolishness are completely unnecessary. (For much more detail on this, see Book 2 of the "Thoughts On" series: *Is It Possible to Stop Sinning?*, available from the sources noted on BibleAuthor.DaveArns.com.)

So it becomes clear after reading the above, that sharing in the sufferings of Christ—that is, following His example, as I Peter 2:21 above points out—is indeed good. But, suffering merely for the sake of suffering, even for foolish reasons, is *not* included in Christ's example. Therefore, we should not suffer for these foolish reasons; that would be just letting the devil walk all over us while we think we're submitting to Christ. That's just unnecessary pain and *not* a good representation of the Father's heart toward us, nor is it good stewardship of the time and resources he has supplied us with to further His Kingdom.

So, let's take a look at what Christ's sufferings actually were, so we'll know which suffering to embrace as a blessing and which suffering to resist as an attack from the enemy.

- He was misrepresented and maligned for ministering ("He casts out demons by the prince of demons"—Matthew 12:24).
- He was misrepresented and maligned for loving people ("Why does He eat with publicans and sinners?"—Matthew 9:11, Mark 2:16, Luke 5:29–30, 15:1–2; "He's a glutton and a drunk"—Matthew 11:19, Luke 7:34).
- His life was threatened multiple times (Matthew 26:4, Mark 14:1, Luke 13:31, 22:2, John 5:18, 7:1, 7:25).
- He was betrayed by friend and partner in ministry, Judas (Matthew 26:14–17, 47–50, Mark 14:10–11, 44–45, Luke 22:3–6, 47–48, John 18:2–5).
- He bore a *very* heavy prayer burden (Matthew 26:38–44, Mark 14:33–34, Luke 22:44).
- He was let down by his closest partners in ministry when He needed support the most (Matthew 26:40–43, Mark 14:35–40, Luke 22:45).

- Underwent false arrest (Matthew 26:50, Mark 14:46, Luke 22:54, John 18:12).
- He was abandoned by all of his friends and ministry partners (Matthew 26:31, 56, Mark 14:50).
- He was falsely accused (False witnesses: Matthew 26:59–61, Mark 14:55–59; Chief priests and scribes: Matthew 26:65–66, 27:12–13, 18; Mark 15:3–4, 10, Luke 23:2, 10, John 18:29).
- He was denied by a close friend and associate, Peter (Matthew 26:70–75, Mark 14:68–72, Luke 22:57–62, John 18:17, 25–27).
- He was mocked (Funeral mourners: Matthew 9:24, Luke 8:53; Chief priests, scribes, and elders: Matthew 26:67–68, 27:41–43, Mark 14:65, 15:31–32, 23:35; the mob: Luke 22:63–65; Herod and his men: Luke 23:11; Soldiers: Matthew 27:29–31, Mark 15:17–20, Luke 22:63–65, 23:36; Passersby: Matthew 27:39–40, Mark 15:29–30; Criminals: Matthew 27:44, Mark 15:32, Luke 23:39).
- He was hated for doing the will of His Father (Matthew 27:22–23, Luke 23:21–23).
- He was unjustly condemned to death (Matthew 27:1, 20, 26, Mark 14:64, 15:13–14, Luke 23:21–24, John 19:6).
- He was slapped, beaten with fists and rods (Matthew 26:67–68, Mark 14:65, 15:19, Luke 22:63–64, John 18:22, 19:3).
- He was humiliated (Matthew 27:28, Matthew 15:1).
- He was scourged with whips (Matthew 27:26, John 19:1).
- He was robbed (Matthew 27:35, Mark 15:24, Luke 23:34, John 19:23).
- He was crucified and killed (Matthew 27:35, 50, Mark 15:25, 37, Luke 23:21–23, John 19:16–18).

That's a lot of suffering that Jesus went through. And it's interesting to note that, in all of these descriptions of how Jesus suffered, *every one* describes Him suffering because of people (motivated by the devil) who got upset because He was obeying the Father in every aspect of His ministry. *Not once* is there a mention of Him being sick with any illness or disease. So when we passively allow sickness in our lives, that does *not* fall into the category of "sharing in Christ's sufferings" because He did not allow sickness into His own life—reread the Scriptures above for confirmation of this. Also, when we passively allow sickness in our lives, we have allowed the devil to deceive us into letting him steal, kill, and destroy various aspects of our lives, and believe we're doing so at Christ's behest. How Satan must laugh at our gullibility!

Now, be assured that there is no condemnation if you are sick and are striving in prayer and faith for your healing. There is a huge difference between *passively* allowing sickness in our lives (described above), which is unnecessary and wasteful, and *actively* resisting the devil, as we are commanded to do (James 4:7).

But—and here is the point of this whole section—the fact that Christ has called us to share in His sufferings does *not* give us a justification to passively accept sickness into our lives. *Sickness was not a part of Christ's sufferings, so it should not be part of ours either.*

One more thing: One of the Scriptures quoted above, in the "good suffering" discussion was this:

> Philippians 3:10 (TEV): All I want is to know Christ and to experience the power of his resurrection, **to share in his sufferings** and become like him in his death. . .

I don't think it's an accident that Paul put the concept of sharing in Christ's suffering together in the same verse with the concept of the power of His resurrection. Why do I say that? Because of something else that Paul wrote, and which has a direct bearing on the topic at hand:

> Romans 8:11: But **if the Spirit of him that raised up Jesus from the dead dwell in you,** he that raised up Christ from the dead **shall also quicken your mortal bodies** by his Spirit that dwelleth in you.
>
> AMP: And if the Spirit of Him Who raised up Jesus from the dead dwells in you, [then] **He Who raised up Christ Jesus from the dead will also restore to life your mortal (short-lived, perishable) bodies** through His Spirit Who dwells in you.

ERV: God raised Jesus from death. And **if God's Spirit lives in you, he will also give life to your bodies that die.** Yes, God is the one who raised Christ from death, and he will raise you to life through his Spirit living in you.

GWORD: Does the Spirit of the one who brought Jesus back to life live in you? Then **the one who brought Christ back to life will also make your mortal bodies alive** by his Spirit who lives in you.

PHILLIPS: Nevertheless once the Spirit of him who raised Jesus from the dead lives within you **he will, by that same Spirit, bring to your whole being new strength and vitality.**

NIRV: The Spirit of the One who raised Jesus from the dead is living in you. So **the God who raised Christ from the dead will also give life to your bodies, which are going to die.** He will do this by the power of his Spirit, who lives in you.

NLV: The Holy Spirit raised Jesus from the dead. **If the same Holy Spirit lives in you, He will give life to your bodies** in the same way.

WE: God raised Christ Jesus from death. Does God's Spirit live in you? Then **God will also give life to your bodies which die.** He does this through his Spirit who lives in you.

YLT: and if the Spirit of Him who did raise up Jesus out of the dead doth dwell in you, **He who did raise up the Christ out of the dead shall quicken also your dying bodies,** through His Spirit dwelling in you.

Fascinating. This is not talking about the Holy Spirit giving life to our *spirits*—that is obviously true also, but it's not what this particular verse is talking about. And, this is not talking about giving life to our glorified, resurrected bodies either. The verse above, in its various translations, say that the Spirit will quicken—give life to—our *mortal* bodies. The bodies we are living in now, here on earth! The ones that will eventually die! Does this also indicate God wants us healthy, and to heal us if we're not? I think so, and we just have to look at Jesus' examples to see what God's will is: 100% of the people who came to Him for healing were healed. See the chapter Jesus' Examples for these stories.

What About Paul's "Thorn?"

Yes, what about Paul's "thorn?" Many people say that Paul's "thorn" was that he was sick or sickly his whole life, and even though he asked God to heal him, God basically said, "No." In essence, Paul was doomed by God to be sick or sickly his whole life. Is this idea supported by Scripture?

Let's look at the passage that actually mentions Paul's "thorn."

> II Corinthians 12:7–10 (NIV): To keep me from becoming conceited because of these surpassingly great revelations, **there was given me a thorn in my flesh,** a messenger of Satan, to torment me. ⁸Three times I pleaded with the Lord to take it away from me. ⁹But he said to me, "My grace is sufficient for you, for my power is made perfect in weakness." Therefore I will boast all the more gladly about my weaknesses, so that Christ's power may rest on me. ¹⁰That is why, for Christ's sake, I delight in weaknesses, in insults, in hardships, in persecutions, in difficulties. For when I am weak, then I am strong.

If we don't read anything *into* the passage above, what does it really say? Actually, quite a few things.

What Does "Thorn" Mean, Anyway?

I have personally heard people on many different occasions talk about something being a "thorn in their flesh," and rarely, if ever, are they referring to an illness or disease; they are virtually always talking about some person, or the actions of some person, being bothersome, very similar to "pain in the neck." Now of course, what I have personally heard doesn't prove anything either way as to what the Bible means by a particular phrase, but it does raise the questions, "Is this a common phrase? Is it an idiom? And if so, what does it mean in general?"

As you may have seen in other books in the "Thoughts On" series, one good way of finding out what the Bible means by a particular word or phrase in some verse is to see if the Bible uses that same word or phrase elsewhere. If it does, then you're more likely to have learned something that Bible actually intended, as opposed to some commentator's opinion on what the Bible meant. And fortunately, such bothersome "thorns" are indeed mentioned elsewhere in the Bible.

In Numbers, God tells Moses to warn the Israelites that when they got to the Promised Land, they were to utterly drive out the Canaanites, because there would be dire consequences otherwise:

> Numbers 33:55 (NIV): But if you do not drive out the inhabitants of the land, those you allow to remain will become **barbs in your eyes and thorns in your sides.** They will give you trouble in the land where you will live.

Note that God is calling the Canaanites "barbs in your eyes and thorns in your sides." But what were the Canaanites? Were they diseases? No, they were the enemies of God's people, and they were entities, sentient beings, personalities—not diseases. And what would they do if the Israelites didn't drive them out? They would become bothersome pests.

One other thing: the very fact that God used the phrases "barbs in your eyes and thorns in your sides" to communicate to the Israelites that the Canaanites would oppose them and be bothersome, is a *strong* indicator that they knew what the phrases meant. A "thorn" in this context, was already a figure of speech, a metaphor, an idiom, all those thousands of years ago.

If the Israelites hadn't already been familiar with such linguistic usage of "thorn," God's statement would not have been very communicative. The Israelites would have thought, "The Canaanites will become pointy little things that grow on bushes? I wonder how they'll do that. . ." No, they understood the symbolism of thorns being enemies who were bothersome and habitually trying to hinder what you're doing.

Later on, Joshua is again warning the Israelites to stay faithful to God:

> Joshua 23:11–13 (NIV): So be very careful to love the LORD your God. ¹²But if you turn away and ally yourselves with the survivors of these nations that remain among you and if you intermarry with them and

associate with them, ¹³then you may be sure that the LORD your God will no longer drive out these nations before you. Instead, they will become snares and traps for you, **whips on your backs and thorns in your eyes,** until you perish from this good land, which the LORD your God has given you.

Here again, Joshua is using the same metaphor or figure of speech: "thorns" representing the enemies of God (and therefore also of His people) constantly being bothersome annoyances, trying to resist or hinder the work of God (and therefore also of His people). Again, notice that the implication of the word "thorn" is not a disease, but an enemy. And again, the fact that Joshua uses the phrase to communicate is a *strong* implication that they knew what he was saying.

Still later, after Israel had moved into the Promised Land, they forgot (or ignored) the command that God had given them—to drive out the Canaanites—so they let them stay:

Judges 1:28–35 (NIV): When Israel became strong, they pressed the Canaanites into forced labor **but never drove them out completely.** ²⁹**Nor did Ephraim drive out the Canaanites living in Gezer,** but the Canaanites continued to live there among them. ³⁰**Neither did Zebulun drive out the Canaanites living in Kitron or Nahalol,** who remained among them; but they did subject them to forced labor. ³¹**Nor did Asher drive out those living in Acco or Sidon or Ahlab or Aczib or Helbah or Aphek or Rehob,** ³²and because of this the people of Asher lived among the Canaanite inhabitants of the land. ³³**Neither did Naphtali drive out those living in Beth Shemesh or Beth Anath;** but the Naphtalites too lived among the Canaanite inhabitants of the land, and those living in Beth Shemesh and Beth Anath became forced laborers for them. ³⁴The Amorites confined the Danites to the hill country, not allowing them to come down into the plain. ³⁵And the Amorites were determined also to hold out in Mount Heres, Aijalon and Shaalbim, but when the power of the house of Joseph increased, they too were pressed into forced labor.

This is not looking hopeful: God tells Israel, "Don't do this because it will be bad," so Israel goes ahead and does it. (It's a good thing *we* never do such things nowadays, isn't it?) So sure enough, God shows up and addresses Israel:

> Judges 2:1–4: And an angel of the LORD came up from Gilgal to Bochim, and said, I made you to go up out of Egypt, and have brought you unto the land which I sware unto your fathers; and I said, I will never break my covenant with you. ²And ye shall make no league with the inhabitants of this land; ye shall throw down their altars: but ye have not obeyed my voice: why have ye done this? ³Wherefore I also said, I will not drive them out from before you; but **they shall be as thorns in your sides,** and their gods shall be a snare unto you. ⁴And it came to pass, when the angel of the LORD spake these words unto all the children of Israel, that the people lifted up their voice, and wept.

Yet again, God uses the "thorn" imagery to communicate the idea of the enemy being a constant annoyance.

Fast-forward a few hundred years. In Proverbs, Solomon weighs in and also says something about thorns:

> Proverbs 22:5 (NIV): **In the paths of the wicked lie thorns** and snares, but he who guards his soul stays far from them.

Now this particular Scripture does not use "thorn" to symbolize enemies of God causing problems, but it does say that such thorns are "in the paths of the wicked," and "he who guards his soul stays far from them." How would you characterize the Apostle Paul: as a "wicked" person, or a person "who guards his soul?" Selah.

So we've seen multiple instances of the Bible using the imagery of thorns, and in the majority of cases (including when God Himself was speaking), "thorns" refer to enemies of God, resisting His work and His will, and not as sicknesses or diseases. In the lone exception, the Bible states that "thorns" were what awaited "wicked" people as a natural fruit of what they had sown as they traveled along their path.

So, could it be that Paul's "thorn" uses the same imagery? Could it be that the One Who inspired the writing of Numbers, Joshua, and Judges also inspired the writing of II Corinthians and used similar words to communicate similar ideas?

Why Did Paul Have His Thorn?

It's been quite a few pages now since we've seen Paul's mention of his thorn, so let's look at it again:

> II Corinthians 12:7–10 (NIV): **To keep me from becoming conceited because of these surpassingly great revelations,** there was given me a thorn in my flesh, a messenger of Satan, to torment me. ⁸Three times I pleaded with the Lord to take it away from me. ⁹But he said to me, "My grace is sufficient for you, for my power is made perfect in weakness." Therefore I will boast all the more gladly about my weaknesses, so that Christ's power may rest on me. ¹⁰That is why, for Christ's sake, I delight in weaknesses, in insults, in hardships, in persecutions, in difficulties. For when I am weak, then I am strong.

According to Paul's own words, the reason *why* Paul was given his thorn in the flesh—regardless of *what* it actually was—is because of all the "surpassingly great revelations" that God had given Him (v. 7) for the benefit of the entire Body of Christ. If we want to use this passage to explain away our illness as just being our "thorn in the flesh, like Paul's," are we saying that we too have had so many surpassingly great revelations for the Body of Christ that we need such a thorn to keep us from getting conceited?

So it doesn't look like the average Christian warrants using the "thorn in the flesh" excuse, regardless of what it was.

What Did Paul Say His "Thorn" Was?

Actually, Paul *does* state what his thorn in the flesh was: he said it was "a messenger of Satan" (v. 7). Something that many people don't apparently notice is that the Greek word translated "messenger" in the KJV and some other translations is ἄγγελος (*aggelos*, G32). In Greek, a double gamma—two "γ" characters in a row—is pronounced like the English "ng" sound, so a better transliteration might be *angelos*. Does that look more familiar? The Greek word is usually translated "angel." For example:

> Matthew 1:20: But while he thought on these things, behold, the **angel** of the Lord appeared unto him in a dream, saying, Joseph, thou son of

David, fear not to take unto thee Mary thy wife: for that which is conceived in her is of the Holy Ghost.

Matthew 2:13: And when they were departed, behold, the **angel** of the Lord appeareth to Joseph in a dream, saying, Arise, and take the young child and his mother, and flee into Egypt, and be thou there until I bring thee word: for Herod will seek the young child to destroy him.

Matthew 4:6: And [Satan] saith unto him, If thou be the Son of God, cast thyself down: for it is written, He shall give his **angels** charge concerning thee: and in their hands they shall bear thee up, lest at any time thou dash thy foot against a stone.

Matthew 4:11: Then the devil leaveth him, and, behold, **angels** came and ministered unto him.

Matthew 13:39: The enemy that sowed them is the devil; the harvest is the end of the world; and the reapers are the **angels**.

Matthew 16:27: For the Son of man shall come in the glory of his Father with his **angels**; and then he shall reward every man according to his works.

Matthew 18:10: Take heed that ye despise not one of these little ones; for I say unto you, That in heaven their **angels** do always behold the face of my Father which is in heaven.

Matthew 22:30: For in the resurrection they neither marry, nor are given in marriage, but are as the **angels** of God in heaven.

Matthew 24:31: And he shall send his **angels** with a great sound of a trumpet, and they shall gather together his elect from the four winds, from one end of heaven to the other.

Matthew 25:41: Then shall he say also unto them on the left hand, Depart from me, ye cursed, into everlasting fire, prepared for the devil and his **angels**. . .

Matthew 26:53: Thinkest thou that I cannot now pray to my Father, and he shall presently give me more than twelve legions of **angels**?

Matthew 28:2: And, behold, there was a great earthquake: for the **angel** of the Lord descended from heaven, and came and rolled back the stone from the door, and sat upon it.

Matthew 28:5: And the **angel** answered and said unto the women, Fear not ye: for I know that ye seek Jesus, which was crucified.

Luke 1:13: But the **angel** said unto him, Fear not, Zacharias: for thy prayer is heard; and thy wife Elisabeth shall bear thee a son, and thou shalt call his name John.

Luke 1:26–27: And in the sixth month the **angel** Gabriel was sent from God unto a city of Galilee, named Nazareth, ^{27}To a virgin espoused to a man whose name was Joseph, of the house of David; and the virgin's name was Mary.

Luke 2:13–15: And suddenly there was with the **angel** a multitude of the heavenly host praising God, and saying, ^{14}Glory to God in the highest, and on earth peace, good will toward men. ^{15}And it came to pass, as the **angels** were gone away from them into heaven, the shepherds said one to another, Let us now go even unto Bethlehem, and see this thing which is come to pass, which the Lord hath made known unto us.

Luke 12:8: Also I say unto you, Whosoever shall confess me before men, him shall the Son of man also confess before the **angels** of God. . .

Acts 10:3: He saw in a vision evidently about the ninth hour of the day an **angel** of God coming in to him, and saying unto him, Cornelius.

II Corinthians 11:14 (NIV): And no wonder, for Satan himself masquerades as an **angel** of light.

II Peter 2:4: For if God spared not the **angels** that sinned, but cast them down to hell, and delivered them into chains of darkness, to be reserved unto judgment. . .

Jude 6: And the **angels** which kept not their first estate, but left their own habitation, he hath reserved in everlasting chains under darkness unto the judgment of the great day.

Revelation 5:11–12: And I beheld, and I heard the voice of many **angels** round about the throne and the beasts and the elders: and the number of them was ten thousand times ten thousand, and thousands of thousands; ^{12}Saying with a loud voice, Worthy is the Lamb that was slain to receive power, and riches, and wisdom, and strength, and honour, and glory, and blessing.

Revelation 9:11: And they had a king over them, which is the **angel** of the bottomless pit, whose name in the Hebrew tongue is Abaddon, but in the Greek tongue hath his name Apollyon.

Revelation 12:7–9 (NIV): And there was war in heaven. Michael and his **angels** fought against the dragon, and the dragon and his **angels** fought back. ⁸But he was not strong enough, and they lost their place in heaven. ⁹The great dragon was hurled down—that ancient serpent called the devil, or Satan, who leads the whole world astray. He was hurled to the earth, and his **angels** with him.

In *all* of the cases above, plus about 150 more omitted for the sake of brevity, the Greek word translated into the English word "angel" was ἄγγελος. And as we can see from Matthew 25:41, II Peter 2:4, Jude 6, Revelation 9:11, and 12:7–9, even the demons (as well as Satan himself) are legitimately called "angels." And indeed they are: they are created beings, and they did not cease to be angels when they rebelled against God; they just ceased to be *good* angels. That is, they became *fallen* angels, also known as demons.

So we can see from the above list of Scriptures, plus a quick confirmation with a Bible concordance, that in the *vast* majority of cases, ἄγγελος refers to a spirit being, and is therefore translated "angel." In only *one* case does ἄγγελος refer to a spirit being but it was *not* translated "angel"—it's where Paul talks about his thorn in the flesh, and in that case it was translated "messenger." Why was it translated "messenger" in that case? I don't know, but it seems that a lot of confusion could have been avoided had it been translated as "angel" in that case, as it was in *every other case* of referring to a spirit being.

Now, granted, ἄγγελος can occasionally refer to a human, and in those cases, it is appropriately translated "messenger." But even in those rare cases, it *always* refers to a sentient, self-aware, choice-making being who was sent on an errand for someone else. *Not once* does it refer to an illness, sickness, disease, or physical infirmity.

Now, lest we get the impression that *all* the modern Bible translators followed suit with the KJV in translating the Greek word ἄγγελος into "messenger" and thus propagated the inconsistency with *every other* reference to a spirit being, let me add that there are translations of the Bible that translated it "angel:"

> II Corinthians 12:7 (CEV): Of course, I am now referring to the wonderful things I saw. One of Satan's **angels** was sent to make me suffer terribly, so that I would not feel too proud.

DOUAY: And lest the greatness of the revelations should exalt me, there was given me a sting of my flesh, an **angel** of Satan, to buffet me.

ERV: But I must not be too proud of the wonderful things that were shown to me. So a painful problem was given to me—an **angel** from Satan, sent to make me suffer, so that I would not think that I am better than anyone else.

NABRE: . . .because of the abundance of the revelations. Therefore, that I might not become too elated, a thorn in the flesh was given to me, an **angel** of Satan, to beat me, to keep me from being too elated.

WYC: And lest the greatness of revelations enhance me in pride, the prick of my flesh, an **angel** of Satan, is given to me, that he buffet me.

So again, the Greek word ἄγγελος *always* refers to a sentient being, a free-will entity, and never as an illness, sickness, disease, or physical infirmity. But the theory of Paul's thorn being a disease or physical infirmity is *very* firmly stuck into the mindset of most of modern American Christendom. So much so that, amazingly, a few recent translations of the Bible put *both* ideas in: they acknowledge that the Greek states it was an angel of Satan—a demon—harassing Paul, but then they also put in the mutually-exclusive verbiage of "painful physical ailment," "physical handicap," "physical condition," "painful physical problem," "pain in my body," or some such, as if to provide an easy theological-sounding escape route for people when they pray and nothing seems to happen. After all, it's faster and easier to say "I have a thorn in the flesh like Paul" than it is to seek God for sufficient faith and understanding of the spiritual power, authority, and blessings Jesus bought for us in the Atonement to overcome and conquer an attack from the enemy.

So it seems that the KJV translation of the Greek word ἄγγελος as "messenger" instead of "angel" in II Corinthians 12:7 was an unfortunate choice during the translation process. It has lulled countless Christians into giving in to demonic attack instead of resisting to the point of victory.

What Did *Not* Paul Say His "Thorn" Was?

In I Corinthians 11—just one chapter before his "thorn in the flesh" statement—Paul is warning the Corinthians against falling for the wiles of false teachers, and specifically, to not be impressed simply because they claim to have suffered for Christ. In this passage, Paul acknowledges that to be proud of such is silly, but he says basically, "You think *they've* suffered a lot? Listen to what *I've* been through!"

> II Corinthians 11:16–28 (NIV) I repeat: Let no one take me for a fool. But if you do, then receive me just as you would a fool, so that I may do a little boasting. ¹⁷In this self-confident boasting I am not talking as the Lord would, but as a fool. ¹⁸Since many are boasting in the way the world does, I too will boast. ¹⁹You gladly put up with fools since you are so wise! ²⁰In fact, you even put up with anyone who enslaves you or exploits you or takes advantage of you or pushes himself forward or slaps you in the face. ²¹To my shame I admit that we were too weak for that! What anyone else dares to boast about—I am speaking as a fool—I also dare to boast about. ²²**Are they Hebrews? So am I. Are they Israelites? So am I. Are they Abraham's descendants? So am I.** ²³**Are they servants of Christ?** (I am out of my mind to talk like this.) **I am more. I have worked much harder, been in prison more frequently, been flogged more severely, and been exposed to death again and again.** ²⁴**Five times I received from the Jews the forty lashes minus one.** ²⁵**Three times I was beaten with rods, once I was stoned, three times I was shipwrecked, I spent a night and a day in the open sea,** ²⁶**I have been constantly on the move. I have been in danger from rivers, in danger from bandits, in danger from my own countrymen, in danger from Gentiles; in danger in the city, in danger in the country, in danger at sea; and in danger from false brothers.** ²⁷**I have labored and toiled and have often gone without sleep; I have known hunger and thirst and have often gone without food; I have been cold and naked.** ²⁸Besides everything else, I face daily the pressure of my concern for all the churches.

Isn't that interesting? In this extensive list of all the things Paul has suffered for the sake of the Gospel, *he doesn't mention sickness once.* If this thorn that he had was actually a disease put on him because of his amazing power and understanding and revelations in the spirit, don't you think he would have mentioned that as one of the things he had suffered?

Not only that, but the things Paul *does* mention are things that Satan habitually does to discourage people, even today. He incites other people rise up in mindless rage against Godly people, just like he did to Job (Job 1:15, 17), and to Jesus before the crucifixion (Luke 23:20–23). Thus, Paul was jailed, beaten, flogged, and stoned either from legal action or mob action, and he had been in danger from bandits, Jews, Gentiles, and false brothers. He was shipwrecked three times, and there is little doubt that Satan provoked the storms that caused the shipwrecks, since we know Satan can change the weather to cause destruction (Job 1:19). And on and on. *But not once* does he mention that he was sick. Hmm. . .

An Eye Disease?

Another thing about Paul's thorn: Some people point to a verse in Galatians as proof that Paul's thorn was an eye disease of some kind:

> Galatians 6:11 (NIV): See what large letters I use as I write to you with my own hand!

The thinking goes like this. Paul usually used an amanuensis (a scribe) to write his letters because he couldn't see as a result of his eye disease and the resulting poor vision. Since he had poor vision as a result of his eye disease, when he wrote things himself, he had to write really large in order to see what he had written. Therefore, the fact that he wrote large shows that he had an eye disease of some kind.

It doesn't take much reflection to see the flaw in the above train of thought: based on the assumption that Paul had an eye disease, one can "prove" he had an eye disease. A classic case of circular reasoning, which is inherently flawed and unreliable.

But even putting aside the circularity of the reasoning above, it still doesn't stand up to scrutiny, because it makes two other assumptions that are also unfounded:

- "People who have others write letters for them have bad eyesight." This of course, is ridiculous, as shown by the millions of secretaries and admin assistants worldwide, who work for bosses who can see just fine.
- "People who write large must have bad eyesight." (And the implied converse: "People who have good eyesight will write small.") This idea falls apart as soon as you look at any newspaper, magazine, billboard, website, and even handwritten notes, and see that large letters more often indicate **emphasis** than poor eyesight. (See how that drew your attention?) Plus, I personally know many people who always write large, and many other who always write small, and in neither case is there a correlation to their visual acuity.

So we see that using Paul's writing with large letters as proof of an eye disease, or even poor eyesight, is really grasping at straws.

Where Did Paul's Thorn Come From?

You may have noticed in the II Corinthians 12 passage quoted above, that Paul says:

> II Corinthians 12:7: And lest I should be exalted above measure through the abundance of the revelations, **there was given to me** a thorn in the flesh, the messenger of Satan to buffet me, lest I should be exalted above measure.

Many people in modern-day American churches read that to say, "*God gave me* a thorn in the flesh. . ." Grammatically, that could be true because that sentence doesn't say *by whom* it was given to him, but does that conclusion hold water, Scripturally speaking?

We saw above that Paul's thorn was, in his own words, an "angel of Satan," based on the definition of the Greek word as "angel." I think it's safe to say that an "angel of Satan" can also be called a "demon." So who sends demons to attack people? Does Jesus? Why would Jesus give us power and authority to cast out demons (Matthew 10:1, Luke

9:1) and power over *all* the power of the enemy, such that evil spirits are subject to us (Luke 10:17–19), and then send demons after us?

And Jesus Himself, our role model, cast out demons throughout His earthly ministry. Doesn't it sound a little suspicious to accuse Him of *sending* demons against Paul or anyone else? What did Jesus say when the Pharisees were confused about where He got the power to cast out demons? He said this:

> Matthew 12:25–26: And Jesus knew their thoughts, and said unto them, **Every kingdom divided against itself is brought to desolation; and every city or house divided against itself shall not stand:** ²⁶And if Satan cast out Satan, he is divided against himself; how shall then his kingdom stand?

What fraction of all kingdoms did Jesus say would be brought to desolation if it were divided against itself? *Every* kingdom. Well, since God has a kingdom, His must be included, since Jesus said "*every* kingdom." And, since we know that His kingdom lasts forever (Isaiah 9:7, Revelation 11:15), we are driven to conclude that His kingdom cannot be divided against itself. Which means, since Jesus gave us power over demons, *He would not also give demons power over us.*

So when Paul said that an angel of Satan—i.e., a demon—"was given" to him, we see that it could not have been given to him by God, because God's kingdom would be divided in doing so. Also, it just doesn't fit *at all* with God's Father-heart. So it must have been given to him by Satan. After all, Satan was the one whose kingdom was being threatened by Paul's revelations of the kingdom of God, of "Christ in you, the hope of glory." So what does that verse say again?

> II Corinthians 12:7: And lest I should be exalted above measure through the abundance of the revelations, **there was given to me** a thorn in the flesh, the **messenger of Satan** to buffet me, lest I should be exalted above measure.

Now someone might say, "Paul says it was a messenger *of* Satan, but couldn't it have come *from* God?" In case the above Scriptural refutations of this idea weren't enough, let's look at some other translations and see if they support this idea:

CEB: . . .It's a messenger **from Satan** sent to torment me. . .

CJB: . . .a messenger **from the Adversary** to pound away at me. . .

ERV: . . .an angel **from Satan,** sent to make me suffer. . .

EXB: . . .This problem was a messenger **from Satan,** sent to beat [torment; harass; trouble] me. . .

TLB: . . .a messenger **from Satan** to hurt and bother me. . .

NCV: . . .This problem was a messenger **from Satan,** sent to beat me. . .

NIRV: . . .It is a messenger **from Satan** to make me suffer. . .

NLT: . . .a messenger **from Satan** to torment me. . .

WE: . . .It came **from Satan [the devil]** to trouble me. . .

So I think we can safely conclude that the demon, the angel of Satan, the messenger of Satan, did *not* come from God. As shown above, it came from Satan.

"My Grace is Sufficient For You. . ."

In this passage about Paul's thorn, we see God saying to him, "My grace is sufficient for thee." But what did God mean by that? We in the modern church all too often interpret God's statement here to be a courteous way of saying, "Tough luck, you're going to have to live with it." Or maybe, "Having Me in your heart should more than compensate for your disease that I won't take away." But is either of those consistent with God's character and His Word?

Here is yet another reason that it seems unlikely that Paul's thorn was a physical disease, illness, or painful bodily condition: Jesus had already given His disciples power over all demons and to heal all kinds of diseases:

Matthew 10:1: And when he had called unto him his twelve disciples, **he gave them power** against unclean spirits, to cast them out, and **to heal all manner of sickness and all manner of disease.**

And of course, Paul knew about this; he was used mightily in healing many people of all sorts of diseases. However, let's assume for the moment that Paul's thorn was indeed a disease (which, as we've seen, seems unlikely, given the preponderance of Scripture). What else could the phrase "My grace is sufficient for thee" mean?

The Parable of the College Student

To help answer that question, let me tell a parable. Suppose a wealthy man is sending his youngest son off to college on the other side of the country, as he had done for his other children earlier. A couple months before the semester starts, he calls his son into his office to talk about the logistics of the cross-country move and the start of the college term.

"Son, you'll be leaving for college soon, and there will be a lot of expenses as you get settled in and get ready to start classes. As I've done for all your brothers and sisters, I have created a college fund account and put enough money in it to cover all your expenses. Here is a credit card that draws from that account. You'll need to buy your plane tickets, get a rental car until you can buy your own, find an apartment, and so forth. Whatever you need, just charge it to that account. I seriously doubt it will run low, but if it does, I'll add to it whatever is necessary to cover your expenses."

So the son thanks his father for all his care and nurturing during his earlier years, and then finishes packing. The young man buys a plane ticket to get to his destination, rents a car, gets a hotel room for a few days until he finds an apartment. Once he finds a suitable apartment, starts up all his utilities, and puts down the deposit and first month's rent, he goes looking for a car. Being a responsible and well-trained young man, he gets a good car but doesn't go over the top, trying to get the hottest thing on wheels. He charges everything to the credit card that draws from the college account his father set up, and sure enough, there's always enough in there to cover his expenses.

Then the young man has to get furniture for his apartment, plus enough food that he won't need to run to the grocery store every day. He pays his tuition and fees, and buys his textbooks (boy, are those expensive!), and puts it all on his father's credit card. He seems to be all set for classes to start next week, and then as he walked past the computer store, he remembers that he needs a computer for his classes.

He walks in, finds exactly what he needs, and excitedly sends his father a text message, and his father responds:

> Dad, I found a really cool computer that I'd like to get, and I'll need it for my classes that start next week. Would you buy it for me, please?

> There's still plenty of money in the college account; just put it on the credit card you've been using for your other purchases.

Several days later, the computer had not shown up, so the young man texts his father again, who promptly replies:

> Dad, classes are starting in a couple days, and I still don't have a computer. Would you please buy me that one I talked about as soon as possible?

> You have sufficient funds for the computer in the credit-card account, just use the same card that you've been using. There's plenty enough money in there to cover the computer.

Several more days pass, and classes have started. The computer had *still* not arrived, and the young man had already gotten two assignments for which he would need the computer, so he nervously texts his father again:

> Dad! Classes started two days ago and I still don't have the computer. Are you going to buy it for me? I really need it...

> Son, you have access to all the money in the college-fund account, so just buy the computer like you've bought everything else you've needed. I don't need to buy the computer here and then ship it; my card is sufficient for you.

So when the father told his son, "My card is sufficient for you," what was he saying? Maybe it's just a courteous way of saying "Tough luck, you're going to have to live without your computer." Or maybe, "Having my credit card in your pocket should more than compensate for the computer I won't buy for you." Is that what the father was saying? Of course not. He was saying to his son, "I've already provided all you need to make the computer a reality in your life. Go use it!"

In the same way—again, we're still assuming for the moment that Paul's thorn actually *was* a bodily disease instead of the angel of Satan that the text clearly states—is it possible that when Paul asked God to take away his disease, could God possibly have meant something similar to the father in the parable? As in, "My grace is sufficient to remove your disease. I don't need to do anything more; use the power I've already granted you."

I think that is exactly what Jesus was saying to him, regardless of what his thorn in the flesh actually was. It seems to me that a perfectly reasonable interpretation of Jesus' words here is, "I've already given you my grace, and that has enough power to take care of the problem, if you apply it. You don't need me to do anything more than I already have."

This interpretation of God's response to Paul makes much more sense Scripturally, because Jesus had indeed given his disciples power over all diseases, as shown above. So, since Paul already had received sufficient power by virtue of God's grace to get rid of diseases, God was not telling him to live with it, but rather, that he already had everything he needed to remove the disease he had, if indeed he had one.

It's like us asking God to go witness to our neighbors and preach the gospel to them. He is entirely justified in saying, "I've already told *you* to do that, and given you the power to do so." Similarly, here is Paul (again, assuming for the moment that his thorn actually *was* a disease) saying, "God, heal my disease," and God replying, "*You* get rid of it; I've already given you more than enough power to do so, and the command to use it."

But someone might say at this point, "God said His *grace* is sufficient for Paul. He didn't say anything about giving Him *power*." True, I am going on the assumption that God's grace includes empowerment to obey Him, even in miraculous, supernatural things. Is it warranted to equate God's grace with miraculous power, or at least to act as if His grace *includes* power? I think so:

> Acts 4:33: And **with great power gave the apostles witness** of the resurrection of the Lord Jesus: and **great grace was upon them all**.
>
> Acts 14:3 (NIV): The apostles stayed there [in Iconium] for a long time, speaking boldly about **the Lord, who proved that their message about his grace was true by giving them the power to perform miracles and wonders.**

In the Scriptures above, grace and power are closely associated. Also, in both Romans 12 and I Corinthians 12, Paul talks about supernatural empowerments, and how we are all members of one body, and have various gifts that only the Holy Spirit can empower us to use:

> Romans 12:6 (WEB): Having **gifts differing according to the grace that was given to us**, if prophecy, let us prophesy according to the proportion of our faith. . .

And when Paul exhorts the Corinthians that when God's grace abounds to them, they should abound in every good work:

> II Corinthians 9:8 (WEB): And God is able to make **all grace abound to you, that you,** always having all sufficiency in everything, **may abound to every good work.**

What kinds of good works? Let's look at the good works Jesus performed, since He is the role model we are to copy; what kinds of good works did He perform? Almost without exception, they were supernatural, miraculous works, and of those, the most common type was restoring health to people. Hmm. We'll need His grace (which includes His power) to do that, won't we?

Paul's "Infirmities"

Another reason that some people think that Paul's "thorn" was a disease is because, in that same passage, Paul refers to his "infirmities" (at least in some translations):

> II Corinthians 12:7–10: And lest I should be exalted above measure through the abundance of the revelations, there was given to me a thorn in the flesh, the messenger of Satan to buffet me, lest I should be exalted above measure. ⁸For this thing I besought the Lord thrice, that it might depart from me. ⁹And he said unto me, My grace is sufficient for thee: for my strength is made perfect in weakness. Most gladly therefore **will I rather glory in my infirmities,** that the power of Christ may rest upon me. ¹⁰Therefore I take pleasure in **infirmities,** in reproaches, in necessities, in persecutions, in distresses for Christ's sake: for when I am weak, then am I strong.

The Greek word ἀσθένεια (*astheneia*, G769) is translated into the English word "infirmity." That word *astheneia* can indeed mean illness or disease, as in:

> Matthew 8:17 (NIV): This was to fulfill what was spoken through the prophet Isaiah: "He took up our **infirmities** and carried our diseases."
>
> Luke 5:15: But so much the more went there a fame abroad of him: and great multitudes came together to hear, and to be healed by him of their **infirmities.**

> Luke 7:21: And in that same hour he cured many of their **infirmities** and plagues, and of evil spirits; and unto many that were blind he gave sight.
>
> Luke 8:2: And certain women, which had been healed of evil spirits and **infirmities**, Mary called Magdalene, out of whom went seven devils. . .
>
> Luke 13:11: And, behold, there was a woman which had a spirit of **infirmity** eighteen years, and was bowed together, and could in no wise lift up herself.

. . .and so forth. So we can see that *astheneia* can mean diseased or ill. *But that is not the only valid definition.* Let's look at some other Scriptures that use exactly the same Greek word, and see how there are several other possible meanings.

In the Scriptures below, the Bible writers use *astheneia* to mean a variety of different things, both literal and figurative: mere weakness, submission, lack of awareness, living in a human body, and so forth. In general, it could be understood to be "the inability to produce desired results" of whatever kind the context calls for. Let's look more closely.

> Romans 6:19 (NIV): I put this in human terms because you are **weak** in your natural selves. Just as you used to offer the parts of your body in slavery to impurity and to ever-increasing wickedness, so now offer them in slavery to righteousness leading to holiness.

In this case, *astheneia* (which is translated "infirmity" in the KJV and some other translations) apparently refers to simply a lack of theological knowledge for the Romans to understand the spiritual underpinnings of his argument. Paul was a highly trained Pharisee, and was well-versed in theological concepts. Of course, before he encountered Christ Himself, that knowledge merely puffed Paul up, and caused him to actually resist the move of God.

When Paul met Jesus, he didn't forget all his theology; he simply realized how it fit into the God's plan. But the church at Rome was not theologically trained, and so Paul needed to speak in ordinary, non-theological terms. Indeed, the TEV renders the first sentence of this verse as: "I use everyday language because of the weakness of your natural selves." So this use of *astheneia* has nothing to do with disease.

Here's another usage of the word "infirmity" from the Greek *astheneia*. In this case, it refers merely to a lack of knowledge:

> Romans 8:26: Likewise the Spirit also helpeth our **infirmities:** for we know not what we should pray for as we ought: but the Spirit itself maketh intercession for us with groanings which cannot be uttered.

So what is Paul saying is our infirmity in this verse? Simply that we don't know what to pray for as we ought. This is why praying in tongues is so important: even when we don't have a clue how to pray for some person or situation, "the Spirit itself maketh intercession for us with groanings which cannot be uttered." Other translations render that final phrase "groanings too deep for utterance" or "groanings too deep for words." So our "infirmity" is merely not knowing how to pray, so we are encouraged to let the Spirit supply the words, while we supply only the willingness to obey and let Him work through us.

Here's another one. In this Scripture, Paul is using *astheneia* (translated "weakness" in the KJV) to simply mean "in our earthly bodies," as opposed to the glorified bodies we'll get later:

> I Corinthians 15:41–44: There is one glory of the sun, and another glory of the moon, and another glory of the stars: for one star differeth from another star in glory. ⁴²So also is the resurrection of the dead. It is sown in corruption; it is raised in incorruption: ⁴³It is sown in dishonour; it is raised in glory: it is sown in **weakness**; it is raised in power: ⁴⁴It is sown a natural body; it is raised a spiritual body. There is a natural body, and there is a spiritual body.

Again, there is no indication or implication of sickness in this use of the word.

Here's another one. In this passage, Paul describes Jesus Himself as having *astheneia*, but to assume that means that Jesus was sick is as preposterous as saying that Jesus sinned. The context shows that it refers to the fact that Jesus let Himself be crucified (John 10:17) for our sake:

> II Corinthians 13:3–4: since you are demanding proof that Christ is speaking through me. He is not weak in dealing with you, but is powerful among you. ⁴For to be sure, he was crucified in **weakness**, yet he

lives by God's power. Likewise, we are weak in him, yet by God's power we will live with him to serve you.

Again, no implication at all of sickness or disease.

The writer of Hebrews uses *astheneia* in yet another way: to express the human propensity to be tempted to sin. He was pointing out that Jesus understands our situation, because He too was tempted during His earthly ministry:

> Hebrews 4:14–15: Seeing then that we have a great high priest, that is passed into the heavens, Jesus the Son of God, let us hold fast our profession. [15]For we have not an high priest which cannot be touched with the feeling of our **infirmities**; but was in all points tempted like as we are, yet without sin.

And there are even more perfectly valid usages of *astheneia* that are completely unrelated to disease, but were omitted here for the sake of brevity. So let's summarize what we've seen from studying Paul's thorn in the flesh:

- In *every other* Bible passage that uses the idiom "thorn in the flesh" or something comparable, it refers to sentient, aware, conscious entities who are deliberately resisting the work of God. So why do we interpret Paul's thorn to be a disease?

- Paul had his thorn—whatever it was—*because* he had such profound and far-reaching revelation for the Body of Christ that there was a potential for pride to arise in his life (II Corinthians 12:7). So why do we so quickly use Paul's thorn as a model for ourselves when it's rather (read: "extremely") unlikely we've had anywhere near the revelation of Jesus that Paul did? Isn't that somewhat presumptuous?

- Paul clearly states that his thorn was a demon—a "messenger of Satan"—sent to harass him (II Corinthians 12:7). Remember that the Greek word *angelos*, translated "messenger" in the KJV, is translated "angel" in *every other case* of that Greek word referring to a spiritual being. So why do we assume *angelos* in Paul's case refers to a disease, when it isn't translated that way *anywhere else* in the Bible?

- When Paul was listing all the things that he had suffered for the sake of the Gospel (II Corinthians 11:22–29), any concept of sickness or disease is conspicuously absent. If his thorn was a disease, why didn't he mention it as one of the things he suffered? And why do we so readily gloss over this fact when reading that passage?
- Paul mentions in Galatians 6:11 that he writes large. Why do we so easily conclude from that fact that he must have had an eye disease? As noted above, that seems to be *really* grasping at straws.
- When Paul states that Jesus responded to him with "My grace is sufficient for you," we readily interpret that to mean "Sorry, you'll have to live with your disease." Why do we not see that that is inconsistent with God's intent and promises, and Christ's examples, commands, and character? And why do we overlook that God's grace includes empowerment to do His will, including His command to heal the sick?
- The Greek word *astheneia* means "weakness" or "frailty" in whatever context is currently being discussed. So why do we assume in Paul's case it must mean "sickness"—one of *many* valid interpretations of that word? As we have seen, any alleged support for this particular interpretation depends on the other (shaky) assumptions listed above.

Taken as a whole, the body of evidence above shows that it is very questionable, to say the least, to say that Paul's thorn in the flesh was a disease—actual Biblical evidence for that belief is slim to none. But looking at it from Satan's point of view, it makes sense that he would want to promote this interpretation, because of its inherent de-motivating effects. Think about the take-away concept from this passage, *if* we assume Paul's thorn was a disease: "Don't let God use you *too* much, because the more you do, the more likely His promises of healing and health will stop working." No wonder Satan pushes it so heavily.

What About Trophimus?

There is a famous Scripture passage at the end of II Timothy, where Paul is closing his letter to Timothy; just the typical stuff: Say hi to these people, these other people say hi, come visit soon, that kind of stuff. But one little phrase in the middle seems to have become, for some, a defining worldview:

II Timothy 4:20b: . . .Trophimus have I left at Miletum **sick**.

I have seen people triumphantly point to this Scripture and say, "See? That proves that it's not always God's will to heal people." Does it indeed prove that? Let's examine it and see.

First of all, we don't know that Trophimus didn't get healed; we only know that Trophimus didn't get healed *by the time Paul left Miletum.* But even granting—for the moment—the unfounded assumption that Trophimus *never ever* got healed, let's look at the other pertinent information:

- In the chapter God's Original Intent, we saw that from the beginning, He designed mankind to be healthy, and at the end of the story, sickness will again be nonexistent.
- In the chapter Biblical Promises, we saw multiple places where God promises health and healing, in both the Old Testament and the New, as well as one of the self-identifying Jehovah-names with which He says health and healing are part of *His very nature.*
- In the chapter Jesus' Examples, we saw 38 people come to Jesus individually or in small groups for healing, and 100% of them get healed. In the places where "great multitudes" of people came to Him, He "healed them all" of "every disease and every sickness among the people." Again, 100%.
- In the chapter Are All Christians Supposed to Heal the Sick?, we saw Jesus empower the disciples—first the Twelve and then the Seventy-Two—and then command them to heal the sick, which they did. Then in the Great Commission, Jesus tells His followers to make disciples of all nations, teaching them to obey

all the commands He gave them, which would have to include the ones about healing the sick.

Okay, now that we've been reminded of the content of the previous chapters, let's look at the preponderance of evidence. On the one hand, we have God's intent, God's promises, Jesus' examples, and Jesus' commands. And on the other, we have an example of someone who (we think) didn't get healed. Which carries more weight in our hearts?

Isn't it interesting that for so many people, it is far easier to base our theology, our beliefs, our worldview, *on one person's experience,* rather than God's clear intent, promises, examples, and commands? Sometimes we need to ask ourselves, very seriously, "Do I really believe God is strong enough to heal? Do I believe God *wants* to heal? Do I believe that God loves me like a father ought to love his children?" And then the hardest question: "*Why* do I believe that way?" If we are more influenced by someone's experience than by God's expressed will, we need to repent and stop sinning against Him.

Many Christians would not admit out loud that they place more credence in so-and-so's experience than in the Bible, but many do in real life. How do we know that? Two different ways:

- *Out of the abundance of the heart, the mouth speaks* (Matthew 12:34). When someone mentions divine healing in a positive light, or asks you to pray for him for healing, do you find yourself readily agreeing, simply because God promised it, and Jesus commanded us to do so? Or do all the "failures" come to mind, and you find yourself saying something like, "Well, you have to be careful with that kind of stuff. . ." to "prepare" them in case God doesn't come through?

- *By their fruits, you shall know them* (Matthew 7:16–20). As many people have noted, it's very easy to answer the question "How do you know if you have faith to pray for the sick?" The answer is "You pray for the sick." Observe your actions: do you pray for the sick? When you see someone who is sick, does your internal response lean toward "Ooh, I'd hate to be that person."? Or more toward "It'll be so cool when he's healed!"?

So-and-So Got Prayed For, But Didn't Get Healed

This is similar to the previous section, but motivated by personal experience of an "unsuccessful" prayer for healing, rather than some obscure person mentioned in the Bible almost 2000 years ago, whose only claim to fame is that he didn't get healed by the time his companions left town. And again, I have seen this excuse used many times, by many people over the years, to explain why God's intent, promises, examples, and commands "don't apply" anymore, at least in the area of healing.

Randy Clark has a worldwide healing ministry that has seen tens of thousands of jaw-dropping miraculous healings over the decades. In one of his teachings, he recalls how, at the beginning of his ministry, he used to be embarrassed by some Scriptures and would de-emphasize them during sermons, because he had rarely or never seen some of the miracles the Scriptures talked about in "heal the sick, cleanse the lepers, raise the dead, cast out demons." When God called him on the carpet about his attitudes, he admitted, "Yes, I *am* embarrassed about those Scriptures. I'm barely seeing the sick healed, let alone the dead raised."

And God gave him one of the strongest rebukes he has ever gotten: "Don't you *dare* lower My Word to the level of your experience. *Don't* you be an experience-based preacher. *Do not* create a theology that excuses your lack. *Do not* create a theology based on your experience of *not* seeing the dead raised or people healed. Preach My Word, and let people's experience rise to it." We would do well to take this rebuke to heart. Whenever we start acting like God's Word is not true, based on what *we've* experienced, we are lowering God's Word to *our* level. This is a seriously bad choice to make.

Basically, we should avoid being like the comic-strip character Garfield the Cat. In the first frame of one comic strip, he's lying in his bed, looking depressed and thinking, "I really shouldn't eat so much." In the second frame he continues, "I really should get more exercise." In the third frame, he considers his long-time nemesis, Odie the dog, "I really should be nicer to Odie." And in the fourth frame, a lightbulb appears above his head, and Garfield excitedly snaps his fingers and cries out, "I've got it! I'll lower my standards!"

While humorous in a comic strip, do we do the same thing when we encounter a Scriptural concept we're not comfortable with? Do we try to interpret God's Word according to *our* level of experience, or do we let His Holy Spirit raise our faith and expectations to the level of His Word?

And if you think about it rationally, it is extremely foolish to assume God doesn't want to heal everybody, simply because someone "didn't get healed." You could use the same logic—no, let's not call it "logic," because it isn't logical. Let's call it a "train of thought" instead. You could use the same train of thought to prove that God doesn't want to save everybody. Never mind multiple, clear statements that He *does* want to save everybody, and therefore offers salvation to all, such as in these Scriptures:

> Ezekiel 18:23 (TEV): "Do you think I enjoy seeing evil people die?" asks the Sovereign LORD. "No, **I would rather see them repent and live.**"
>
> Ezekiel 18:32 (NIV): For **I take no pleasure in the death of anyone,** declares the Sovereign LORD. **Repent and live!**
>
> Ezekiel 33:11 (NLT): As surely as I live, says the Sovereign LORD, I take no pleasure in the death of wicked people. **I only want them to turn from their wicked ways so they can live.** Turn! Turn from your wickedness, O people of Israel! Why should you die?
>
> Matthew 18:11 (WEB): For **the Son of Man came to save that which was lost.**
>
> Matthew 18:14 (NIV): In the same way **your Father in heaven is not willing that any of these little ones should be lost.**
>
> Luke 19:10 (NASB): "For the Son of Man has come to seek and **to save that which was lost.**"
>
> John 1:7–9 (BBE): He [John the Baptist] came for witness, to give witness about the light [Jesus], **so that all men might have faith through him.** ⁸He himself was not the light: he was sent to give witness about the light. ⁹**The true light, which gives light to every man,** was then coming into the world.

- John 3:16–18 (WEB): For God so loved the world, that he gave his one and only Son, that **whoever believes in him should not perish, but have eternal life.** ¹⁷For God didn't send his Son into the world to judge the world, but **that the world should be saved through him.**

- John 12:32 (GWORD): When I have been lifted up from the earth, **I will draw all people toward me.**

- Acts 17:30 (GWORD): God overlooked the times when people didn't know any better. But **now he commands everyone everywhere to turn to him and change the way they think and act.**

- Romans 5:18 (AMP): Well then, as one man's trespass [one man's false step and falling away led] to condemnation for all men, so one Man's act of righteousness [leads] to **acquittal and right standing with God and life for all men.**

- I Timothy 1:15 (AMP): The saying is sure and true and worthy of full and universal acceptance, that **Christ Jesus (the Messiah) came into the world to save sinners,** of whom I am foremost.

- I Timothy 2:3–6 (AMP): For such [praying] is good and right, and [it is] pleasing and acceptable to **God our Savior,** ⁴**Who wishes all men to be saved** and [increasingly] to perceive and recognize and discern and know precisely and correctly the [divine] Truth. ⁵For there [is only] one God, and [only] one Mediator between God and men, **the Man Christ Jesus,** ⁶**Who gave Himself as a ransom for all** [people, a fact that was] attested to at the right and proper time.

- Titus 2:11 (DARBY): For the grace of God which carries with it **salvation for all men** has appeared. . .

- II Peter 3:9 (HCSB): The Lord does not delay His promise, as some understand delay, but is patient with you, **not wanting any to perish but all to come to repentance.**

- I John 2:1–2 (NIV): My dear children, I write this to you so that you will not sin. But if anybody does sin, we have one who speaks to the Father in our defense—Jesus Christ, the Righteous One. ²He is the atoning sacrifice for our sins, and **not only for ours but also for the sins of the whole world.**

So, out of the mouth two or three (or sixteen) witnesses shall every word be established: if you're lost—if you are a sinner—He came to save you. The sixteen Scriptures above prove beyond a shadow of a doubt that God wants *all* people to be saved. But if we use here the same train of thought used by so many people in the area of healing, we could "prove" that God doesn't want all people to be saved because "I prayed for so-and-so to get saved, and he didn't get saved. That proves that God didn't want him to."

Here's another potentially disturbing thought. Consider the following scenario: I pray for someone and he (apparently) doesn't get healed, so I feel like I've failed. *I* feel like I've failed? If I feel like *I've* failed when someone (apparently) doesn't get healed, doesn't that imply that I consider the healing power is coming *from* me?

Now consider this scenario: I pray for someone and he does get dramatically healed, so I feel like I'm pretty hot stuff. *I* feel like I'm hot stuff? If I feel like *I'm* hot stuff when someone *does* get healed, doesn't that imply that I consider the healing power is coming *from* me? The answer, in both cases, is Yes, and (to coin a phrase), my brethren, these things ought not so to be.

In the same way we shouldn't take the *credit* when a miraculous healing takes place, neither should we take the *blame* when a miraculous healing (apparently) does *not* take place. Why? Because *we* don't supply the miraculous power to make it happen; we merely supply the willingness to obey. So if nothing perceptible happens, the problem does not lie with God, because we know from the mounds of Scriptures above that He wants to heal us, and He has more than enough power to do so. The problem could be any number of things, so our proper response is to seek God in our prayer closet to find out what the hindrance is, so we can address it, and not be hindered by the same problem when we run across it in the future.

The Common Thread

If you read through the previous sections in this chapter, you'll find that all the arguments against praying for healing have one thing in common: All of them elevate someone's experience *above* the plain, clear word of God. We have seen dozens, scores, even hundreds of Scriptures that show it is God's will to heal, but one person's undesirable outcome tends to completely derail it for so many people.

Why is it so easy to believe that the devil is stronger than God? And even the people who would indignantly sniff and say, "I would *never* say that!" often portray it with their actions, even if they don't say it in so many words. We become like the Pharisees, to whom Jesus said:

> Matthew 15:6b: Thus have ye made the commandment of God of none effect by your tradition.

By looking through the Old Testament, we can clearly see that God is not fundamentally against tradition. But He *is* against the idea of putting tradition on a higher plane than His Word, like the Pharisees did.

"The Healing Didn't Last Very Long"

This is one of the reservations that some people may have when presented with the opportunity to pray for someone's healing. The situation goes something like this:

1. People pray in faith for someone for healing, and speak God's promises. The healing comes: the symptoms subside, the pain vanishes completely, the range of motion is restored, or whatever. Everybody is thrilled.
2. A few days later, the healed person feels a twinge of pain, or notices a familiar symptom again. A pang of fear grips his heart, and he wonders if the prayers were as effective as he had thought.
3. A few more days pass, and he has felt a few more twinges of pain, or sees some more evidences of old symptoms, and he gets

more and more convinced that the healing didn't happen after all; it must have been all in his mind.

4. A few more days pass, and all the original pain and symptoms are back in full force, and he concludes that healing isn't for today, or at least that God sometimes chooses not to heal people who ask for it.

5. Months later, someone else who is in pain and has some symptoms asks him to pray for his healing, to which the first man says, "No, I tried that. It only lasts a few days, if that long."

So what was going on behind the scenes, in the spiritual realm? The healing happened, because people believed for it. It is important to speak God's Word on the matter; it builds faith, and God's Word by itself has the power to heal:

Psalm 107:20: **He sent his word, and healed them,** and delivered them from their destructions.

Matthew 8:8: The centurion answered and said, Lord, I am not worthy that thou shouldest come under my roof: but **speak the word only, and my servant shall be healed.**

Matthew 8:16: When the even was come, they brought unto him many that were possessed with devils: and **he cast out the spirits with his word, and healed all that were sick. . .**

Romans 10:17 (NIV): Consequently, **faith comes from hearing the message, and the message is heard through the word of Christ.**

So God's Word, and faith in it, caused the healing. But then the enemy comes—you know, that enemy who doesn't even show up unless he's there to steal, kill, and destroy—and causes a symptom. Satan is trying to remove the healing Word from your heart and your body; read the following excerpt from the Parable of the Sower:

Luke 8:5, 12 (NIV): A farmer went out to sow his seed. As he was scattering the seed, **some fell along the path; it was trampled on, and the birds of the air ate it up. . ..** [12]Those along the path are the ones who hear, and then **the devil comes and takes away the word from their hearts,** so that they may not believe and be saved.

What? Satan can take the Word out of our hearts? Yes, *if we let him*. But we would be wise not to let him do so:

James 4:7: Submit yourselves therefore to God. **Resist the devil, and he will flee from you.**

Ephesians 6:11–13 (NIV): **Put on the full armor of God so that you can take your stand against the devil's schemes.** ¹²For our struggle is not against flesh and blood, but against the rulers, against the authorities, against the powers of this dark world and against the spiritual forces of evil in the heavenly realms. ¹³Therefore put on the full armor of God, so that **when the day of evil comes, you may be able to stand your ground, and after you have done everything, to stand.**

II Corinthians 10:3–5 (NIV): For **though we live in the world, we do not wage war as the world does.** ⁴The weapons we fight with are not the weapons of the world. On the contrary, they have divine power to demolish strongholds. ⁵We demolish arguments and every pretension that sets itself up against the knowledge of God, and **we take captive every thought to make it obedient to Christ.**

The point is that the enemy is trying to convince us that God's Word is not true; if he can get us to give up, it's a lot easier for him than fighting us when we have God's full armor on. If, when we feel a symptom and the devil whispers to us that the healing didn't work after all, we agree with the devil, we do exactly what Adam did in the Garden of Eden. The serpent whispers "Hath God said. . .?" and when we choose to go his way, the results are of the same type. We need to *resist* the devil, and soak in God's Word and His Presence long enough to get our proper perspective back.

What we need to realize is that the phrase "According to thy faith be it unto you" works both ways. If we believe God's Word, our faith is in His love and goodness as a Father; and if we believe the enemy (who happens to be the father of lies—John 8:44), our faith is in a devil who is, in our estimation, bigger than God can handle.

If It Be Thy Will

Chapter 8:

The Atonement

There are few concepts in the Bible more important and far-reaching than the Atonement that Jesus makes available to us. Surely no Christian would deny that the forgiveness of sins was made available in the Atonement, but the current question is: Is healing also included in the Atonement?

But even the statements above—about the Atonement including forgiveness of our sins—might not be obvious if we don't know what atonement is. The word "atone" comes from the older phrase "at one." When we are "at one" with God, that means we are united with Him, or reconciled with Him.

When Adam sinned by disobeying God, that broke the intimate fellowship humans had with God, and introduced spiritual death, physical death, sickness, decay, strife, hatred, every other sin you can think of, and many that you can't. At that point, we, as humans, were definitely *not* "at one" with God. On the contrary, our sinful nature and worldly minds (minds that do not care what God wants) caused us to be enemies of God:

> James 4:4 (NIV): You adulterous people, don't you know that friendship with the world is hatred toward God? **Anyone who chooses to be a friend of the world becomes an enemy of God.**

So atonement, by its very definition, is some event or process that changes a state of war to a state of peace; it brings the two parties into a state of being "at one" with each other. In the context of what Jesus did, this reconciliation is between us and God; the Atonement unites us with Him; it reconciles us to Him.

Since it was our sin that broke the peace and made us enemies of God in the first place, the Atonement would certainly have to deal with sin in order to be effective. But the question under consideration now is: Did the Atonement accomplish more than just the forgiveness of our sins?

Let me be quick to point out that when I say "just" the forgiveness of sins, I am not in any way belittling it. It is of paramount importance, and without it, we would all be destined to an eternity of unimaginable torment in hell, and justly so. We will no doubt be plumbing the depths of the profound and far-reaching effects of the forgiveness of our sins for all eternity.

But what I *am* saying is this: If you have been with the Lord any length of time, you have likely discovered that when He does something, He does it well in *so* many ways that we never would have imagined. And because of this, it would not at all be out of character for God to include, along with the amazingness of the forgiveness of our sins (as if that weren't enough), *even more* blessings and goodness in the Atonement. And when we search the Scriptures, that is indeed what we find.

So the specific question at hand is this: Was physical healing one of the things that Jesus included (bought for us and paid for by His blood) in the Atonement? Let's look through some relevant Scriptures, and then you make up your own mind.

The Passover Lamb

When Israel was about to leave Egypt, and the tenth and final plague—the death of the firstborn—was about to be unleashed, God told Moses how the people were to prepare the Passover Lamb, and how to apply the blood of the Lamb, so that the plague would not affect them:

> Exodus 12:12–13 (NIV): "On that same night I will pass through Egypt and strike down every firstborn—men and animals—and I will bring judgment on all the gods of Egypt. I am the LORD. ¹³The blood will be a sign for you on the houses where you are; and **when I see the blood, I will pass over you. No destructive plague will touch you** when I strike Egypt."

The Passover Lamb is a type—a symbol—of Christ, and the symbolism is truly astonishing. It is outside the scope of this book to go into details on all the parallels between the Passover Lamb and Jesus, the Lamb of God Who takes away the sin of the world, but I would encourage you to investigate it. Many churches host Seder meals around Passover; these are re-enactments of the Passover meal that the Israelites ate on the eve of their departure from Egypt. As you participate in such a Seder meal, you will notice that the number of parallels between that meal and Christ's atoning work on the Cross is amazing.

Now just in case you're thinking that interpreting the Passover lamb as a symbol of Christ is an unwarranted stretch, the Apostle Paul apparently didn't think so:

> I Corinthians 5:7 (NIV): Get rid of the old yeast that you may be a new batch without yeast—as you really are. **For Christ, our Passover lamb, has been sacrificed.**

So, getting back to the Exodus Scripture above, notice that when the blood of the Lamb is applied, God said that "no destructive plague will touch you." I don't know for sure, but that kinda sounds like He will protect us from destructive plagues. And this is not merely theoretical or spiritualized; the Israelites experienced this in real life: as we saw above in the section None of These Diseases, *all* the millions of Israelites left Egypt healthy; there was not *one feeble person* among their tribes!

So we see, like the Israelites did, that we can apply the blood of the Passover Lamb, and therefore we can be protected from the plagues that are afflicting the people around us.

The Healing of the Leper

In Leviticus 14, God prescribes how a person with leprosy is officially and ceremonially declared to be healed. The first seventeen verses describe various steps in the cleansing procedure, and then it ends with this:

> Leviticus 14:18–22 (NIV): The rest of the oil in his palm the priest shall put on the head of the one to be cleansed and **make atonement for him** before the LORD. [19]Then the priest is to sacrifice the sin offering and **make atonement for the one to be cleansed from his uncleanness.** After that, the priest shall slaughter the burnt offering [20]and offer it on the altar, together with the grain offering, and **make atonement for him,** and he will be clean. [21]If, however, he is poor and cannot afford these, he must take one male lamb as a guilt offering to be waved to **make atonement for him,** together with a tenth of an ephah of fine flour mixed with oil for a grain offering, a log of oil, [22]and two doves or two young pigeons, which he can afford, one for a sin offering and the other for a burnt offering.

In the above passage, atonement seems to "clinch the deal" on the leper's healing; to declare him officially and ceremonially clean. Isn't it interesting that "atonement" is the word God uses to describe the process of declaring a person that used to be sick, now healthy? A person that used to be unclean—to the point that he was not even allowed inside the camp where the presence of God was—to now be clean?

Again, "atone" means to become "at one" with another party, so when we are "at one" with God, something or Someone has atoned for our differences and now we are reconciled—united—with God.

Korah's Rebellion

The story of Korah's rebellion is amazing in its portrayal of a stiff-necked and rebellious group of people. The story is told in Numbers 16, but rather than include the whole chapter here, I'll just highlight the important points, but I encourage you to read the whole story yourself:

1. Korah, Dathan, Abiram, plus 250 other people basically staged a coup against Moses, and told him "You have no right to tell us what to do." (vv. 1–7).
2. Moses told Korah, "Let's gather before the Lord tomorrow, and let Him decide" (vv. 8–11).
3. Moses also invited Dathan and Abiram, who said, "No," which really irritated Moses (vv. 12–15).
4. Moses told Korah again, "You and your gang be there tomorrow," which they did (vv. 16–19).
5. God was not amused either, and He told Moses and Aaron, "Stand back while I burn down the whole nation." Moses and Aaron fall on their faces and intercede on their behalf (vv. 20–22).
6. God relented, but then told Moses to warn the rest of the nation to stand back from the (new, unauthorized) tabernacle that Korah and his cohorts had built (vv. 23–27).
7. Moses announced to the children of Israel, "If these rebels die of old age, you'll know God didn't send me. But if the ground opens up and swallows them, you'll know He did" (vv. 28–30).
8. The ground opened up and swallowed Korah, Dathan, and Abiram and their families (vv. 31–34).
9. Then a fire came out from the LORD and consumed the 250 cohorts (v. 35).
10. God told Moses to do some ceremonial cleanup (vv. 36–40).
11. The next day, the Israelites complained about how Moses and Aaron had killed "the people of the LORD." Then they rose up against Moses and Aaron (vv. 41–43).

12. God again told Moses and Aaron, "Stand back while I take out the whole nation." Moses and Aaron fall on their faces and intercede on their behalf (vv. 44–45).

Right here in the story, is the point I am making. Note what Moses and Aaron do to avert the judgment of God that was beginning at that moment:

> Numbers 16:46–50 (NIV): Then Moses said to Aaron, "Take your censer and put incense in it, along with fire from the altar, and **hurry to the assembly to make atonement for them.** Wrath has come out from the LORD; the plague has started." ⁴⁷So Aaron did as Moses said, and ran into the midst of the assembly. The plague had already started among the people, but **Aaron offered the incense and made atonement for them.** ⁴⁸He stood between the living and the dead, and **the plague stopped.** ⁴⁹But 14,700 people died from the plague, in addition to those who had died because of Korah. ⁵⁰Then Aaron returned to Moses at the entrance to the Tent of Meeting, for the plague had stopped.

I think it's very interesting and significant that when the atonement was made, the plague stopped, and the rest of the people were protected from the completely justified anger of the Lord. The Bible doesn't say what kind of plague it was, but apparently, it was some kind of fast-moving disease. The word "plague" here was translated from the Hebrew word נֶגֶף (*negeph*, H5063), whose meaning is "an infliction of disease." But in any case, the atonement not only afforded them forgiveness of their rebellious, complaining attitude, it also *stopped whatever bodily disease* it was that made this plague.

The Caduceus

A few chapters later, the Israelites are complaining—again. Why were they complaining? God had just given them victory over their enemies simply because they had asked. *Now* what were they complaining about?

> Numbers 21:3–9 (NIV): The LORD listened to Israel's plea and gave the Canaanites over to them. They completely destroyed them and their towns; so the place was named Hormah. ⁴They traveled from Mount

Hor along the route to the Red Sea, to go around Edom. But the people grew impatient on the way; ⁵they spoke against God and against Moses, and said, "Why have you brought us up out of Egypt to die in the desert? There is no bread! There is no water! And we detest this miserable food!" ⁶Then the LORD sent venomous snakes among them; they bit the people and many Israelites died. ⁷The people came to Moses and said, "We sinned when we spoke against the LORD and against you. Pray that the LORD will take the snakes away from us." So Moses prayed for the people. ⁸The LORD said to Moses, **"Make a snake and put it up on a pole; anyone who is bitten can look at it and live."** ⁹So Moses made a bronze snake and put it up on a pole. **Then when anyone was bitten by a snake and looked at the bronze snake, he lived.**

Do you see the symbolism here? The snake represents Satan (Genesis 3:1–19), and when we are "bitten" by Satan; i.e., when we do his bidding instead God's bidding, that sin invokes God's justified curse on us, and we start dying. But Jesus took our sin, our curse, upon Himself when He was hung on the cross, which is why the snake being hung on a pole, in this instance, also represents Christ:

> Galatians 3:13 (NIV): Christ redeemed us from the curse of the law by becoming a curse for us, for it is written: "Cursed is everyone who is hung on a tree."

But again, someone might think it is a bit far-fetched to say that Moses hanging a bronze serpent on a wooden pole to heal people of poisonous snakebites represents Christ on the cross to heal our diseases. But what did Jesus Himself say?

> John 3:14–15 (NIV): Just as Moses lifted up the snake in the desert, so the Son of Man must be lifted up, ¹⁵that everyone who believes in him may have eternal life.

And notice that when the Israelites looked to the serpent on the pole, they were not only forgiven of their sinful, rebellious attitudes, they were *physically healed*. The fact that the Israelites were physically healed is so plain, that the snake on a pole has been used as a symbol for medicine for millennia; basically, ever since this incident where God gave healing to everyone who looked to the serpent on the pole. It is still is very common use today at doctors' offices, in hospitals, on ambulances, and so forth.

The "caduceus," a symbol for the field of medicine for millennia.

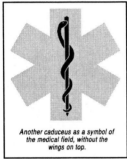

Another caduceus as a symbol of the medical field, without the wings on top.

Almost two thousand years after the Israelites were healed by looking at the serpent on the pole, the Greeks incorporated the concept into their pantheon, as those familiar with Greek mythology are aware. The Greek god Asclepius is portrayed as carrying a rod with a snake wrapped around it. And Hippocrates, the legendary "father of medicine," invoked the name of Asclepius in his famous Hippocratic Oath, which includes the concept of "do no harm."

Not all caducei have the wings on the top, as shown above. You may be wondering where the wings on the top came from in the first place, since that is not part of the story from Numbers 21. It is likely that they came from a printer's device in the front of a medical book published by Johann Froben in the sixteenth century, as shown below. At the bottom of his artwork, Froben wrote, in Greek, Jesus' command to be "be as wise as serpents, and harmless as doves" from Matthew 10:16. So apparently, in this artwork as the printer's device, Froben combined the dove—a symbol of not doing harm—

Sixteenth-century caduceus as a printer's device for Swiss medical printer Johann Froben.

with the serpent on the pole from Numbers 21—a symbol of doing good, actively promoting healing.

Froben apparently also included the concept of the Glory Cloud (for much detail on this, see the chapter "The Glory Cloud" in Book 4 of the "Thoughts On" series: *Gold Dust, Jewels, and More: Manifestations of God?*, available from the sources on BibleAuthor.DaveArns.com), since he portrayed the pole as being held by two hands protruding from clouds.

Unfortunately, we humans, as is our wont, have this annoying habit of worshipping the thing created, when we should be worshipping the Creator. And that is what happened to the bronze snake on the pole. After God healed the Israelites, they kept the bronze snake, and after a while, people started thinking that it was bronze serpent—the hunk of metal itself—instead of God that had healed them. So they began to worship it, and it became an idol to them. In a wise move, King Hezekiah saw the snake for what it was—a hunk of metal that symbolized God's healing blessing in the wilderness—so he destroyed it to prevent people from worshipping it any longer:

> II Kings 18:4 (NIV): He [Hezekiah] removed the high places, smashed the sacred stones and cut down the Asherah poles. **He broke into pieces the bronze snake Moses had made, for up to that time the Israelites had been burning incense to it.** (It was called Nehushtan.)

So using the bronze snake as an idol is wrong, of course, but the point of this story is that the bronze snake on the pole was a *type*—a figure, a foreshadowing—of Christ on the cross, and Jesus stated as much in John 3:14–15. And if the *foreshadowing* had enough power to provide physical healing, it's ludicrous to think that the real thing, to which the foreshadowing pointed, would be *less* effective. Jesus' work on the cross purchased a "better covenant, established on better promises" (Hebrews 8:6), so to claim it wouldn't even work as well as the old one is a slap in God's face. Let us *not* be guilty of that.

Forgiveness and Healing Together

It's intriguing to note how forgiveness and healing are mentioned together in the Bible. Here is one:

> Isaiah 33:24 (NIV): **No one living in Zion will say, "I am ill"; and the sins of those who dwell there will be forgiven.**

Why would *nobody* say, "I am ill"? The only answer that makes sense is that everyone living in Zion will be healthy. Here's another one, which we briefly addressed much earlier in the book:

> Psalm 103:2–3 (NIV): Praise the LORD, O my soul, and forget not all his benefits— ³**who forgives all your sins** and **heals all your diseases.** . . .

In this one verse, God says (since He inspired the Bible—II Timothy 3:16 and II Peter 1:21) that He forgives all our sins *and* heals all our diseases. Both. So, in practical terms, it doesn't really matter whether it is technically the Atonement itself that purchased healing for us, or some other merciful act or attribute of God. This verse says He does both, and for that, we should be thankful. To accept one half of this verse and reject the other half would be intellectually dishonest, and it would reveal just how far we are willing to go to prioritize our own preconceived notions above God's Word. And, it would require us to reject the hundreds of other supporting Scriptures shown earlier in this book.

And we already saw in great detail how Isaiah 53:4–5—one of the greatest Messianic passages in the Bible—includes both forgiveness of sins and healing of bodies in the same passage; see Wounded For Our Transgressions above for details.

It is fascinating that forgiveness and healing are clumped together so closely in these verses; it makes you wonder if they are connected somehow. Let's look at yet another passage that connects them and see what we can learn on this topic.

This next passage was partially covered above in The Paralytic with Four Good Friends, but we'll get some more nuggets out of the story here:

> Matthew 9:2–8 (NIV): Some men brought to him a paralytic, lying on a mat. When Jesus saw their faith, he said to the paralytic, "Take heart, son; your sins are forgiven." ³At this, some of the teachers of the law said to themselves, "This fellow is blaspheming!" ⁴Knowing their thoughts, Jesus said, "Why do you entertain evil thoughts in your hearts? ⁵**Which is easier: to say, 'Your sins are forgiven,' or to say, 'Get up and walk'?** ⁶But **so that you may know that the Son of Man has authority on earth to forgive sins. . .**" Then he said to the paralytic, "Get up, take your mat and go home." ⁷And the man got up and went home. ⁸When the crowd saw this, they were filled with awe; and they praised God, who had given such authority to men.

Did you see v. 6? That is earth-shaking! Look what Jesus said in these various translations of the Bible:

> Matthew 9:6: But **that ye may know that the Son of man hath power on earth to forgive sins,** (then saith he to the sick of the palsy,) Arise, take up thy bed, and go unto thine house.
>
>> CJB: "But look! **I will prove to you that the Son of Man has authority on earth to forgive sins.**" He then said to the paralyzed man, "Get up, pick up your mattress, and go home!"
>>
>> CEV: "But **I will show you that the Son of Man has the right to forgive sins here on earth.**" So Jesus said to the man, "Get up! Pick up your mat and go on home."
>>
>> vv. 5–6, ERV: "The Son of Man has power on earth to forgive sins. But **how can I prove this to you?** Maybe you are thinking it was easy for me to say, 'Your sins are forgiven.' There's no proof that it really happened. **But what if I say to the man, 'Stand up and walk'? Then you will be able to see that I really have this power.**" So Jesus said to the paralyzed man, "Stand up. Take your mat and go home."
>>
>> EXB: "**But I will prove to you [so that you may know]** that the Son of Man [a title for the Messiah; Dan. 7:13–14] has authority on earth to forgive sins." Then Jesus said to the paralyzed man, "Stand up, take [pick up] your mat [cot; bed], and go home."

GNT: "**I will prove to you, then, that the Son of Man has authority on earth to forgive sins.**" So he said to the paralyzed man, "Get up, pick up your bed, and go home!"

PHILLIPS: "But **to make it quite plain that the Son of Man has full authority on earth to forgive sins**"—and here he spoke to the paralytic—"Get up, pick up your bed and go home."

vv. 5–6, TLB: "I, the Messiah, have the authority on earth to forgive sins. But talk is cheap—anybody could say that. **So I'll prove it to you by healing this man.**" Then, turning to the paralyzed man, he commanded, "Pick up your stretcher and go on home, for you are healed."

MSG: "Which do you think is simpler: to say, 'I forgive your sins,' or, 'Get up and walk'? Well, **just so it's clear that I'm the Son of Man and authorized to do either, or both. . .**" At this he turned to the paraplegic and said, "Get up. Take your bed and go home."

NCV: "But **I will prove to you that the Son of Man has authority on earth to forgive sins.**" Then Jesus said to the paralyzed man, "Stand up, take your mat, and go home."

NLT: "So **I will prove to you that the Son of Man has the authority on earth to forgive sins.**" Then Jesus turned to the paralyzed man and said, "Stand up, pick up your mat, and go home!"

VOICE: "**To make clear that the Son of Man has the authority on earth to forgive sins** (turning to the paralytic man on the mat), Get up, pick up your mat, and go home."

Read the corresponding verses in Mark 2:10 and Luke 5:24 as well. Do you see what Jesus did here? He offered healing—physical healing—as *proof* that He had the power to forgive sins! He didn't consider it "beneath Him" to offer proof that God was backing Him up. And here is not the only place where Jesus used healing and other miracles to prove that He was on the level:

John 14:11 (NIV): Believe me when I say that I am in the Father and the Father is in me; or **at least believe on the evidence of the miracles themselves.**

Jesus' reasoning is sound (surprise, surprise). He knew that there are many voices out there, all claiming to speak The Truth. So how do we know who is speaking for God? They are the ones that God backs up with supernatural evidence as proof, as Nicodemus points out:

> John 3:2 (NIV): He [Nicodemus] came to Jesus at night and said, "Rabbi, we know you are a teacher who has come from God. For **no one could perform the miraculous signs you are doing if God were not with him.**"

As mentioned earlier, Jesus *gave people explicit permission* to reject His verbal claims if He didn't back them up with supernatural signs. In fact, it's even stronger than that: Jesus *commanded* people *not* to believe Him unless He backed it up with the miraculous:

> John 10:37: If I do not the works of my Father, **believe me not**.

So Jesus offered physical healing and other miraculous signs as *proof* that God was with Him, endorsing His ministry, and authenticating His message. And remember, Jesus did only what the Father told Him to do, so God the Father also wanted the proof to be presented to the listeners, along with the verbal statements the miracles were verifying.

A poignant question we need to ask ourselves again: What proof are *we* offering to those who hear our message? If Jesus, the Lamb of God Himself, felt it was appropriate—decent and in order—to prove, through physical healing and other miraculous signs, that God was backing Him up in His ministry, *how arrogant* we must be to think we wouldn't need that as well!

The Curse of the Law

Paul says some very profound stuff to the church in Galatia, and part of that is where he talks about Christ redeeming us from the curse of the law. That sounds cool, being redeemed from a curse and all, but what does it mean?

Let's look at what Paul said in Galatians, as well as the Old Testament passages he was quoting, to find out what he was talking about.

> Galatians 3:10–14 (NIV): All who rely on observing the law are under a curse, for it is written: "Cursed is everyone who does not continue to do everything written in the Book of the Law." [11]Clearly no one is justified before God by the law, because, "The righteous will live by faith." [12]The law is not based on faith; on the contrary, "The man who does these things will live by them." [13]Christ redeemed us from the curse of the law by becoming a curse for us, for it is written: "Cursed is everyone who is hung on a tree." [14]He redeemed us in order that the blessing given to Abraham might come to the Gentiles through Christ Jesus, so that by faith we might receive the promise of the Spirit.

Note that Paul goes through a very logical train of thought to show from the Old Testament why Christ did what He did in the Redemption. In v. 10, Paul quotes from Deuteronomy (part of the Law of Moses), which says:

> Deuteronomy 27:26 (TEV): "'**God's curse on anyone who does not obey all of God's laws** and teachings.'" And all the people will answer, 'Amen!'

This says that people will be under God's curse if they don't obey all His laws. Then Paul quotes from Habakkuk:

> Habakkuk 2:4 (NIV): See, he is puffed up; his desires are not upright— but **the righteous will live by his faith**—

So we live with God's favor because we believe in Him, not because we followed a bunch of rules. Next, Paul quotes from the Law again:

> Leviticus 18:5: Ye shall therefore keep my statutes, and my judgments: which **if a man do, he shall live in them**: I am the LORD.

This basically states the same things as Deuteronomy 27:26 above, except it says it from the opposite point of view: Instead of saying you'll be cursed if you *don't* obey His laws, it says you'll be blessed if you *do*. But it also points out that if you obey God's Laws completely, you will have *earned* God's favor. That is, a right relationship with God would not be a matter of faith in His goodness anymore, but an obligation He *owes* us—a paycheck, so to speak.

Next, Paul again quotes from Deuteronomy:

> Deuteronomy 21:22–23 (NIV): If a man guilty of a capital offense is put to death and his body is hung on a tree, ²³you must not leave his body on the tree overnight. Be sure to bury him that same day, because **anyone who is hung on a tree is under God's curse.** You must not desecrate the land the LORD your God is giving you as an inheritance.

Because Christ, Who perfectly fulfilled the Law, hung on a tree, He was cursed. But since He didn't break the Law Himself, it wasn't *His* curse, so where did the curse come from? It was *our* curse, the results of our *not* having followed the Law of God. He *redeemed* us from the curse that was headed our way—a curse we deserved—and He took the curse of the Law upon Himself so we wouldn't have to. We must accept that by faith, but because He has shown Himself to be extremely reliable and dependable, that should not be difficult.

Okay, all of the above sounds cool, but it doesn't really mean anything to us in the practical realm until we find out what exactly the "curse of the law" entailed. Are there Scriptures that spell out what exactly was included in the curse of the law? As a matter of fact, yes.

We saw above where God says that anyone who does not obey God's law would be cursed. If we keep reading from that point onward, it states the blessings that follow people who obey the Law, and the curses that follow people who don't. Since we're trying to figure out what the curses are, from which Jesus redeemed us, let's skip to that portion of the passage. I realize that this is a rather long passage, but please read at least the verses in which I have emphasized the words; those specifically pertain to the topic at hand.

> Deuteronomy 28:15–68 (NIV): However, if you do not obey the LORD your God and do not carefully follow all his commands and decrees I am giving you today, **all these curses** will come upon you and overtake you: ¹⁶You will be **cursed** in the city and **cursed** in the country. ¹⁷Your basket and your kneading trough will be cursed. ¹⁸The fruit of your womb will be cursed, and the crops of your land, and the calves of your herds and the lambs of your flocks. ¹⁹You will be **cursed when you come in** and **cursed when you go out.** ²⁰The LORD will send on you

curses, confusion and rebuke in everything you put your hand to, until you are destroyed and come to sudden ruin because of the evil you have done in forsaking him. ²¹The LORD will plague you with **diseases** until he has destroyed you from the land you are entering to possess. ²²The LORD will strike you with **wasting disease, with fever and inflammation,** with scorching heat and drought, with blight and mildew, which will plague you until you perish. ²³The sky over your head will be bronze, the ground beneath you iron. ²⁴The LORD will turn the rain of your country into dust and powder; it will come down from the skies until you are destroyed. ²⁵The LORD will cause you to be defeated before your enemies. You will come at them from one direction but flee from them in seven, and you will become a thing of horror to all the kingdoms on earth. ²⁶Your carcasses will be food for all the birds of the air and the beasts of the earth, and there will be no one to frighten them away. ²⁷The LORD will afflict you with **the boils of Egypt and with tumors, festering sores and the itch,** from which you cannot be cured. ²⁸The LORD will afflict you with **madness, blindness and confusion of mind.** ²⁹At midday you will grope about like a blind man in the dark. You will be unsuccessful in everything you do; day after day you will be oppressed and robbed, with no one to rescue you. ³⁰You will be pledged to be married to a woman, but another will take her and ravish her. You will build a house, but you will not live in it. You will plant a vineyard, but you will not even begin to enjoy its fruit. ³¹Your ox will be slaughtered before your eyes, but you will eat none of it. Your donkey will be forcibly taken from you and will not be returned. Your sheep will be given to your enemies, and no one will rescue them. ³²Your sons and daughters will be given to another nation, and you will wear out your eyes watching for them day after day, powerless to lift a hand. ³³A people that you do not know will eat what your land and labor produce, and you will have nothing but cruel oppression all your days. ³⁴**The sights you see will drive you mad.** ³⁵The LORD will afflict your **knees and legs with painful boils that cannot be cured,** spreading from the soles of your feet to the top of your head. ³⁶The LORD will drive you and the king you set over you to a nation unknown to you or your fathers. There you will worship other gods, gods of wood and stone. ³⁷You will become a thing of horror and an object of scorn and ridicule to all the nations where the LORD will drive you. ³⁸You will sow much seed in the field but you will harvest little,

If It Be Thy Will

because locusts will devour it. ³⁹You will plant vineyards and cultivate them but you will not drink the wine or gather the grapes, because worms will eat them. ⁴⁰You will have olive trees throughout your country but you will not use the oil, because the olives will drop off. ⁴¹You will have sons and daughters but you will not keep them, because they will go into captivity. ⁴²Swarms of locusts will take over all your trees and the crops of your land. ⁴³The alien who lives among you will rise above you higher and higher, but you will sink lower and lower. ⁴⁴He will lend to you, but you will not lend to him. He will be the head, but you will be the tail. ⁴⁵**All these curses** will come upon you. They will pursue you and overtake you until you are destroyed, because you did not obey the Lord your God and observe the commands and decrees he gave you. ⁴⁶They will be a sign and a wonder to you and your descendants forever. ⁴⁷Because you did not serve the LORD your God joyfully and gladly in the time of prosperity, ⁴⁸therefore in hunger and thirst, in nakedness and dire poverty, you will serve the enemies the LORD sends against you. He will put an iron yoke on your neck until he has destroyed you. ⁴⁹The LORD will bring a nation against you from far away, from the ends of the earth, like an eagle swooping down, a nation whose language you will not understand, ⁵⁰a fierce-looking nation without respect for the old or pity for the young. ⁵¹They will devour the young of your livestock and the crops of your land until you are destroyed. They will leave you no grain, new wine or oil, nor any calves of your herds or lambs of your flocks until you are ruined. ⁵²They will lay siege to all the cities throughout your land until the high fortified walls in which you trust fall down. They will besiege all the cities throughout the land the LORD your God is giving you. ⁵³Because of the suffering that your enemy will inflict on you during the siege, you will eat the fruit of the womb, the flesh of the sons and daughters the LORD your God has given you. ⁵⁴Even the most gentle and sensitive man among you will have no compassion on his own brother or the wife he loves or his surviving children, ⁵⁵and he will not give to one of them any of the flesh of his children that he is eating. It will be all he has left because of the suffering your enemy will inflict on you during the siege of all your cities. ⁵⁶The most gentle and sensitive woman among you—so sensitive and gentle that she would not venture to touch the ground with the sole of her foot—will begrudge the husband she loves and her own son or daughter ⁵⁷the afterbirth from her womb and the children she bears. For she intends to eat them secretly during the siege and in the distress that your enemy will inflict on you in your cities. ⁵⁸If you do not carefully follow all **the words of this law, which are written in this book,** and do not revere this glorious and awesome name—the LORD your God— ⁵⁹the LORD will send **fearful plagues** on you and your descendants, harsh and prolonged disasters, and **severe and lingering illnesses.** ⁶⁰He will bring upon you **all the diseases of Egypt** that you dreaded, and they will cling to you. ⁶¹The LORD will also bring on you **every kind of sickness and disaster not recorded in this Book of the Law,** until you are destroyed. ⁶²You who were as numerous as the stars in the sky will be left but few in number, because you did not obey the LORD your God. ⁶³Just as it pleased the LORD to make you prosper and increase in number, so it will please him to ruin and destroy you. You will be uprooted from the land you are entering to possess. ⁶⁴Then the LORD will scatter you among all nations, from one end of the earth to the other. There you will worship other gods—gods of wood and stone, which neither you nor your fathers have known. ⁶⁵Among those nations you will find no repose, no resting place for the sole of your foot. There the LORD will give you an anxious mind, eyes weary with longing, and a despairing heart. ⁶⁶You will live in constant suspense, filled with dread both night and day, never sure of your life. ⁶⁷In the morning you will say, "If only it were evening!" and in the evening, "If only it were morning!"—because of the terror that will fill your hearts and the sights that your eyes will see. ⁶⁸The LORD will send you back in ships to Egypt on a journey I said you should never make again. There you will offer yourselves for sale to your enemies as male and female slaves, but no one will buy you.

At this point, you might feel that's pretty heavy; pretty oppressive. And indeed it is. But the whole point here is that Jesus redeemed us from it. Let's look into it with more detail, as it applies to the subject of this book.

This passage is a statement of general, overall, and pervasive curses for rebellion against God. It uses several *merisms* to describe its ubiquitous nature. In case you're not familiar with the term "merism," it is a figure of speech that uses two or three examples from a certain context to represent *all* members of that context. This is a common part of speech, and some examples in English are:

- "I searched *high and low*," which means, "I've searched everywhere." The two locations "high" and "low" represent all possible locations.
- "He fell for it *lock, stock, and barrel*," which means "He fell for it completely" or "in every way." The three parts of a rifle—the lock, the stock, and the barrel—represent *all* parts of the rifle: lock, stock, barrel, trigger, trigger guard, bolt, safety, front sight, rear sight, magazine, recoil pad, hammer, and so forth. In other words, *everything*.
- "She swallowed the sales pitch *hook, line, and sinker*," which means "she swallowed (believed) it, entirely, completely, utterly." The three parts of a fisherman's equipment represent all other parts as well.
- "The king invited to the feast his subjects *young and old*," which means "The king invited everybody to the feast." The two age descriptors "young" and "old" represent all possible ages.

. . .and there are many more English merisms. Unsurprisingly, Hebrew and Greek have merisms as well:

- Psalm 139:2 (NIV): "You know *when I sit and when I rise;* you perceive my thoughts from afar." In other words, "You know everything about me all the time."
- Psalm 139:3 (NIV): "You discern *my going out and my lying down;* you are familiar with all my ways." In other words, "You discern everything I do."
- Revelation 1:8: "I am *Alpha and Omega,* the *beginning and the ending,* saith the Lord, which is, and which was, and which is to come, the Almighty." In other words, Jesus is the creator of everything that exists, and its maintainer from its inception through every nanosecond to its destruction.

. . .and again, there are many more, but you get the idea. I mention the concept of merisms here because this passage from Deuteronomy—the one that describes the curse of the law—uses some of them very deliberately. Verse 16 says "in the city and in the country," which is a Hebrew merism that means "in *every* location." Verse 19 says "when you come in and when you go out," which is a Hebrew merism that means "at *all* times." Verse 20 doesn't use a merism, but it says plainly that the people will be cursed in *everything* they put their hand to. In other words, because of their rebellion against God, they would be cursed everywhere, all the time, whatever they were doing. The point here is that sin is supremely dangerous.

Now keep in mind, lest you be swallowed up with overmuch sorrow from dwelling on all these curses of the law, that the first section of Deuteronomy 28 has a list of very cool blessings of the law that result from following God. Jesus has not redeemed us from the *blessings* of the law; in fact, He has increased and improved upon them:

> Hebrews 8:6 (NIV): But the ministry Jesus has received is as superior to theirs as the covenant of which he is mediator is **superior to the old one**, and it is **founded on better promises.**

So the first section of Deuteronomy 28 is definitely a good read, and I encourage you to study it, but I won't get into detail on it here, because it is not the topic of this book.

So, in the context of this book, note that sickness and disease are a large part of the overall curse for rebelling against God. Diseases were mentioned in several places, and quite a few by name:

- Generic "diseases" (v. 21).
- "Wasting disease, fever, and inflammation" (v. 22).
- Incurable "boils of Egypt and with tumors, festering sores and the itch" (v. 27).
- "Madness, blindness and confusion of mind" (v. 28).
- "Knees and legs" with incurable and "painful boils" which spread to the entire body (v. 35).
- "Fearful plagues" and "severe and lingering illnesses" (v. 59).
- "All the diseases of Egypt" (v. 60).

This is quite an intimidating list, is it not? That makes it all the more wonderful that Jesus redeemed us from it. But what if you have a disease that isn't specifically mentioned in the above list? Did Jesus cover that also? Yes!

Very significantly, almost as if God knew someone would ask that question, He covered that potential exception. Note v. 61 also includes in the curse "every kind of sickness and disaster *not* recorded in this Book of the Law." That is huge! In this context, there are two categories of sicknesses (or diseases or illnesses):

- Those whose names were recorded, and
- Those whose names were *not* recorded.

Putting those two categories together, how many sicknesses (or diseases or illnesses) does that cover? *All of them!* Every disease that could ever exist is either mentioned in this passage, or it is not; there is no third option. When Jesus redeemed us from the curse of the law, He redeemed us from *all* sicknesses and diseases as part of the package!

Now at this point, someone will say, "But *that's* not part of the curse that He redeemed us from." Never mind that God includes sicknesses in the list of things He calls "curses"—He *introduces* the list (which includes sicknesses) with "all these curses will come upon you" in v. 15, and then *within* the list (which includes sicknesses), He says, "All these curses will come upon you" again in v. 45. So sickness is part of the curse. And notice the sentence structure: it's like saying, "All these relatives will attend the party: Bob, Mary, and Jane." Are Bob, Mary, and Jane relatives? Yes. How do we know? Because they're included in the list identified as "all these relatives." This is *so* clear that you need to do some very imaginative and contorted mental gymnastics to *mis*understand what is being stated here.

And never mind that this passage is in the Pentateuch, also known as the Torah, which is defined as "the Law of God as revealed to Moses and recorded in the first five books of the Bible." So by virtue of its being in the Pentateuch, this passage is in, and is a part of, The Law.

And never mind that in the Pentateuch/Torah, the Law is presented and explained twice—firstly in Exodus and secondly in Deuteronomy—and that "Deuteronomy" literally means "Second Law." So again, by virtue of its being in Deuteronomy (i.e., the "Second Law"), this passage is seen to be part of The Law.

And never mind that *that very passage*, which categorizes sicknesses as a "curse" (vv. 15, 45) identifies itself as "this Book of the Law" (v. 61). Note the specificity: not just *any* old Book of the Law, but *this* Book of the Law. It conveys to the reader, "the Book of the Law you are reading at this very moment." So yet again, this passage that characterizes sickness as a curse is confirmed to be part of The Law.

And never mind that the apostle Paul, in his teaching that Christ redeemed us from the curse of the law, *quotes this very passage* as part of his exhortation in Galatians 3:10 (see above). But in spite of all that, some people still think Paul (or the Bible, or the Holy Spirit) did not consider sickness to be included in the curse from which Jesus redeemed us. Curious, isn't it?

Wounded for Our Transgressions, Take 2

I covered this in great detail above, so I won't cover it again, I'll just refer you to the section Wounded for our Transgressions. That section has some very relevant information on whether Jesus included physical healing in the Atonement prophesied about in Isaiah 53. And we don't even need to wonder how to interpret the potentially ambiguous words in Isaiah, because Matthew interprets them for us.

It Just Makes Sense

If you think about where sickness and disease came from, you quickly realize they came in when Adam and Eve sinned: sin was the doorway through which sickness came to this world. So doesn't it just make sense that, since Jesus did away with sin and its consequences in our lives, that sickness would have to be one of those consequences He did away with? Doesn't it just make sense that, since the "doorway" through which sin enters is closed, it would also be closed to those things that came in with sin? If you're wondering about the whole idea of whether Jesus' work on the cross could get rid of sin in our lives, see Book 2 of the "Thoughts On" series: *Is It Possible to Stop Sinning?*, available from the sources noted on BibleAuthor.DaveArns.com.

Since sickness came in with sin, it should go out with sin too. Just makes sense, doesn't it?

If It Be Thy Will

Chapter 9:

Personal Testimonies

The Scriptures in the previous chapters and the concepts they state are not just "theological facts." Indeed, if they *were* just theological facts, they would be pretty useless in real life. Any revelation of truth, be that from us reading God's written Word in the Bible, or from hearing God's Spirit speak to us directly, should lead us to an encounter with Christ. And if it doesn't, it only serves to make us proud (I Corinthians 8:1), and we become the very Pharisees we've been shaking our heads at.

So, below are some testimonies from my own life. They're not as dramatic as some of the testimonies you hear from Bill Johnson, Randy Clark, James Maloney, Ian Andrews, and the like, but they are mine, and God has shown me that He is just as eager to work miracles through me as He is the "big name" preachers. He will use anyone who will seek Him and obey Him, and as we get better at hearing Him, our faith grows, and so does the size and impact of the miraculous works He does through us.

Aspergillosis

As a dance instructor, I meet and talk to lots of people. This one particular lady I often dance with is in her early twenties, and once when we were talking at a dance, I don't exactly remember how it came up, but she mentioned that she had "aspergillosis." I had no idea what that was, so she explained that it was basically mold growing in her lungs. That sounded pretty nasty, and she went to say that she had grown up in Texas in a very humid environment when she inhaled the mold, and because of the high humidity, it flourished in her lungs. The result was severe asthma-like symptoms, so severe that she was hospitalized with life-threatening shortness of breath almost once a week.

Her doctors told her she should move to a drier climate, so she moved to Colorado, which is where I met her. She said that the drier climate had helped a lot, but she still had way too many bouts with the asthma-like symptoms, but now, more annoying and intrusive than life-threatening, and she wasn't hospitalized nearly as often as she had been in Texas.

So, a little irritated at the whole idea of mold growing in lungs, I prayed for her during my quiet time one morning. The prayer time was a good one, although I didn't have heavenly visions open up or anything. Then a few weeks later, I saw her at another dance. Her hair was still wet from a recent shower, so every time she spun fast, her braid would send a fine spray of water in every direction.

As we danced, I asked her how she was feeling, and she beamed and said, "I've been doing really well lately! In fact, right before I came to the dance, I just got done with a seven-mile run, and I beat my best time!" It looked like her smile was wider than her whole head. "As soon as I got home, I jumped in the shower and then came here; that's why my hair is still wet," she grinned.

I rejoiced with her and said "That's wonderful! I was praying for you." She, not yet a believer, didn't know what to do with that, and so after a few seconds of speechlessness said, "Oh. Thanks." I rejoiced again, knowing that God's Spirit was busily working on her heart.

Neuropathy of the Feet

At one particular dance I went to a couple years ago, there was a group lesson before the open dancing time started, and to maximize the skill-building of the newbies, the ladies rotated from one gentleman to the next every few minutes, whenever the instructor said to. This one lady came by, and since the dance itself was not new to us, we were quietly chitchatting while the other students were figuring out how to do the step they were currently working on. During the chitchat, she casually mentioned that she couldn't feel her feet.

That was unexpected, so I asked her to elaborate, and she said she had neuropathy in her feet and lower legs. Immediately, God said to me, "You need to pray for her." She added that her feet and lower legs tingled and hurt most of the time, and when she got tired, they went completely numb. And this tingling was not the good anointing-of-the-Spirit kind of tingling, but the bad, nerve-damage kind of tingling. Then the instructors told everyone to rotate, so I was not able to talk to her further. After a while, the dance ended, and I still hadn't prayed with her, so I left the dance, feeling condemned for letting fear get the better of me. I *could have* made the time to pray for her, but was afraid. So, after asking for forgiveness, I asked God to set up another time when I could pray for her.

Two weeks later, at another dance, another opportunity came. I told her of my conversations with God the previous time around, and asked her if I could pray for her about the neuropathy. She was very open to it and told me a story of her granddaughter who had had a miraculous healing of her own. So, at the end of the dance, we went into the little coffee shop at the health club at which the dance was held, talked for a while, and then I held her hands, and started praying for her feet, for her to be healed of the neuropathy.

Almost immediately, she started punctuating the prayer with little gasps of astonishment and squeals of excitement, because a little part of her left foot, in one of the toes, suddenly stopped hurting. The pain-less area grew, and soon a significant part of her left foot was pain-free, and part of her right foot started growing a pain-free area. She was *very* excited. She had to leave after 15 minutes or so to meet some other people, so the healing was not yet complete when we parted ways, but it was definitely underway, and she was giddy with excitement. I advised her to use her authority over the enemy if he ever tried to talk her out of the healing, and she acknowledged that would be a good idea. I told her I would continue to pray with her for continued healing, as long as it took to get it done.

About a month later at a different dance, I saw her again, and asked how her feet were doing, and she said the healing of the tips of her toes was still there, and she was still in amazement and very grateful. I asked her if she wanted me to pray with her again for further healing. She said yes, so we went upstairs to get away from the crowd and prayed. The portions of her feet that didn't hurt grew, and included all her toes and all the way back to her arches, and she started getting normal feeling back in her shins and calves as well. She was very excited and grateful again.

Kidney Failure

At my public large-group dance classes, we always start and end with a word of prayer. One night, one of the students asked for prayer for her sister-in-law in Alaska who was suffering from renal failure: her kidneys were not filtering toxins out of her blood, so they were building up in her body and causing blockages and other problems. She had lesions on her legs, where calcifications were blocking blood flow, and the doctors were considering amputation of her legs (if she lived long enough).

So we all prayed, and asked God for a miracle: a dramatic, obvious, supernatural intervention on behalf of the sister-in-law. Then we continued with the dance class.

Four days later, my student texted me a message saying that her sister-in-law had apparently received a miracle! She quoted the sister-in-law's doctor as having said, "We don't know where the disease went." The lesions on her legs disappeared, and she was released from the critical-care section of the hospital to go to another much-less-critical care facility for observations and/or care before going home. You can imagine that my student was happy about that, plus her brother being "ecstatic," and their mother was "overwhelmed with joy." God is good! And His power is not limited by distance.

Left Ankle and Back

As I write this, I think back to last Monday night when I was on a prayer team with the Healing Rooms chapter in Loveland, Colorado (for more details, see HealingRooms.com). A woman came in who had had surgery on her left ankle because one of her tendons had, to quote her doctor, "shredded." During the surgery, the doctor had put two long screws into her ankle to compensate for absence of tendon; these screws severely restricted her foot's range of motion (she couldn't point her toes), but because of the absence of viable tendons, the surgeon didn't have much choice. After the surgery, she could walk, though not without pain, and the inability to extend her left foot caused her to walk asymmetrically; she limped. This, over time, led to back pain from the uneven movement when she walked.

We told her about various ways that God has healed people, and then laid hands on her and prayed. After a few minutes, I asked her if she could feel anything, and she said, "My ankle tingles." I told her that was a good sign, and we prayed a little longer. Then I asked her again, and this time she said, "My ankle's hot." We kept praying for a few more minutes, and when we felt a release in the Spirit, we stopped praying and I asked her to do something she couldn't do before.

She stood up, balanced on her right foot, and cautiously extended her left foot—she pointed her toes. First tentatively, then repeatedly and energetically, she flexed, extended, flexed, extended, staring in amazement at her foot. "I couldn't do that!" she gasped. "I couldn't do that!"

Then she walked around behind the chair she had been sitting in during the prayer, leaned heavily on the chairback, and slowly stood on her tiptoes. Her eyes got very wide, and she repeated, "I couldn't do that! This is awesome!" She relaxed her feet, and then stood on her tiptoes again, several times. Then she let go of the chairback, putting all her weight on her feet, and continued going up on her tiptoes and back down, all the while muttering, "This is awesome! I couldn't do that!" Then she started pacing back and forth across the room, not from nervousness, but from the joy of having a foot that worked again.

We asked her if there was any pain left, and she said "No! This is awesome! This is awesome!" She paced a bit more and then, almost as an afterthought, she added, "Oh, and my back doesn't hurt anymore either!" I don't know if God miraculously removed the screws, converted them into tendon, made them flexible, or what He did; all I know is that she couldn't walk without pain and limping, and then she could. She fairly *floated* out of the prayer room, she was so overjoyed.

Frozen Neck, Internal Organs, and Asthma

The following testimony was given to me by a woman who is on the prayer team for the Healing Rooms of Loveland. It pertains to a friend of hers whom I had prayed for in 2014. Honestly, I don't even remember praying for this particular woman—lots of people come through the Healing Rooms—but the woman who is on the prayer team assures me that I did indeed pray for her friend; she remembers it well.

This is the prayer-team member's written testimony of her friend's healing:

> My best friend from California came to the Healing Rooms in Loveland, Colorado. For decades she suffered from neck pain. She had to drive and sleep with certain pillows. She could not turn her head side to side; she had to move her entire body to face you.
>
> For decades she suffered from asthma. She could not go anywhere without her inhaler or go on trips without her breathing machine in case a bad attack occurred. She also had a problem with her internal organs after her last child was born; it felt like they had shifted and dropped.

But all that changed after coming to the Healing Rooms. Her neck was instantly healed and she could feel her organs realigning themselves, raising up inside her as they prayed over her. She had no idea that her asthma had been healed until she returned to California and things that had previously brought on an asthma attack now had no effect. She no longer carries her inhaler or uses her machine.

Praise God for the Healing Rooms of Loveland!

Receiving this testimony reminded me all over again that when we make ourselves to God's leading, He uses us so much more than we realize. We should never assume God is not working through us simply because we don't see or hear about the results of any particular prayer!

Others

The above testimonies are some of the more dramatic miracles in which God has used me, but there are also "smaller" miracles. I am not in any way belittling these so-called "smaller" miracles, because they were immensely important to the people getting healed. They include headaches, stomach cramps, chronic coughing in a baby, knee and ankle pain from a car accident, a heel spur, plantar fasciitis, torn shoulder muscles, broken pinky finger, neuropathy of the thighs, chronic chest pains, torn meniscus in knee, floaters in the eyes, frozen shoulder, stiff neck, and more. I am including them because they are good places to start when you're beginning to pray for people.

If It Be Thy Will

Chapter 10:

What Shall We Say, Then?

The mountains of Scriptures above have been collected, organized, and presented in this book form to make a point, obviously. What point would that be? The point is to show, regardless of individual people's experiences, that God's Word clearly shows that it is His desire, His will, His pleasure to provide physical healing for mankind.

The Kingdom of God

A very well known Scripture is this one, from the Sermon on the Mount:

> Matthew 6:33: But **seek ye first the kingdom of God**, and his righteousness; and all these things shall be added unto you.

The point I'm making here is not concerned with what "all these things" refers to, but the command to seek first "the kingdom of God."

What is the kingdom? What does it entail? Let's look at some other Scriptures and see what we discover:

> Matthew 4:23: And Jesus went about all Galilee, teaching in their synagogues, and **preaching the gospel of the kingdom, and healing all manner of sickness and all manner of disease** among the people.
>
> Matthew 9:35: And Jesus went about all the cities and villages, teaching in their synagogues, and **preaching the gospel of the kingdom, and healing every sickness and every disease** among the people.
>
> Matthew 10:7–8: And as ye go, **preach, saying, The kingdom of heaven is at hand. ⁸Heal the sick, cleanse the lepers, raise the dead, cast out devils:** freely ye have received, freely give.
>
> Luke 9:2: And he sent them to **preach the kingdom of God, and to heal the sick.**
>
> Luke 9:11: And the people, when they knew it, followed him: and he received them, and **spake unto them of the kingdom of God, and healed them** that had need of healing.

Well, isn't *that* interesting? These verses seem to imply that healing is a very real and important part of the Kingdom. Which kingdom is that? The Kingdom of God, which we are commanded to seek above all else. But is it really true that one of the rights of the citizens of the Kingdom of God is healing? Yes, this is confirmed yet again by the following verses:

> Luke 10:9: And **heal the sick that are therein, and say unto them, The kingdom of God is come** nigh unto you.
>
> Luke 11:20: But **if I with the finger of God cast out devils, no doubt the kingdom of God is come** upon you.

So the two Scriptures above point out that healing is indeed part of the Kingdom, regardless of whether the sickness was directly caused by demonic activity, or was just a side-effect of living in a fallen world.

The Lord's Prayer

Remember the Sermon on the Mount, where Jesus told people how to pray? He showed them what kinds of things to include when He gave them what we now call The Lord's Prayer:

> Matthew 6:9–13: After this manner therefore pray ye: Our Father which art in heaven, Hallowed be thy name. ¹⁰**Thy kingdom come. Thy will be done in earth, as it is in heaven.** ¹¹Give us this day our daily bread. ¹²And forgive us our debts, as we forgive our debtors. ¹³And lead us not into temptation, but deliver us from evil: For thine is the kingdom, and the power, and the glory, for ever. Amen.

We already saw that when the Kingdom comes, healing and deliverance take place. But here, in this prayer that Jesus says to use as a model (though not a rote formula), we are supposed to pray that His Kingdom come, with the implied healing and deliverance based on the previous Scriptures. But not only that, we see here that *we are supposed to pray that His will be done on earth, as it is in heaven.* So something we need to ask ourselves is this: How much sickness is there in heaven? How much sickness does God's will allow in heaven? *Jesus is telling us here to pray that that same amount of sickness be allowed here on earth.* This passage, all by itself, is enough to show God's will on healing, even without the hundreds of others we've seen already. But He gives us the hundreds of others as well, just to completely wipe out any tenable objection or misunderstanding.

Applying God's Will In Our Lives

A huge part of understanding this point about God's will to heal us is realizing God's Father-heart of love toward us that is more rich, strong, and intense than we could ever hope to comprehend in its fulness. This is what Jesus was saying, when He told the people a little bit later in the Sermon on the Mount:

> Matthew 7:9–11: Or what man is there of you, whom if his son ask bread, will he give him a stone? ¹⁰Or if he ask a fish, will he give him a serpent? ¹¹If ye then, being evil, know how to give good gifts unto your children,

how much more shall your Father which is in heaven give good things to them that ask him?

Is physical healing a "good thing?" When you're sick, there are few things that are *better* than physical healing. But, as shown above, it's difficult to have faith to pray for something if you don't know whether God would want to answer you in the affirmative.

And that's what all the Scriptures above are intended to do, when collected into a single work like this: they are intended to make people realize that it *is* God's will to heal us physically, in *all* cases. That's what the apostle John was saying in his first epistle:

> I John 5:14–15: And this is the confidence that we have in him, that, **if we ask any thing according to his will, he heareth us:** [15]**And if we know that he hear us, whatsoever we ask, we know that we have the petitions that we desired of him.**

Do you see the simple logical progression here?

1. If we ask anything according to His will, *we can be confident* that He hears us.
2. If He hears us (and we know He did, because we asked something according to His will), *we know* that we have what we asked Him for.

So what we need to do is to meditate on the Scriptures above until we realize that God *really does* want to heal us, and has already made provision for it. If we have leftover doubt from whatever source—stories we read on the internet, apparently unsuccessful prayers for healing of friends or relatives, the doctrinal persuasion of various churches or organizations we've attended, or whatever—we need to repent of placing more faith in people's experiences (or *lack* of experiences) than we do in God's Word.

· Soak in the Scriptures above until you understand that God wants to remove sickness from us just like *any* loving earthly father would want to remove sickness from his beloved children, if he could. The good news is that God *can* remove sickness from us, and when you understand that He also *wants to* do so, faith arises. And then the logical progression shown above (which is based on I John 5:14–15) becomes, in this particular application:

1. We know that physical healing is in His will (see the first eight chapters of this book for confirmation). This also applies to salvation, emotional healing, deliverance from demonic oppression, and everything else that the Bible clearly states is His Will.
2. If we ask for physical healing (which, as we've seen, is according to His will), *we can be confident* that He hears us.
3. Since He hears us (based on v. 14), *we know* that we have what we asked Him for, which was physical healing.
4. Therefore, we believe Him, agree with Him, and are not ashamed to say so. This is not living in denial, as some say; it is acknowledging that there is a problem of sickness, but that God is bigger than that problem, or any other.

So, from all of the Scriptural evidence above, we can now confidently change any "*...if it be* Thy will" that we may have been praying, to "*...since it is* Thy will" when we are petitioning God for physical healing for ourselves or someone else. Glory to God!

If It Be Thy Will

About the Author

David Arns was raised in church, but didn't start actually serving the Lord until his sophomore year of high school, in 1972. Being of a rather analytical turn of mind, he was delighted to see that there is a Biblical mandate for all Christians to be analytical: I Thessalonians 5:21 (NIV) says "Test everything. Hold on to the good." That, coupled Paul's exhortation to teach what "the Holy Ghost teaches," not depending on man's wisdom (I Corinthians 2:11–14), and with the commendation of the Bereans, who "searched the scriptures daily, whether those things were so" (Acts 17:11), pretty much define Dave's life, in the spiritual realm, as well as the natural realm.

In the mid-1970s, Dave heard a sermon in which he was exhorted to "know *what* you believe and *why* you believe it," and he has been trying to put that into practice ever since. He has been known to abandon long-held beliefs when someone showed him that they were incompatible with Scripture; that attitude seems to be necessary if we want to continue to grow in the Lord.

The "THOUGHTS ON" Series of Books

This book is a member of the "THOUGHTS ON" series of books. The phrase "Thoughts On" is deliberately ambiguous, because it is meaningful and accurate either way you interpret it. First, it indicates where the seeds of the whole series came from: they were from a large list of informal Bible studies Dave had put together for his own interest and edification as a result of his "thoughts on" various topics that occurred to him during his quiet times with the Lord. And second, it indicates one of Dave's goals as a teacher: to persuade people to turn their "thoughts on" and consider logically what God has said in His word, and how it is very much to our benefit to take heed to what He says.

When reading *The Chronicles of Narnia* to his son Matthew when he was little, Dave came across the Professor's exasperated musing: "'Logic!' said the Professor half to himself. 'Why don't they teach logic at these schools?'" Oh, did that ring true with him! Many are the times

Dave has heard a preacher or Bible teacher make a statement from the pulpit, and the crowd responds with a hearty "Amen!" Dave looks around astonished, thinking, "That statement's not true! I can think of three Scriptures off the top of my head that refute it!" And he just grieves for the complacency evident in most Christians; there is *so* much God wants to bless them with, and they miss out because they don't check the Bible to verify statements they hear.

To see the other books in the "THOUGHTS ON" Series, and the sources from which they are available, or to contact the author, see the website BibleAuthor.DaveArns.com.

So, Dear Reader, please turn your Thoughts On. . .

If It Be Thy Will

If It Be Thy Will